INFORMATION MANAGEMENT

D0169094

INFORMATION MANAGEMENT

The Strategic Dimension

Edited by
MICHAEL EARL

CLARENDON PRESS · OXFORD

Oxford University Press, Walton Street, Oxford OX2 6DP
Oxford New York Toronto
Delhi Bombay Calcutta Madras Karachi
Petaling Jaya Singapore Hong Kong Tokyo
Nairobi Dar es Salaam Cape Town
Melbourne Auckland
and associated companies in
Berlin Ibadan

Oxford is a trade mark of Oxford University Press

Published in the United States
by Oxford University Press, New York

© Oxford University Press 1988

Reprinted 1989, 1990

British Library Cataloguing in Publication Data
Information management: the strategic
dimension.
1. Business firms. Information systems.
Management.
I. Earl, Michael J.
658.4'.038
ISBN 0–19–828592–2

Library of Congress Cataloging in Publication Data
Information management: the strategic dimension/edited by Michael
Earl
p   cm.   Includes index.
Papers from a conference jointly sponsored by the Oxford Institute
of Information Management, Templeton College, Oxford and PA
Computers and Telecommunications.
1. Management information systems—Congresses.   I. Earl, Michael J.
II. Oxford Institute of Information Management.
III. PA Computers and Telecommunications.
T58.6.I47 1988   658.4'038—dc19   88-6605
ISBN 0–19–828592–2

Printed and bound
in Great Britain by Biddles Ltd,
Guildford and King's Lynn

PREFACE

Information Technology has become a strategic resource. Whilst observers and forecasters describe and predict the oncoming of an information society, or information economy, firms and their managements have been investing in information technology (IT) to seek strategic advantage. A number of well known exemplars have had headline impacts as they create apparent competitive edge, produce significant productivity and performance gains, or provide new ways of managing and doing business. The exploits of Merill Lynch, American Hospital Supply, or American Airlines in the USA, and Reuters, Thomson Holidays, and the Nottingham Building Society in the UK have excited or alerted even the sternest critic of computing and IT.

Behind this 'hype' and vision however, lie a multitude of management challenges—issues which worry IT professionals and general managers alike, and questions which puzzle researchers and consultants. It was obvious therefore that the first annual Oxford PA Conference on information management should address 'the strategic dimension'. Jointly sponsored by the Oxford Institute of Information Management and PA Computers and Telecommunications, the conference brought together 40 leading IT Directors and academics from around the world to share and discuss the state of the art in IT and strategy. A principal objective was to identify areas in need of further research; perhaps where business and the universities could work together. An important step therefore was to publish the papers.

I believe we have produced a valuable collection of theoretical, practical, and investigative papers which not only document the state of the art, but also suggest the ways ahead for research and practice. The papers are organized in thematic sessions. To begin, the connection between IT and strategy is examined, together with the emerging conceptual frameworks for understanding it. Next, the reality rather than the rhetoric of strategic exploitation of IT is presented, based on empirical studies and accounts of IT in use. In the third section, the core problem of how to formulate IT strategies is examined, including the issue of how to discover competitive advantage opportunities via IT. The practical problems of managing and implementing IT strategies are discussed in the next section, with prescriptions on how to succeed. Some of the organizational issues arising in the strategic era of IT are analysed in the next section, at the levels of the firm, the department, and the individual. Finally, the editor, some months after the conference itself, reflects on what might be the major issues and lessons which may guide practitioners, consultants, and researchers in their endeavours—

particularly looking to distinguish between ephemeral and substantial matters and seeking those questions which might have been kept in the background so far.

It is the intention that annual Oxford PA Conferences on Information Management produce a series of benchmarking and direction-setting books on important themes concerned with managing IT and information systems. The sponsors and editor trust that this volume begins to achieve this aim.

Michael Earl
Templeton College, Oxford
July 1987

CONTENTS

Section 5: IT Strategy and Organization

Section 6: IT and Strategy: Reflections and Directions

LIST OF CONTRIBUTORS

MICHAEL EARL
Oxford Institute of Information Management, Templeton College, Oxford

DAVID FEENY
Oxford Institute of Information Management, Templeton College, Oxford

ROBERT GALLIERS
School of Computing and Quantitative Studies, Western Australian Institute of Technology

GRAHAM GOODING
Ford In Europe

VARUN GROVER
Graduate School of Business, University of Pittsburgh

RUDI HIRSCHHEIM
Oxford Institute of Information Management, Templeton College, Oxford

KARL-HENRIK HUBINETTE
Volvo Data AB

ELLEN HUFNAGEL
Graduate School of Business, University of Pittsburgh

PETER KEEN
International Center for Information Technologies, Washington DC

WILLIAM KING
Graduate School of Business, University of Pittsburgh

MARTIN LOCKETT
Oxford Institute of Information Management, Templeton College, Oxford

STEVE MATHESON
Inland Revenue

JOHN McGEE
Templeton College, Oxford

DAVID RUNGE
Oxford Institute of Information Management, Templeton College, Oxford

MICHAEL SCOTT MORTON
Sloan School of Management, MIT

DEREK SEDDON
Imperial Chemical Industries plc

HOWARD THOMAS
Department of Business Administration, University of Illinois at Urbana-Champaign

Strategy and Information Technology

FOREWORD

Ten years ago, claims that there were important connections between information technology (IT) and strategy, however well argued, were thought mostly to be pretentious and 'academic'. Although some, such as Kantrow (1980), began a little later to argue more persuasively that technology and strategy were inseparable, the strategic role of *information* technology was still barely appreciated. Today, few chief executives or IT directors of leading companies would take such a sceptical or dispassionate view. They see and hear of firms using IT for strategic advantage and strive to emulate them, both feeling threatened by a new IT Age and invigorated by the opportunities.

Many case studies of exploiting IT for strategic advantage are documented in the academic and professional literature, and various frameworks connecting strategy and IT have been proposed. Some of these exemplars have become shorthand in daily discourse. Lister-Petter, the UK diesel engine manufacturer, by investing in flexible manufacturing systems and computer integrated manufacturing, maintained their profit levels on 60% of their previous volume, as they fought for survival in a global and diminishing market place. American Hospital Supply increased market share dramatically by setting up computer-based ordering links with customers and suppliers and making a strength out of a large product range. American Airlines and United Airlines used reservation systems to dominate the channel of distribution—travel agents—and outwit their competitors in the use of their new databases in the deregulated US airline industry. Indeed American Airlines derives a major proportion of its earnings from selling on reservation system use to agents and other airlines. Merrill Lynch helped forge the concept of financial services and break down industry barriers with the introduction of its computer- and telecommunications-based product, the Cash Management Account. The provider of much of the data processing behind this product, Banc One of Columbus, Ohio, diversified into information processing from banking by this and similar moves. Indeed we have seen both Dun and Bradstreet, and Reuters build on their information networks and data bases to demonstrate that an information services sector really exists. Furthermore, as some of these firms realize how information and IT cross conventional boundaries, they seek alliances—as Wiseman has emphasized—with technology firms and others to implement their strategic visions. Thus Merrill Lynch has a joint venture with IBM to provide personal computer users with financial data and software. The Nottingham Building Society collaborates with a bank, a stockbroker, and a travel agent in providing its videotext-based home banking service. On the other hand the joint venture between IBM UK Ltd and British Telecom PLC to develop the JOVE network was vetoed by the UK government, probably for reasons for competition policy above anything. Thus policy-makers as well as business executives realize the strategic potential of IT.

Several driving forces have prompted this transformation. Techno-logical change certainly has been significant. The convergence of data processing, communications, and automation has opened up possibilities of integration, of inter-organizational information processing and of changing the ways of doing business. The continuous cost reduction in hardware, improvement in data storage capabilities, and advances in software have rendered computing more accessible, easier to use, and more exciting to develop. However the context of computing and IT has changed. Smokestack industries look to technology to drive down costs, improve performance, and revolutionize traditional systems of produc-tion. Firms facing global competition, pressures of customization, and restructured market places hope that IT can help them differentiate, be more flexible, and create niches. Sectors undergoing deregulation and liberalization see telecommunications as a means of overcoming time and space constraints, and data and knowledge bases as a means of developing new services and customer sets. Entrepreneurs may see IT and information processing as the new resources available for creating monopoly profits, or at least for yielding long-term 'rents' from sustain-able comparative advantage.

Thus in the late 1970s theorists might have stated that information systems should support business strategy. More than likely this was advocated with a concern that use of IT should be aligned with business needs. Probably the vision of applications was internal and back office in orientation. Today, a second strategic role is argued for information systems. It is argued that IT provides strategic opportunities, that IT can be exploited for competitive advantage and therefore that IT can create strategic options. The vision of applications becomes external as well as internal and front office and beyond the organization as well as back office.

It is therefore not surprising that Porter (1980) asserts that 'the power of technology as a competitive variable lies in its ability to alter com-petition through changing industry structure'. Many writers have built upon Porter's work on competitive strategy to examine the strategic potential of IT. Indeed Porter and Millar (1985) suggest that IT is affecting competition in three vital ways:

1. it changes industry structure and, in so doing, alters the rules of competition,

2. it creates competitive advantage by giving companies new ways to out-perform their rivals, and
3. it sponsors whole new businesses, often from within a company's existing operations.

In the first effect, IT can be used to help implement one of Porter's three generic strategies: it can drive down costs in a lowest cost producer strategy, it can be exploited to distinguish a firm's products or services in a differentiation strategy, or it can be applied in both ways to create or reinforce a focus strategy. In the second effect, IT can be analysed for its potential in limiting or reinforcing Porter's five competitive forces operating in any sector. These comprise new entrants, suppliers, rivals, customers, and new products. In the third effect, IT and information processing can be exploited to 'make a business of information' as a recent UK Government publication proposed. Here the main power comes from information and information services rather than technology and automation.

This suggests an important distinction. The 'technology' of IT provides the information processing and thus is only a facilitator or enabler, *but* it also allows us to automate data-dependent tasks and improve physical processes. The 'information' of IT allows us to improve performance by better control, co-ordination, and decision-making *and* it also allows us to provide and sell new or added value services. Then together tech nology and information provide a potentially huge array of new ends and new means, where strategy uses may grow out of support applications as well as be explicitly developed with competitive advantage in mind.

It seems likely therefore that the perspectives, frameworks, and theories of Data Processing (DP) and Information Systems (IS) which evolved in the 1960s and 1970s will be of limited value in connecting IT and strategy. We now have to understand much more about strategy, the connection and potential of IT and the new business environment that the IT entrepreneurs and innovators are creating today. Both practitioners and researchers need to be aware of an understand these issues, and appreciate both what is new and what has not changed. The three papers in this section seek to provide a backcloth and foundation for this process.

McGee and Thomas present the strategists' view. They examine the nature of the technology–strategy connection, review recent research, and highlight the policy questions which arise. Whilst they are concerned with technology in general, much of their comment can be applied to IT. They conclude by suggesting new directions for research and, by implication, for policy and practice. Interestingly, their recommendations are beginning to be followed by scholars in information management. Indeed some later papers in this volume testify to this claim.

Earl summarizes, from an information management perspective, the work on IT and Competitive Advantage to date. He evaluates the principal frameworks for analysis and suggests their uses and abuses. The intent is to document and discuss the normative literature which has been influential through rhetoric and education. Section Two then provides empirical evidence.

In the third paper, Scott Morton provides a historical perspective on IT and strategy to provide a model of the complexities of strategy formulation. He also exhorts companies to embrace the technologies simultaneously with the knowledge concepts that are emerging in the late 1990s. As a lead into the next two sections, Scott Morton states that strategy formulation is a complex matter and reminds us of the totality of approaches that seem to be required.

References

ITAP (1983), *Making A Business Of Information: A Survey Of New Opportunities*, Information Technology Advisory Panel, HMSO.

Kantrow, A. M. (1980), The Strategy-Technology Connection, *Harvard Business Review*, July–August.

Porter, M. E. (1980), *Competitive Strategy*, The Free Press, New York.

—— and Millar, V. E. (1985), 'How Information Gives You Competitive Advantage', *Harvard Business Review*, July–August.

1

Technology and Strategic Management: A Research Review[1]

JOHN McGEE* and HOWARD THOMAS†

*Templeton College, Oxford

†Department of Business Administration, University of Illinois at Urbana-Champaign

Introduction: the Relevance of Technology

For many years, technological change has been the subject of discussion and research, but only in the last decade have we witnessed the rapid emergence of technology as a major change agent in markets and industries around the world. The scale and pervasiveness of technological change has led to a wide acceptance of technology as a major strategic variable both for corporations and for national governments. Traditionally the strategy literature treats technology as an implementation issue. The firm determines its strategy and this, in turn, defines how technology will be used (Birnbaum et al., 1984). This ignores two problems; how does technology enter into the strategy formulation process, and how are technological capabilities fostered and managed so as to create the basis for competitive advantage? To make progress along these dimensions requires addressing several points; (1) what is the relationship between technology and economic conditions within which strategy is formulated, (2) what characteristics of technology and innovative activity affect the choice and implementation of strategies, (3) how might technological issues be incorporated into strategic planning practice, and (4) how does technology affect the underlying capabilities of firms and how is this translated into competitive advantage? These issues are the agenda of this paper.

Harris, Shaw, and Sommers (1984) focus upon the influence of technology-driven events causing a lack of competitiveness and competitive edge in United States industry. They suggest that in the 1980s 'technology will continue to trigger major market shifts as a new set of trends emerges' (Harris et al., 1984). The trends they foresee are first, continuing technological transformations in low-growth, mature industries such as automobiles, banking, manufacturing, and retailing; second, continuing technological revolutions in high-tech industries

[1] Earlier drafts of this paper were presented to the ESRC Workshop on New Technology at Windsor, UK, May 1985, and the Academy of Management, San Diego, August 1985.

such as semi-conductors; and third, technology will continue to radically change the nature of business definitions and market segmentation. This will in turn lead to the increasing globalization of markets and offer opportunities for organizations to use technological advantages to consolidate their long-term market positions and competitive edge.

Mackenzie and Hesselman (1984) explore the reasons why Western Europe has fallen behind both Japan and the USA in electronics. In terms of the European position they put up for debate three propositions; the fragmented nature of the market in Europe, the nature of corporate strategies required, and the role of public policy. Technology issues are now a matter for debate and decision by governments as well as corporations. The ability of technology to change industry and market conditions is now unquestioned. For recent examples concerning telecommunications and the insurance industry in the UK see Sciberras (1986) and Barras and Swann (1983).

These debates contain elements of frustration because technology is a highly complex activity not amenable to neat generalizations. Technological innovation is a process made up of diverse parts, varied participants, complicated patterns of evolution and information feedback loops, potentially long time duration, and very high cost. The sheer variety of types of technological innovation is the key distinctive characteristic of the subject. This is mirrored (Horwitch and Sakakibara, 1983) by different types of organizations which have distinctive ways of approaching and managing innovation. His own classification distinguishes between three 'pure' modes of innovation; mode 1—innovation in the small high technology firm, mode 2—innovation in the large, multi-product, multi-market, and multi-divisional corporation, and mode 3—innovation in huge multi-organization enterprises that usually involve public and private sector collaboration on mission-oriented, large scale programmes. Table 1.1 summarizes some of the features of this taxonomy and relates them to corporate processes.

Because of the importance of the issues and their inherent complexity many commentators (including Horwitch, Harris and their associates) stress the importance of links between technology, top management, and strategic management. Rumelt (1984) in his thought-provoking paper on the strategic theory of the firm captures the essence of this linkage extremely well:

A firm's strategy may be explained in terms of the unexpected events that created (or will create) potential rents together with the isolating mechanisms that will act to preserve them.

Rumelt judges that successful strategies adapt to unexpected events by capturing available economic rents and preserving them through 'isolating mechanisms' which are firm-level barriers erected to prevent exploitation by others. For Rumelt, key sources of potential rents are changes in technology and discoveries and inventions which may be capitalized and stabilized through patents and trademarks and reputation and image.

Rumelt and others (e.g. Kantrow, 1980; Cooper and Schendel, 1976) have emphasized the technology–strategy connection and have provided the impetus for other strategic management researchers to explore the technology–strategy interface albeit from a wide range of alternative perspectives.

Some observers have remarked on how highly Balkanized is the literature on R&D and Technology. However it is becoming clear that a competitive strategy orientation to the analysis of technological change requires:

1. a prime focus on the ways in which key strategic decisions affect or are affected by changes in technology (not a focus on the changes themselves).
2. the realization that technological change is not merely a company's ability to elevate its technological capabilities, but should be linked with the innovation process and the elaborate system of foresight, planning and application through which abstract capabilities are transformed into saleable products.
3. A view of technology as a central part of the company's thinking at all levels and not as some kind of alien ritual serviced only by the high priests of technology.

This reflects a relatively recent consensus which stems from a number of different research antecedents some of which we discuss in subsequent sections of this paper. We begin with the extensive literature on the economics of technical change. The writings of economists traditionally focus on the nature of competition and markets and the ways in which different technological regimes affect the competitive outcome and the allocation of resources. Much of the literature is disappointing in that it treats technology as given and the firm as some kind of black box thus assuming away some of the most interesting problems of how firms themselves initiate, sponsor, and react to technological change. However, more recent writings take the firm as the unit of analysis (rather than the market) and seek to identify firm-specific skills and competences from which profit streams can be derived. However, this stream of thought is rather silent about particular characteristics of technology and the difficulties of managing them.

So we look briefly at the operations management literature whose direct concern is very often with the specific ways in which technological change affects the production process and the requisite control and management apparatus surrounding the process. This provides some insights into the considerations which lead to technologies being absorbed into firms changing the production boundaries (e.g. through vertical integration) of forming new replacement technology cores in the firm. Some of the lessons from this lead to issues of managing the internal learning process and lead directly to the problems of managing innovation, the subject of the next section.

The management of innovation literature focuses much more on the micro character of technological change in contrast for example; to the contributions of economists which suffer in general from being too macro (and therefore not knowing enough about technology). As a consequence, however, it is very hard to generalize from a scattered literature which does not contain a central theoretical model or frame of reference. The empirical findings seem to support a number of propositions about desirable decision processes within firms. Part of the 'desirable' set of management practices is the entrepreneurial role in championing and sponsoring technological innovation—the subject of the next section. This literature is also rather formless because it lacks a central theoretical core. The role of purposeful management is stressed by expert commentators but we take the discussion back into strategic planning as the arena in which organization and management issues are placed against the environmental and technological contexts.

The strategic planning literature is macro in style and therefore somewhat uncomfortable with the details inherent in technology and struggles with over general caricatures of technology. This section concentrates primarily on ways in which technology might be formally incorporated into a strategic planning logic and specifies in particular those arenas of decision concerning technology with which general managers must be concerned. This leads directly into the next section which discusses the relationship between competitive advantage and technology. At this point we have come full circle from the economists' concerns with competition and markets, through operations management and the very micro nature of innovation management and leadership, through planning processes which should bring together the demands of the market place with the internal capabilities and processes of the organization, and finally to the issue of competitive advantage to which the process of strategic management is directed.

The final section makes some brief comments about the research issues arising out of the earlier discussion concluding with an observation that the abiding problem with research in this area is the lack of empirical content allied to some suitably robust theoretical framework.

The Economics–Technology Interface

Schumpeter (1934) emphasized in his *Theory of Economic Development* that technology and the processes of innovation are important change agents in the structure of industries and competition. Schumpeter also stressed that firm-level issues, such as entrepreneurship and the diffusion of innovations, are important influences in analysing the bases of competition and changes in the structure of competition.

What emerges clearly from the literature on the economics of innovation (Freeman, 1983; Mansfield, 1968; Norris and Vaizey, 1973) is the micro character of innovative activity. This is emphasized very strongly in the scholarly NBER volume (Nelson, 1962) on the rate and direction of inventive activity, Unfortunately it is equally apparent that lack of knowledge stemming from an inadequate framework of enquiry about this micro character inhibits a full understanding of the relationship between invention, innovation, and economic growth. This has seemingly forced many economists to fit the process of innovation and invention into a classical input–output type of economic analysis. Thus, technology is regarded as one of the set of inputs in the mix of productive factors available to the firm or economy which will produce an inventive output in the form of new or improved products and processes.

Among earlier writers Nordhaus (1964), Klein (1962), and Arrow (1969) emphasize some of the distinctive features of the inventive process and suggest that different approaches must be adopted to explain and understand the economic characteristics of the process at the micro level. More recently, writers such as Nelson and Winter (1982), Porter (1983), Rumelt (1984), and Teece (1984) have examined inadequacies involving the treatment of technology in both accepted industrial organization paradigms and the theory of the firm.

Porter states (1983):

Missing in both fields (*the management of technology and industrial economics*) is a comprehensive view of how technological change can affect the rules of competition, and the ways in which technology can be the foundation of creating defensible strategies for firms.

Porter then uses his (1980) competitive strategy framework—the structural analysis of industries—to assess the impacts of technology on industry structures and to help formulate strategy choice for firms in terms of whether it should be a 'first-mover' or innovator in technology or alternatively a 'follower' or imitator. The value of Porter's contribution is that he focuses upon the firm as the appropriate unit of analysis and upon the impact of technology in changing the rules of the competitive game for the firm.

While Teece (1984) concentrates upon the tensions between orthodox economic theory and strategic management, many of his arguments can be applied directly to the debate about the economics–technology linkage at the firm level. For example, in examining the treatment of 'know-how' in orthodox economic theory, he states (p. 89),

The production and utilization of technological and organizational knowledge is a central economic activity that is handled in a most cavalier way within economic theory. By far the most common theoretical approach is simply to take technology as a given, ignoring entirely the fact that the options open to a manager almost always include an attempt at some degree of innovative improvement in existing ways of doing things.

Further weaknesses of existing economic theory which are relevant to the specification of the economics/technology linkage are its *focus on static analysis* whereas innovation is a dynamic process, its *suppression of entrepreneurship* even though some entrepreneurs may provide strong direction and leadership for innovatory processes, and its assumption of *stylized markets* which ignores effects such as reputation and image which characterizes successful innovative firms. To overcome some of these difficulties Teece uses Williamson's (1979) transactions cost approach to link organizational design issues to the adoption of innovations by organizations.

Nelson and Winter's (1982) evolutionary theory of the firm also suggests a framework for the strategic management of technology. The authors propose that a firm has a relatively well-defined and narrow set of strategic capabilities which evolve through experience and learning during its business history. Therefore, firms develop routines or repertoires which reflect the organization's ability to adapt changing circumstances and establish distinctive capabilities and skills. Innovation (arising from a so-called 'technological trajectory') may be one such skill which can provide continuing profitability for the organization if it cannot be readily imitated by its competitors. As noted earlier in the introduction section, Rumelt (1984) provides a theoretic linkage between sources of rents (i.e. changes in technology) and firm-level 'isolating mechanisms' (i.e. patents, discoveries) which reinforce and capture long-term economic rents for the organization. While competitors may wish to imitate the successful firm's policies, they may be impeded both by the presence of isolating mechanisms and their inability to replicate the successful firm's strategy because of lack of knowledge of the idiosyncrasies of its internal decision processes and routines. In Rumelt's terms 'uncertain imitability' may characterize the competitor's tacit state of knowledge about the successful firm's strategy.

In summary, the more recent literature on the economics–technology interface has sought to identify the distinctive firm-level technological competences which may subsequently translate into a sustainable competitive advantage. This competitive advantage may also require the exploitation of firm-level management skills and the ability to recognize the increasing globalization of markets.

The Operations Management–Technology Interface

Many recent writers have stressed the value of co-operation between engineering-oriented technologists and operations strategists in implementing such technological breakthroughs as computerized design and manufacture, flexible manufacturing systems and just-in-time manufacturing philosophies. Wheelwright (1981), Miller *et al.* (1981), and Hax (1981) point to the success of Japanese operations strategy which is often achieved without becoming overly technically oriented. For example, the objectives of automation in Japan were clear and easy to comprehend, both by management as well as the workforce. This led to quick implementation and solid gains in productivity. Compare this with the bad experience of the implementation of Materials Requirement Planning in the United States. The major fault in this situation lay in not educating the management and personnel involved as to its effects and consequences.

Other writers from the manufacturing and operations management area have also stressed the linkages between technology and its implementation in organizational contexts. Starting from Skinner's (1978) work on 'top down' strategic management of manufacturing, Abernathy (1978), Abernathy and Utterback (1978), and Utterback (1978) suggest that operations management and the management of technological innovation are inextricably linked and moreover that operations and technology are themselves an integral part of the strategic thinking of the firm. In general, the writing on operations management leads to an interesting set of propositions about technological change:

1. novel and radical change gives way to incremental cost-reducing refinements
2. external stimuli are replaced by internal learning and development (technology becomes endogenous and controllable)
3. higher degrees of vertical integration and/or coordination are needed to balance successive, technology-intensive stages of production
4. Skinner's (1974) 'focused factory' (tightly integrated operations) as well as the more recent flexible manufacturing systems each require strategic investments in distinctive technology-intensive manufacturing capacity.

However, Cusumano's (1987) study of software production facilities in Japan and the USA gives a much wider meaning to the accepted notion of 'factory'. His concept requires a physical and technological infrastructure, policies and controls to integrate the infrastructure and its driving concepts with the people involved, and above all 'a strategy relying on manufacturing concepts' which would determine the engineering and production concepts that would distinguish the facility from job shop or batch processing organizations. The linkages between manufacturing concepts, overall strategy, internal processes and innovation are particularly clear here.

The Management of Innovation

Research on the management of innovations originally focused on specific projects and firms (Pavitt 1986). The focus of such studies was upon the measurement of the financial costs associated with the development and commercialization of innovations as distinct from the routine expenditures on plant and equipment to produce an established product (Kamin *et al.*, 1982). The findings from such studies indicate that innovative activity is multifunctional and results in highly specific and differentiated technological knowledge relating to specific product or process innovations. Other studies have shown that companies regularly underestimate costs and timescales of innovative activities and show significant variation in the returns on such investment. Both of these features underline the fact that innovative activities remain difficult both to predict and to manage (Downs and Mohr, 1976). Some of the most significant work done in this area was carried out by the Science Policy Research Unit (1971, 1972) under Project SAPPHO. Evidence was collected on the histories of more than forty paired innovations and distinctions were made between factors which contributed to success and those which did not. The key findings of the SAPPHO Project were that successful innovating companies had a better understanding of user needs, paid more attention to marketing and public relations activities, performed their development work more efficiently, made more use of outside science and technology in the specific areas concerned, and were driven by a product champion who normally held varied functional management experience and a relatively senior position in the organization (Rothwell *et al.*, 1974).

More recent empirical studies have confirmed the importance of the conjunction of technological strengths with relevant market demand conditions. In Canada, Cooper (1983) identified new product success as being a result of 'having technical and production synergy and proficiency'. In a similar study in the USA, Maidique (1983) showed that 'new products were more likely to be successful if they were close to the company's existing strengths'.

From such studies as these, there do appear to be consistent findings, namely successful and innovating firms

1. have direct strong in-house R&D;
2. use patents for protection and bargaining;

3. pay careful attention to the market for the innovation;
4. exhibit entrepreneurship in integrating R&D, production and marketing. (Mansfield's (1971) studies on innovation strongly support this and Maidique's (1983) Stanford Hi Tech Project finds a strong coupling between marketing and product-technological developments.)
5. have good communications with the scientific world and their customers.

SAPPHO has not yet found conclusive evidence that *size* of the firm is a necessary prerequisite for innovative activity. Further, the evidence on 'readiness to take risks' being valuable for innovative activity is not yet conclusive, though SAPPHO gives some strong positive indications about risk-taking propensity and innovation. Freeman seems also to speculate that there is an interactive effect between size and risk-taking; small firm environments seem to foster entrepreneurial activity.

Research on project selection approaches (e.g. Thomas, 1973) and the management of innovation, concludes that it will be difficult to reduce the failure rate of innovations by mechanistic use of project selection and control techniques. It suggests strongly that the social context of project 'estimation' is a process of political advocacy and clash of interest groups rather than a sober assessment of probabilities. Using this research evidence in terms of a strategic management paradigm leads towards a hypothesis that strategy towards R&D innovation is more often a matter of advocacy and political debate than of rational analysis. The role of project selection, control, and estimation techniques, such as technological forecasting in strategy evaluation is rather like that of tribal war-dances; they play a very important part in mobilizing, energizing, and organizing for the strategic innovation decision process. In other words, *evaluation* is a prerequisite for the formulation and implementation process.

The role of other elements in this process needs to be better understood and researched through in-depth investigation of firms' decision processes. In particular the following issues ought to be addressed:

1. What is the role of venture capital, sources of finance, and risk-taking in the financing of innovation?
2. Is 'bigness' (in terms of firm size) better in generating innovations at the firm level?
3. How should organizational systems be designed to allow for the moulding together of R&D, production, and marketing in the innovation process (there is abundant evidence that successful innovations combine technical with marketing knowledge)?
4. The design of more flexible strategy evaluation approaches.

5. The communication processes in innovation, e.g. where is information obtained? how is technology transferred? who are the technological gatekeepers?

Doz and Prahalad (1983) are currently undertaking a major cross-national program on the management of innovation which addresses many of the issues raised in the above paragraphs.

Kantrow (1980) summarizes this strand of writing in the following terms:

innovative success appears to be a function of good communication, purposeful allocation of resources, top-level support within the organization, and careful matching of technology with the market.

Entrepreneurship and Technology

Although many have proposed complex multi-stage processes for evaluating and screening innovative activities, others reject this notion:

For those who believe that the organisation structure, control mechanisms, formal decision-making processes, delegation of authority, and other formal aspects of a so-called well-run company are sufficient conditions for successful technological innovation, we can say with confidence that this is not so ... Certain individuals had played (often informal) roles in their initiation, progress and outcome. The role of product champion (or similar designation) is a necessary condition for project success (Rubinstein *et al.*, 1976).

The importance of product champions is acknowledged within Project SAPPHO particularly in modern large firms where their role involves attempting to match technological capabilities with market opportunity. Such individuals are seen as being highly political animals, capable of orchestrating the co-ordination of funds, people, and know-how across different functions and at different levels of the organization. Pavitt (1986) refers to the role of such professionals as being entrepreneurial.

Maidique (1980) makes three principal arguments about the relationship between entrepreneurs and technological innovations as follows:

First, that the entrepreneurial role is essential for radical technological innovation, but that it manifests itself differently depending on the firm's stage of development; second, that radical technological innovation, to be successful, requires top management participation in the entrepreneurial network; third, that in addition to the independent entrepreneur and the product-champion, there is an important intermediate entrepreneurial role especially prominent in diversified firms; that is, the executive champion.

A number of other writers also reflect on the need for entrepreneurs and leaders in the innovation process. Indeed, from a theoretical perspective, Rumelt (1984) and Teece (1984) champion the understanding of the entrepreneurial role at the firm level. The SAPPHO project also indicated the significance of the 'business innovator'. Roberts (1968) concluded that 'enthusiastic sponsorship by entrepreneurially minded individuals' is of key importance. Kantrow (1980) summarizes: 'what makes technology go is exactly what makes business go: coherent strategy and managers closely committed to it.' Rosenbloom (1978) argues the case more extensively, reminding us that strategy formulation calls for a perspective that cuts across functional boundaries, but provides integration by matching capability to opportunity. This echoes Cooper and Schendel's (1976) discussion of the 'strategic responses to technological threats'. Rosenbloom (1978) reminds us also that within the organizational context, strategy provides a guide for translating abstractions (such as competitive advantages) into concrete, implementable terms. Strategy is thus a basis for seeing the linkage of organizational context and process to the environmental and technological context.

The proliferation of formal strategic planning approaches has helped make strategy more 'explicit' and communicable in the face of an increasingly more complex and uncertain environment. But, as a consequence, the other side of strategy, the 'implicit' side, receives less attention.

Implicit strategy, with its focus on people, implementation, ambiguity, structure and system, and instinct, often seems less important than formal strategic planning and to be even more difficult to maintain in good working condition. A key challenge, therefore, for modern corporate strategy is to nurture effectively Implicit Strategy behaviour while also developing relevant Explicit Strategy approaches (Horwitch, 1973).

However, in large multinational enterprises it is not always easy to foster entrepreneurial drive, quick appreciation of and adaptation to change, individual creativity, and all the other hallmarks of 'championing'.

Strategic Planning and Technology

Writers on strategy and strategic planning are united in agreeing that technological choices are quintessentially business decisions. However, managers wishing to incorporate technology explicitly into their corporate planning policies find little help in the traditional literature (e.g. Andrews, 1971). Frohman (1984) observes that

R&D activities are not driven by factors consistent with the strategic priorities of the business. R&D projects are stopped and started, and resources are allocated based not on the company's strategic plan, but rather on history or the R&D manager's interpretation of what would be in the best interests of the business. In the absence of a business framework for decision making, the R&D manager must develop a personal set of criteria.

There appears to be little empirical basis in much of the planning literature. Indeed, it tends towards normative propositions illustrated by pertinent examples. A summary of supposed 'good practice' might run as follows:

The first and most critical step in strategic planning for R&D is for the organization to define clearly the nature of its business. For many firms their history and shared experiences have established the broad outlines of that definition, but the definition needs to be sharpened and articulated before it can be used in formal planning systems. In part, the role of R&D is determined by the industries in which the firm competes. However within a given industry, business have strategy alternatives. A firm may choose to be an industry leader or it may choose to be follower; that choice is important for R&D planning. The firm may choose to pursue primarily offensive or defensive strategies. An offensive strategy is characterized by aggressive search for new products and processes, either within the current product/market family or for new ventures. A defensive strategy focuses on maintaining the marketability of current product or on the improvement of production processes in order to cut costs and increase operating efficiency. A defensive strategy will almost certainly be narrow in scope, but an offensive strategy can either be limited to current products and markets utilizing the company's past experience and strengths, or it may have a clear objective of expanding the current scope of business.

Frohman (1984) proposes the following four step framework for incorporating technological issues into business strategy. In doing so, he leans heavily on the traditional SWOT (Strengths, Weaknesses, Opportunities, Threats) framework.

1. identify the organization's distinctive technical competence,
2. identify technology that contributes or will contribute to business success,
3. co-ordinate business goals and their technological implications
4. align systems for implementation, ensuring that the systems necessary to implement the business strategy support the execution of that strategy.

This reflects a traditional style of planning but calls for an explicit recognition of technology. Perhaps the more significant issue is the recognition that rational frameworks for planning rest critically on good communications between departments, groups, and individuals—more on this below. Frohman's framework has the merit of being explicit in saying that 'knowing your distinctive technical competences allows formulating realistic business goals based on the technological competitive edge.' The essence of 'distinctive technological competence' lies not just in the complexity and minutiae of the technology, the area in which the technologist is rightly the king; it lies also in the output and performance of the technology and it is here that the business discipline should be imposed on the technologist. Frohman breaks down the competence into three areas. First is the technical skill or discipline. The second is the type of work for which the skill can be used. This can be described as a continuum from contract research, preliminary development, design, field testing, and so on, right through to new products. The third aspect is the product or the problem worked upon, the conventional starting point for most product oriented companies.

The value of this approach lies in the identification of *how* the technology affects the other parts of the business (not in *what* the technology is) and in the nature of the process by which it eventually impacts the business (the technology 'production function'). Maidique and Patch (1978) illuminate the technology production function in Porteresque style, as shown in Fig. 1.1.

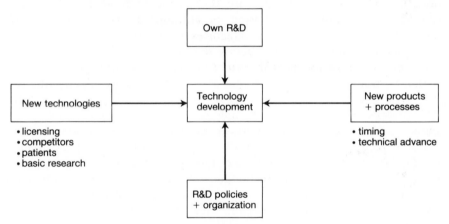

Fig. 1.1. A Framework for Technological Policy (Source: Maidique and Patch, 1978)

The horizontal line reflects the conventional technology flow along which technological criteria condition the decision-making process. The firm's own decisions about the organization of R&D affect the technical efficiency (in the economic sense) of this process—a substantial literature illustrates this. The firm's strategic intent and the reflection of this in its R&D policies and the nature of its R&D activity are intended to discipline and shape the horizontal technology flow.

An understanding of the technology production function helps general managers to understand technology better, and provides a basis for more effective direction and control. The decisions about technology in which general managers should have at least an equal voice include the following:

1. how technology choices should be evaluated
2. what technologies to invest in
3. how technologies should be embedded in new products
4. what level of technical competence is desired
5. what balance should be struck between basic, development, and applied research
6. whether technology should be from internal or external sources
7. organizational and budgetary procedures or R&D departments
8. marketplace strategies in terms of leading, following, and lagging in innovations and product features.

Only after these fundamental objectives are known can R&D planning proceed. This is said clearly recognizing that past and present R&D performance and capabilities are very important considerations in setting the corporate objectives. Once the primary corporate objectives are established, the next steps are the setting of more specific R&D objectives and policies, choosing organizational arrangements, and allocating resources to broad categories of R&D activities. Logically these decisions must be made before questions of project management are even raised. In much of the literature on R&D, strategy answers to major corporate strategy questions are assumed to be given and the emphasis is on project strategy (Bemelmans 1979, Menke *et al.*, 1981). This perspective in the literature may well reflect the kind of corporate thinking which almost unconsciously assumes that the answers to the major strategy questions, based on history, are known to all participants in the planning process. However, mistaken assumptions about corporate objectives can result in the generation of costly useless research. The introduction of formal long-range planning or organizational crisis may serve as a trigger for bringing these fundamental assumptions to the surface.

Effective planning for R&D, or any other function, requires the interaction of a number of contributors. Senior R&D managers must provide strategic planners and decision makers with realistic evaluations of current and potential contributions that their units can make to the business and the amount of resources required to carry out these activities. At the same time other units need to describe their R&D needs (Collier, 1981). These two streams of planning should not be carried out in isolation, but rather there needs to be direct communication between operating units and R&D about needs and capabilities. Marketing strategies will also make an impact on R&D strategies. Attempts to increase market share or to displace a competitor's product may require accelerated R&D. A decision to harvest and perhaps exit from a declining business may make certain lines of research unnecessary.

The most important consideration is to match R&D objectives and programs to other components of the firm's capabilities and objectives. Large scale R&D requires major capital investments and heavy ongoing expense. Unless there are adequate resources; financial, production, marketing, etc., to utilize effectively R&D outputs, resources devoted to R&D will be wasted. Licensing, sale of patents, and other income-producing disposal of R&D outputs are often overlooked returns, but at best they usually only salvage a small portion of the real costs of unused R&D. Unless the broad objectives of the R&D enterprise and its magnitude are matched to the corporate strategic plan, no tinkering with the project portfolio will prevent misuse of resources or compensate for inadequate support of established corporate objectives (Rosenbloom and Kantrow, 1982).

Given the diversity of interests that have a stake in R&D planning, the use of any of a variety of normal processes for policy dialogue would appear to be desirable. While there is a wealth of literature on the use of quantitative decision analysis for project evaluation, there appears to be little or no recorded use of such techniques for setting the overall R&D objectives (Thomas, 1985). Mason and Mitroff's (1981) technique for strategic assumption surfacing would seem to be appropriate given the diversity of interest groups. Although at this stage of planning it may be impossible to assign quantitative outcome measures, techniques for establishing objective hierarchies might be applicable. Keeney and Nair (1976) have described a simple semi-quantitative procedure for goal setting using planning participants' weighting of possible organizational goals. The process would be useful in identifying and resolving goal conflicts.

Strategic Management and Technology

Strategic management researchers in areas such as corporate diversification and organization structure have identified important technological dimensions. In very broad terms, companies have evolved towards a diversified, multidivisional form of organization. Research has been directed towards the nature of the strategic logic that holds such organizations together. Some underlying principle of activity relatedness or synergistic fit is usually specified involving complementarities of financial structure, managerial skills, markets, and technological capabilities. Didrichsen (1982), for example, distinguishes between companies with an 'extensive central technology' (e.g. Du Pont in organic chemicals with seemingly endless potential for generating new product) and a 'branching technology' (e.g. 3M with limited initial expertise in abrasives developed step by step in progressively unrelated directions). Rumelt (1974) provides working definitions for technology relatedness.

Biggadike (1979) and also Salter and Winhold (1979) have followed in the same vein. These studies drive towards the relationships between technological capability, organization structure, and corporate structure and treat this tri-partite relationship as the key to strategic thinking within the company. In the organizational literature, linkages between technology and organizational structure are examined. Burns and Stalker (1961) make a valuable distinction between mechanistic and organic structures where the latter is appropriate to unstable conditions in which, for example, technology is changing rapidly and problems cannot be automatically anticipated and dealt with routinely. Williamson's (1979) transactions cost and control loss ideas can be linked with theories of the multi-product firm (Teece, 1984; Kay, 1983) to examine the nature of transactions costs and property rights of different technologies as firms seek to deal with uncertainty and to collaborate with other firms.

Whereas the 'corporate' level of analysis seeks to understand the issues of relatedness between products and between business units, the 'business' level returns to more conventional territory in asserting that R&D strategy is a function of market characteristics and competitive strengths. Conventional theories of competitive strategy hold that decisions on 'how to compete' determine the shape and direction of resource allocation in functional areas, with an emphasis on the key areas of endeavour and on the co-ordination across those areas to achieve the desired competitive advantage. R&D strategy is one of these functional strategies determined in concert with other functional strategies to obtain a competitive edge.

As a practical matter, however, there are considerable difficulties to be overcome.[2] Following Freeman (1983), one of the salient features of industrial innovation is that both markets and technologies are continually and sometimes rapidly changing. Moreover, as much of the work of the Science Policy Research Unit at Sussex shows, there are considerable stochastic elements in both market changes and in the sources of innovation. Herein lies the fascination with technology and one of the most important reasons for the diversity of literature—the successful innovation is the result of both plain chance and of a range of purposeful efforts. From the viewpoint of the strategy analyst the seemingly random character of the innovative process arises from the high complexity of the interfaces between advancing science, technology, and a changing market. Firms which lie at the nexus of these forces are as much victims as progenitors of the innovative processes. A conclusion from this (again following Freeman) is that the test of successful entrepreneurship and management is the capacity to link together these

---

[2] We are indebted to Ruth Raubitschek for stimulating the thoughts in this section.

technical and market possibilities by managing the information flow within the firm.

This viewpoint complements the current notions of implementation of competitive strategy which focus on 'linkage mechanisms'. Porter (1985) portrays technology as a major source of linkages within the value chain. For Porter, technology strategy is the firm's approach to the development and use of technology and is broader than the role of the formal R&D process because of technology's pervasive impact on the composition of the value chain. Some attempts have been made to link technology strategies at the business unit level with location within the growth-share matrix but these suffer from the familiar problems of over-generality and lack of empirical content. More useful are the relationships drawn between technological leadership and competitive advantage (for example, Maidique and Patch (1978) and Porter (1985)). Maidique and Patch illustrate these interactions by reference to four distinct competitive stances, namely: 'early first-to-market'; 'fast-follower'; 'cost minimizer, late-to-market'; and 'market segmentation, specialist'. Table 1.1 shows the requirements of each strategy for R&D and for other functional strategies.

The power of this approach can be seen by the way in which it calls forth distinctively different R&D strategies. The first-to-market strategy requires strong, almost state-of-the-art, commitments to R&D. Fast following places more emphasis on 'strong and nimble development and engineering ability' with less priority attached to basic research. Late-to-market strategies are based on product and process engineering skills and less exposure to the risk of R&D. Specialization strategies require a cherry picking approach to basic technology and probably needs applied engineering talents and flexibility in manufacturing. Strategies in the market (leading versus following) are reflected in technological choices (leading versus following). To lead requires strengths and capabilities in invention, in innovation, and in large scale product development. Following in product and process technology calls for listening-post activity, development and applied engineering capability, and specialized market (client support) activities. The nexus between competitive strategy and technological policy thus becomes product/process strategy. The product and the process of product development is the 'hinge' between the user on the one side and the value added chain of the firm on the other side.

While this approach at least has some degree of richness and descriptive power it nevertheless is more of a normative guideline than a research paradigm. Nevertheless empirical studies are beginning to emerge (for example, Ghazanfar (1984), and McGee, Ghazanfar, and Thomas (1986)). These and other studies focus on the role of the 'players' intermediating between the technology and the market place

John McGee and Howard Thomas

Table 1.1. *Characteristics of Different Market Strategies*

	R&D	Manufacturing	Marketing	Finance	Organization	Timing
First-to-market	Requires state of the art R&D	Emphasis on pilot and medium-scale manufacturing	Emphasis on stimulating primary demand	Requires access to risk capital	Emphasis on flexibility over efficiency; encourage risk taking	Early entry inaugurates the product life cycle
Second-to-Market	Requires flexible, responsive, and advanced R&D capability	Requires agility in setting up medium scale manufacturing	Must differentiate the product; stimulate secondary demand	Requires rapid commitment of medium to large quantities of capital	Combine elements of flexibility and efficiency	Entry early in growth stage
Late-to-Market or Cost Minimization	Requires skill in process development and cost effective product	Requires efficiency and automation for large-scale production	Must minimize selling and distribution costs	Requires access to capital in large amounts	Emphasis on efficiency and hierarchical control; procedures rigidly enforced	Entry during late growth or early maturity
Market-Segmentation	Requires ability in applications, custom engineering, and advanced product design	Requires flexibility on short to medium runs	Must identify and reach favourable segments	Requires access to capital in medium to large amounts	Flexibility and control required in serving different customers' requirements	Entry during growth stage

Source: Maidique and Patch, 1982

and the nature of the causalities that connect market structure, corporate strategies, and technological change. This cross-linkage between the firm's decisions, the nature of technological change, and competitive advantage can be a fruitful source of hypotheses about the way in which market structures might change. The two matrices in Fig. 1.2 illustrate the possibilities.

Trying to comprehend technological change in terms of its scale and focus (as in Fig. 1.2) has interesting parallels with recent work by Tushman and Anderson (1986). According to them,

Technological change is a bit-by-bit cumulative process punctuated by infrequent discontinuities. These major technological shifts can be classified as *order-breaking* or *order-creating*. Order-breaking discontinuities are those that fundamentally alter either the core product or process of a product class.

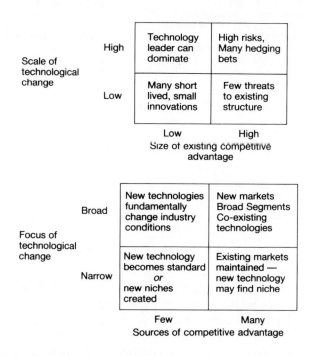

Fig. 1.2. Linkages between Technology and Competitive Advantage

Figure 1.3 illustrates their typology of technological change.

Pavitt (1980) pays more attention to the commitment inherent in insulative activities and provides a link between partial and strategic perspectives within the firm.

Two of the most important points to emerge from Pavitt relate to

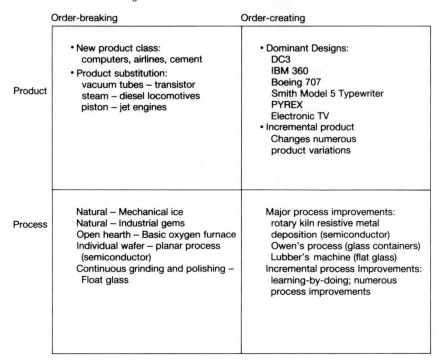

Fig. 1.3. A Typology of Technological Change

1. the capability of the innovation with the firm's existing skills, technology, and product range; and
2. the classification of three types of firm relating to broad sectoral regularities.

According to Steffens (1987) the significance of this lies in the change of perspective from tactical, project level issues to strategic issues through the linkage between technological skills embodied within a particular company and its strategic moves into new products, markets, and technologies. Pavitt suggests that a firm's entry through innovation into a new product class involves once-for-all learning costs which reduce the profitability of earlier product generations compared to those which come later. In particular he suggests that basic designs when entering a product market can be 'robust' in the sense that they are capable of being stretched and adapted to developments in market needs. Thus entry and exploitation of new product markets based upon technological skills will create significant short term costs and such innovations are most likely to be successful when they are used on core technologies close to the existing product market and technology mix of the firm. Therefore the most important conclusion drawn from Pavitt's analysis is that the firm's potential for innovation and for economic return is strongly conditioned by the historical trajectory of innovative activity in the past. Because technology is cumulative and differentiated in nature, firms tend to have different and in many respects unique technological trajectories. Pavitt shows that broad sectoral regularities in the sources and directions of technological progress do emerge as a result of the principal activities of innovation-dominated, production-intensive, and science-based firms. These classifications are suggestive but require further validation and elaboration.

The large scale case studies by Ghazanfar (1985) and Steffens (1987) take Pavitt's work further by concentrating on the interactions of two levels. Firstly between the market place and the firm, and secondly, within the firm. Thus Ghazanfar shows the dynamic interactions between corporate strategy and technological change in reprographics. Steffens traces the development of the personal computer industry and explains the dynamics of the industry in relation to different levels of technological and strategic 'trajectories' (which he calls 'wargame strategies').

Research Issues

Clearly many previous researchers, from economic, production management, decision process, entrepreneurship, and strategy perspectives have grappled with identifying the nature of the relationships between industry-specific and firm-specific characteristics relating to technology on the one hand and strategic choices and organizational processes on the other hand. They are particularly interested in the way in which technological conditions shape the framing of strategy and the nature of the internal implementation processes that are required for 'success'.

It follows from the previous discussion and synthesis of the literature that the link between achieving sustainable competitive advantage in the market and exploiting the information derived from technological change depends on a number of factors including most importantly:

1. coherent strategy (purposeful allocation of resources together with top management commitment);
2. good intra-organizational communications;
3. the nature of the technological change; and
4. the technological capabilities of the firm.

We define technology as information—the specifications for a product or a process which when built will 'work'. Thus technology at any time is merely a set of blueprints (following Hay and Morris, 1979). The general proposition maintains that broadly focused, more 'basic' research (the 'R' of R&D) is from the firm's point of view a quite different animal than narrowly focused, more incremental development work (the 'D'). The former can be said to be an investment in 'key' and 'enabling' technologies and represent an entry fee into certain market segments. The outcome of 'basic' research can be seen as the acquisition of intangible assets which are highly differentiated from firm to firm. Such assets represent the base from which product-market selection and product development takes place. Basic research or new knowledge diffuses over time and development work may be carried out by firms who have not been involved in the basic research. Development proceeds from a different skill or asset base and represents an ability to capture existing knowledge in varieties of detailed forms to meet specific market needs. The outcome of development is product (or process) placed against market requirements. 'Research' decisions, therefore, are of a different kind than 'Development' decisions. There are greater technological uncertainties about the nature and cost of final outcomes, and about the chances of appropriating the benefits. By contrast, development decisions are more explicitly commercial and are more highly appropriable by the firm involved. Consequently, one expects to observe differences in the conditions under which firms would commit themselves to knowledge acquisition rather than product development. The formal decision-making procedures would be different, involving different people, using different information, and emphasizing different features. Furthermore the organizational processes of initiation and innovation would also involve different personnel, employ different information and control systems, and have different linkages into the rest of the organization. As far as the firm itself is concerned, there are issues of 'confidence' and issues of 'emergence'. Issues of confidence concern the *decision* to commit resources to technological change and reflect the coherence of its strategy. This involves analytic questions of competitive position, market intelligence, and internal capabilities. It also involves vision, foresight, and entrepreneurial spirit. Here can be observed decisions of commission/omission, decisions of scale, and decisions calibrated against the competitive environment. These decisions reflect the firm's judgement of its external competitive position, its own abilities to innovate, and the nature of opportunities and threats posed by the technological environment in which it operates.

Whereas issues of confidence relate to the nature of competitive advantage obtainable through technological change, issues of emergence focus much more on the nature of the internal processes which shape the decision-making and carry technological change through to the market. There exists a significant literature in this general area. At a high level of abstraction the Burns and Stalker (1961) discussion points to broad organizational characteristic (e.g. organic versus mechanistic) and their relationship to degrees of turbulence in the environment.

More recently and at a more practical level, the work of the Science Policy Research Unit, SPRU (1971, 1972), has highlighted the need for communication between different parts of the organization in the pursuit of innovation. Thus specific links between market intelligence and product development are recommended, and more generally co-ordination across functional boundaries is deemed more important than vertical, efficiency-driven divisions between functions. A simple but central proposition here is that intra-organizational linkages will be stronger in more successful firms, will vary according to closeness of the technological effort to market, and also according to the scale of the effort.

Our major concern in this paper has been the way in which technology shapes the strategic decisions of firms. In this context we see the existing literature as either too 'macro' or too 'micro' in character. Where we see firms as the critical intermediators between science and the marketplace, some of the literature omits the players and looks only at the reduced form relationship of inputs and outputs. Other literature concentrates on units of analysis that lie within the players and thus loses sight of the essential patterning in the allocation of resources that is quintessentially the strategic element. The lack of empirical content to which we have repeatedly referred varies because the unit of analysis ought to be the firm (in some cases, the business unit)—a charge to which the SAPPHO studies may be held honourably free.

References

Abernathy, W. J. (1978), *The Productivity Dilemma: Roadblock to Innovation in the Automobile Industry*, Johns Hopkins University Press, Baltimore, Md.

—— and Utterback, J. M. (1978), 'The Evolution of Innovation', *Technology Review* MIT Alumni Association, June–July.

Andrews, K. (1971), *The Concept of Corporate Strategy*, Irwin, Homewood, Ill.

Arrow, K. J. (1969), 'Classificatory Notes on the Production and Transmission of Technological Knowledge', *AER Papers and Proceedings* **LIX**.

Barras, R., and Swann, J. (1983), *The Adoption and Impact of Information Technology in the UK Insurance Industry*, Technical Change Centre, London.

Bemelmans, T. (1979), 'Strategic Planning for Research and Development', *Long Range Planning* **12**, pp. 33–44.

Biggadike, E. R. (1979), *Corporate Diversification: Entry, Strategy and Performance*, Division of Research, Harvard Business School, Boston, Mass.

Birnbaum, D. H., Weiss, A. R., Steavas, T. M., and Offenaneger, E. J. (1984), *Strategic Management of Technology*, unpublished working paper, Indiana, June

Burns, T., and Stalker, G. M. (1961), *The Management of Innovation*, Tavistock Publications, London.

Collier, D. (1981), 'Linking R&D and Strategic Planning', *Journal of Business Strategy* **2, 2**, pp. 71–81.

Cooper, A. C., and Schendel, D. E. (1976), 'Strategic Response to Technological Threats', *Business Horizons* **19, 1**, pp. 61–9.

Cooper, R. (1983), 'A Process Model for Industrial New Product Development', *IEEE Transactions on Engineering Management* **EM-30**.

Consumano, M. (1987), *The Software Factory Reconsidered: Strategy–Technology Implementation*, unpublished working paper, MIT, January.

Didrichsen, J. (1982), 'The Development of Diversified and Conglomerate Firms in the United States, 1920–1970', *Business History Review* **46, 3**.

Downs, G. W. jun., and Mohr, L. B. (1976), 'Conceptual Issues in the Study of Innovation', *Administrative Science Quarterly* **21**, pp. 700–14.

Doz, Y., and Prahalad, C. K. (1983), *The Management of Innovation in Large Complex Firms*, Research Proposal, Joint INSEAD–University of Michigan Research Programme.

Freeman, C. (1983), *The Economics of Industrial Innovation* (2nd Edn.), MIT Press, Cambridge, Mass.

Fruhman, A. L. (1984), 'Meshing Technology with Strategy', *Research Management* **XXVII, 6**.

Ghazanfar, A. (1984), *An Analysis of Competition in the Office Reprographics Industry in the UK, 1880–1980*, Ph.D. thesis, University of London.

Harris, J. M., Shaw, R. W. jun., and Sommers, W. P. (1984), 'The Strategic Management of Technology', in *Competitive Strategic Management* (ed. Lamb, R. B.) Prentice-Hall, Englewood Cliffs, N.J., pp. 530–56.

Hax, A. C. (1981), 'Commentary on "Production/Operations Management: Agenda for the 80s"', *Decision Science* **12, 4**, pp. 574–7.

Hay, D. A., and Morris, D. (1979), *Industrial Economics: Theory and Evidence*, Oxford University Press.

Hayes, R. H., and Abernathy, W. J. (1980), 'Managing our Way to Economic Decline', *Harvard Business Review*, July–August, pp. 67–77.

—— and Garvin, G. A. (1982), 'Managing as if Tomorrow Mattered', *Harvard Business Review*, May–June, pp. 71–9.

Horwitch, M., and Sakakibara, K. (1983), *The Changing Strategy–Technology Relationship in Technology-Based Industries: A Comparison of the United States and Japan*, paper presented at the Annual Conference of the Strategic Management Society, Paris, October.

Kamin, J., Bijarni, I., and Horesh, R. (1982), 'Some Determinants of Cost Distributions in the Process of Technological Innovation', *Research Policy* **11, 2**.

Kantrow, A. M. (1980), 'The Strategy–Technology Connection', *Harvard Business Review*, July–August, pp. 6–21.

Kay, N. (1983), *The Innovative Firm*, Macmillan, London.

Keeney, R. L., and Nair, K. (1976), 'Setting Goals in a Professional Service Firm', *Long Range Planning* **9**, pp. 54–9.

Klein, B. (1962), 'The Decision-Making Problem in Development', in Nelson, R. R. (ed., op. cit).

Mackenzie, I., and Hesselman, L. (1984), 'European Electronics in an Era of US–Japanese Competition', working paper, Centre for Business Strategy, London Business School.

Maidique, M. A. (1980), 'Entrepreneurs, Champions, and Technological Innovation', *Sloan Management Review* **21, 2**, pp. 59–76.

—— (1983), *The Stanford Innovation Project: A Comparative Study of Success and Failure in High Technology Product Innovation*, Management of Technology Conference Proceedings, Worcester Polytechnic Institute.

Maidique, M. A., and Patch, P. (1978), 'Corporate Strategy and Technological Policy', in Tushman, M. L., and Moore, W. L. (eds.) *Readings in the Management of Innovation* Pitman.

Mansfield, E. (1968), *Industrial Research and Technological Innovation*, Norton, New York.

—— *et al.* (1971), *Research and Innovation in the Modern Corporation*, Norton, New York.

Mason, R. O., and Mitroff, I. I. (1981), *Challenging Strategic Planning Assumptions*, John Wiley, New York.

Menke, M. M., Gelzer, J., and Pezier, J. P. (1981), 'Evaluating Basic Research Strategies', *Long Range Planning* **14**, pp. 44–57.

Miller, J. G. *et al.* (1981), 'Production/Operations Management: agenda for the 80s', *Decision Science* **12**, **4**, pp. 547–71.

Nelson, R. R. (ed.) (1962), *The Rate and Direction of Inventive Activity*, National Bureau of Economic Research, Princeton, N.J.

—— and Winter, S. G. (1982), *An evolutionary Theory of Economic Change*. Harvard University Press, Cambridge, Mass.

Nordhaus, W. (1964), 'An Economic Theory of Technological change', *AER Papers and Proceedings*, **LXIV**.

Norris, K., and Vaizey, J. (1973), *The Economics of Research and Technology*, Allen and Unwin, London.

Pavitt, K. (1984), *Technology, Innovation and Strategic Management*, working paper, SPRU, University of Sussex, May. Also published in *Strategic Management Research: A European Perspective*, (eds. McGee, J., and Thomas, H.) John Wiley, New York 1986.

Porter, M. E. (1980), *Competitive Strategy*. Free Press, New York.

—— (1983), 'The Technological Dimension of Competitive Strategy', in Rosenbloom, R., (ed.), *Research on Technological Innovation, Management and Policy*, **I**, JAI Press, Greenwich, CT.

—— (1985), *Competitive Advantage: Creating and Sustaining Superior Performance*, Free Press, New York.

Roberts, E. B. (1968), 'Entrepreneurship and Technology', *Research Management*, **XI**, **5**.

Rosenbloom, R. S. (1978), 'Technological Innovation in Firms and Industries: An Assessment of the State of the Art', in Kelly, P., and Kranzberg, M. (eds.) *Technological Innovation*, San Francisco Press, San Francisco.

—— and Kantrow, A. (1982), 'The Nurturing of Corporate Research', *Harvard Business Review* **60**, pp. 115–23.

Rothwell, R. *et al.* (1974), 'SAPPHO Updated—Project SAPPHO Phase II', *Research Policy* **3**.

Rubenstein, A. H. (1976), 'Factors Influencing Innovation Success at the Project Level', *Research Management* **XIX**, **3**.

Rumelt, R. P. (1974), *Strategy, Structure and Economic Performance*, Division of Research, Harvard Business School, Boston.

—— (1982), *Towards a Strategic Theory of the Firm*, paper prepared for conference on 'Non-traditional Approaches to Policy Research', University of Southern California, November.

Salter, M. S., and Winhold, W. A. (1979), *Diversification through Acquisition: Strategies for Creating Economic Value*, Free Press, New York.

Scherer, F. M. (1984), *On the Current State of Knowledge in Industrial Economics*, discussion paper, IIMU/Struktrupolitik—IIM/Industrial Policy, Berlin, August.

Schumpeter, J. A. (1934), *The Theory of Economic Development*, Harvard University Press, Cambridge, Mass.

Sciberras, E. (1986), 'Changing Competitive Strategies in the Telecommunications Subscriber Equipment Industry', *Omega* **14, 5.**

Science Policy Research Unit, University of Sussex (1971), *Report on Project SAPPHO* (2 volumes), Centre for the Study of Industrial Innovation, London.

—— (1972), *Success and Failure in Industrial Innovation*, Centre for the Study of Industrial Innovation, London.

Skinner, W. (1974), 'The Focussed Factory', *Harvard Business Review*, May/June, p. 113.

—— (1978), *Manufacturing in the Corporate Strategy*. John Wiley, New York.

Steffens, J. (1987), *Entry Behaviour and Competition in the Evolution of the United States Personal Computer Industry 1975–1983*, Ph.D. Thesis, University of London.

Teece, D. J. (1984), 'Economic Analysis and Strategic Management', *California Management Review* **26, 3,** pp. 87–110.

Thomas, H. (1985), 'Decision Analysis and Strategic Management of Research and Development: A Comparison Between Applications in Electronic and Ethical Pharmaceuticals', *R&D Management* **15, 1,** pp. 3–21.

Thomas, H. (1973), 'The Assessment of Project Worth with Applications to Research and Developments', in J. N. Wolfe (ed.), *Cost-Benefit and Cost-Effectiveness* Allen and Unwin, London.

Tushman, M. L., and Anderson, P. (1986), *Technological Discontinuities and Organisation Environments*, paper presented to ESRC/Coopers and Lybrand International Research Seminar: The Management of Strategic Change at University of Warwick.

Utterback, J. M. (1978), 'Management of Technology' in Hax, A. C. (ed.), *Studies in Operations Management*, North-Holland.

Wheelwright, S. C. (1981), 'Japan—Where Operations Really are Strategic', *Harvard Business Review*, July–August, pp. 67–74.

Williamson, O. E. (1979), 'Transactions cost Economics: the Governance of contractual Relations', *Journal of Law and Economics* **22,** pp. 223–61.

2

IT and Strategic Advantage: A Framework of Frameworks

MICHAEL J. EARL

Oxford Institute of Information Management, Templeton College, Oxford

It is widely argued today, and is the theme underpinning this volume, that IT is becoming a strategic resource. The introduction to this section paints a scenario of the capabilities of IT continually increasing and the political, social, and economic context of its use undergoing simultaneous radical changes. This combination of contextual forces for change and technological advance has created considerable rhetoric, if not 'hype', about the strategic potential of IT. A stream of persuasive articles has emerged to make the case (Parsons, 1983; McFarlan, 1984; Benjamin *et al.*, 1984; Porter and Millar, 1980) and academics, consultants and practitioners alike are constantly searching for the latest exemplar application of IT which has yielded competitive advantage.

We can generalize that IT can be applied strategically in at least four different ways:

1. to gain competitive advantage,
2. to improve productivity and performance,
3. to facilitate new ways of managing and organizing,
4. to develop new businesses.

Of course, the boundaries between these uses are imprecise and the categories overlap, but they each represent different *intents*. However, it could be claimed that computing, DP, IS, etc. have always been pursuing such goals. This is partially true; the difference today is that the multiplication and convergence of information technologies provide more potential and the structural changes in economies, industries, and organizations more opportunities. Thus some writers, such as Wiseman (1985), argue that a new breed of information systems—'strategic information systems'—has arrived. Various workers therefore draw new systems pyramids to represent this phenomenon as in Fig. 2.1.

A strategic information system presumably either supports or facilitates a particular business strategy or some facet of it. To a degree, an information system may be strategic only in the eye of the beholder since one can envisage a decision support system being used as a

Michael Earl

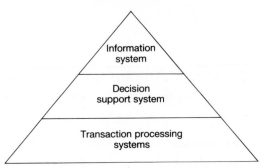

Fig. 2.1.   The 'New' IS Pyramid

strategic tool or product and since many well known strategic information systems also would be classified as transaction processing systems.

It is therefore perhaps the strategic perspective on IT and information
systems which is new. In a few years time, the concepts and practice will
be quite normal. In the meantime influential articles continue to appear,
demonstrating that IT can yield strategic gains and suggesting where
opportunities can be found. Mostly they provide frameworks for
analysis. None of them offers a complete answer; equally, most of them
are helpful if used appropriately. Accordingly this paper presents several
of the well-known frameworks (a) as a way of overviewing the evidence
for strategic information systems and (b) to try and suggest their relative
purposes and merits. A framework of frameworks is presented therefore
to help guide users and researchers through the maze. This analysis is
based on experimentation with available models and frameworks in
management education, research, and consulting.

The framework of frameworks is presented in Fig. 2.2. Three classes of
framework are proposed: awareness, opportunity, and positioning, each
having its own purpose, character, and use. These three classes are
subsequently subdivided into three further subclasses to reflect differences of analysis or approach. The implication of the framework of
frameworks is that a selection of frameworks works best, whether for
education or practical use, but that the right framework must be used
for the right purpose in the right context.

Framework Quality	Awareness	Opportunity	Positioning
Purpose	Vision	Ends	Means
Scope	Possibility	Probability	Capability
Use	Education	Analysis	Implementation

Fig. 2.2.   A Framework of Frameworks

Awareness Frameworks

What these frameworks seem best to achieve is executive appreciation and understanding of the strategic potential and impact of IT. Awareness frameworks are more conceptual and pedagogic than prescriptive and instrumental. Extremely useful in the workshop or classroom, they hint at strategic possibilities of IT, may begin to paint a vision for specific executives, firms, or industries, and help reorient thinking and delimit the scope. In short, their primary use turns out to be educational.

Three subclasses of awareness frameworks may be identified:

1. refocusing frameworks which help change mind-sets,
2. impact models which suggest the scale of strategic change that may be possible, and
3. scoping models which indicate what might be the overall strategic scope of IT for a business or sector.

An early example of a *refocusing framework* is that of Benjamin *et al.* (1984) reproduced in Fig. 2.3. Their strategic opportunities matrix is, like many of the frameworks, a rationalization of recent clever uses of IT. It is founded on two searching questions which they suggest each senior manager should ask:

Can I use IT to make a significant change in the way we are doing business so my company can gain a competitive advantage?

Should we, as a company, concentrate on using IT to improve our approach to the market place? Or should we centre our efforts on internal improvements in the way we currently carry out the activities of the firm?

The four-cell matrix in Fig. 2.3 reflects these questions and reminds companies that strategic advantage can be gained from traditional systems as much as from revolutionary approaches—whether applied in the market place or internally.

The cases quoted by Benjamin *et al.* demonstrate their refocusing

	Competitive marketplace	Internal operations
Significant structural change	Merrill Lynch	Digital Equipment
Traditional products and processes	American Hospital Supply	United Airlines

Fig. 2.3. Strategic Opportunities Framework (Benjamin *et al.*)

model very effectively, Merrill Lynch's Cash Management Account exploited computing and telecommunications in a strategic alliance with Banc One of Ohio to create a new product market which they dominated, erect barriers to entry, and break the conventional boundaries of the financial sector. American Hospital Supply used terminal-based order entry facilities in their customers to make a virtue out of a large product range and increase market share dramatically in a very competitive sector. DEC developed 'XCON', an expert system, to create computer configurations for customers, building on the knowledge of design and field service engineers. This reduced costs of rework, reduced installation delays, and thus improved both DEC's cash flow and their customers' satisfaction. It also provided a sales tool for their sales engineers. United Airlines used teleconferencing in operations management to co-ordinate across airports in emergency situations, daily briefings, and labour negotiations.

The Benjamin *et al.* framework, by demonstration therefore, is valuable in raising executive awareness and refocusing perspectives on IT. It is less satisfactory as a searching framework for a firm because it is not specific enough by application or technology or analytical enough in terms of business strategy or management process. However it could be used to place existing IT initiatives in the firm to derive a general picture of progress.

A detailed example of an *impact model* is the contribution of Parsons (1983). It is based on a recognition and analysis of the competitive environment and strategies of business and focuses on the possible opportunities of firms to exploit IT for strategic advantage. Summarized in Table 2.1, Parson's model reminds us that IT can be influential at the industry, firm or strategy levels.

Table 2.1.   *Strategic Impact of IT (after Parsons)*

Level of impact	Effect of IT
Industry level	Changes fundamental nature of the Industry
Firm level	Influences competitive forces facing the firm
Strategy level	Supports the generic strategy of the firm

At the industry level, Parsons points out that IT can affect the nature of an industry's products and services, the industry's markets, and/or the industry's economics of production. For example, electronic publishing, computer graphics, and communications have substantially affected the product life-cycle and distribution possibilities in publishing. The power of both the technology and the information of IT have been demonstrated dramatically in the newspaper sectors of both the USA and the UK.

At the firm level, Parsons draws on Porter's five competitive forces model of competitive strategy. This model is discussed later but the key message of Parsons is that IT can be used either to limit or enhance the power of rivals, competitors, suppliers, new entrants, or new products in the firm's wider competitive arena.

Parsons also borrows from Porter in his strategy level impact analysis. Here he is concerned with the positioning that successful firms adopt relative to industry structure and competitive forces. Parsons argues that IT can support each of the possible three generic strategies that Porter suggests are available to firms. These are:

1. Overall cost leadership—pursuit of lowest cost production on an industry-wide basis
2. Differentiation—differentiating a product or service on an industry-wide basis
3. Focus—concentration on a particular market or product niche.

Clearly many technologies can be applied to cost reduction, for example substituting robotics for labour, driving down inventory costs with stock control systems, or automating effort-intensive or inefficient manufacturing with CAD/CAM or process control. A packaging company sought to become the lowest cost producer in Europe. Relatively late in development of information systems it had the opportunity to explicitly align investment in IT with its lowest cost strategy. Inventory control systems to reduce working capital costs, instrumentation and process controllers to monitor and reduce inefficiencies, cost control reports to target variances, optimization models to improve throughput, and an automated warehouse to reduce stockholding costs were the main foci for investment.

Differentiation is concerned with creating uniqueness in the eyes of the customers. This may be achieved through product features, customer service, added value services, technological sophistication, brand image, flexibility, quality, or customization. Both information content or technological innovation can be exploited to enhance the product or its distribution; online ordering, computerized quotation systems, or expert system advice are examples. Friends Provident, the UK Insurance company, introduced FRENTEL, an online quotation service to brokers. The objective was to differentiate in an intensely competitive market place where the leading market share does not exceed five per cent. The quotation, query, policy producing, and support facilities of FRENTEL soon earned broker loyalty in the market.

Focus strategies often combine low cost and differentiation, targeting a particular niche. The rationales vary, but technology can be used to reach special niches, information systems can be developed to be better informed about them, and combinations of IT support of low cost and differentiation strategies can be applied when focus becomes necessary in very competitive markets. An accounting firm which has identified high-value niche markets for specialist advisory services, builds databases on clients, experiences, leads, and specialist knowledge all as a foundation from which they can create an image of being the unique player in that niche.

Parsons's impact framework therefore becomes a tool of persuasion. It argues that IT truly does have strategic influence. It can be tailored to a particular industry or firm to explore current trends of future potential, but at a preliminary stage of analysis. It can also be used, particularly at his strategic level, to test if current IS investments in a firm are supporting its generic strategy. Essentially, however, the strength of Parsons's framework is pedagogical—to argue through whether IT is strategic.

Porter and Millar (1985) provided a useful example of a *scoping model*. It is not always easy to see how information can be developed and exploited for competitive advantage. Information processing concepts can be vague and we still tend to see business and industries as providers of products and occasionally services, where information is a peripheral concern. Porter and Millar's information intensity matrix brings the information dimension to industry analysis with useful examples, and can be used as a preliminary assessor of overall potential for exploiting IT for strategic advantage in a particular sector. For whilst a general trend in the strategic importance of IT is evident, at the industry level the direction and pace of change differ. Their matrix in Fig. 2.4 can be used to predict the scope, degree, and rate of change induced by IT for different industries, and thus also can help position a firm accordingly.

The vertical dimension of the matrix measures the information intensity of the value chain—discussed later but briefly defined as the 'Company's technologically and economically distinct activities it performs to do business'. The horizontal axis represents the information content in the product. The publishing industry discussed above rates high on both dimensions—as would most financial services. The oil

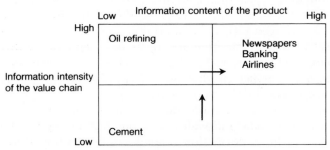

Fig. 2.4.   Porter and Millar's Information Intensity Matrix

industry has high information processing in its production and distribution, but little information content in its product. The cement industry is essentially a physical, process industry producing bulk, industrial product and IT unlikely to have any dramatic impact on it. Thus we see many exemplars of strategic information systems in the finance sector, the oil and petrochemical industries striving for competitive advantage and making small but not major gains, and one UK cement company recently running down much of its DP capability. However, as the capability of IT increases and the cost decreases, we can expect industries to move towards ever higher information content in both process and product, as the arrows in the matrix imply.

Thus awareness frameworks tend to have high pedagogic value in raising the vision of executives, and IT professionals, for strategic use of information technologies. They show broadly what are the possibilities afforded by IT—but they are generally too high level and too descriptive to guide users to specific opportunities for strategic information systems. That is the purpose of opportunity frameworks.

Opportunity Frameworks

These frameworks are designed explicitly to be analytical tools which lead to firm-specific strategic advantage opportunities and/or clarify business strategies in order to demonstrate options for using IT strategically. They are more instrumental and practical than awareness frameworks, but do have an educational role too. Indeed many of the judgements made in this section are derived from using these opportunity frameworks in workshops during management education programmes at the Oxford Institute of Information Management. In principle, however, opportunity frameworks aid the process of analytical discovery of ideas for strategic information systems—probabilities to be examined further by feasibility studies.

Three subclasses may be identified:

1. Systems analysis frameworks—which provide analytical techniques to apply across a business.
2. Applications search tools—which probe the characteristics of specific application areas for good fit with the potentials of IT in general or of specific technologies.
3. Business strategy frameworks—which evaluate the business strategy context and suggest where IT has a payoff.

Systems Analysis Frameworks

Systems analysis frameworks which investigate the information flows, impediments, gaps, and opportunities in business processes and

activities are valuable because they are not confined to any particular
application area or technology. They are generic. Thus even traditional
methods of systems analysis and more recent methodologies of information requirements analysis may help. However they rarely have a
strategic perspective. Porter and Millar's value chain analysis is more
promising as it focuses on competitiveness and the role of technology.

Value chain analysis divides a company's activities into the technologically and economically distinct activities it performs to do business.
These are called value activities because they should add value for
which customers are willing to pay when they buy the final product or
service being supplied. A business is profitable if the value it creates
exceeds the cost of performing the value activities. To gain competitive
advantage over its rivals, a company must either perform these activities
at a lower cost or perform them in a way that leads to differentiation
and a premium price.

Figure 2.5 displays the nine typical activities of the value chain,
comprising five primary activities involved in the production, marketing,
distribution, and after-sales servicing of the product plus four support
activities which provide the inputs and infrastructure that allow the
primary activities to take place. A firm's value chain is a system of
interdependent activities which are connected by linkages. Linkages
exist when one activity affects another in terms of cost or effectiveness;
trade-offs and optimization are sought to find the right blend to achieve
competitive advantage. Also linkages require co-ordination. One firm's
value chain, of course, is embedded in the collective value chains of both

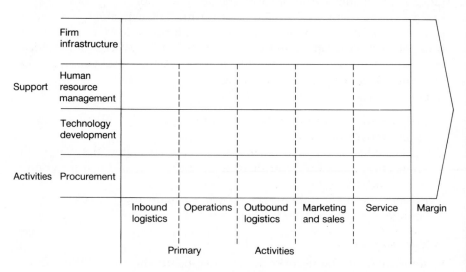

Fig. 2.5. Porter and Millar's Value Chain

suppliers and customers in the industry. This industry stream of activities is termed the 'value system' by Porter and Millar.

The scope for exploitation of IT in the value chain is fourfold, applying either technology directly, or its information processing capability, to either value activities or their linkages:

1. The technology can automate and improve the physical tasks in any activity e.g. computer controlled machine tools in assembly operations.
2. The technology can physically connect and control activities across linkages, e.g. communications links between production and distribution centres.
3. Information systems can help perform, support, or manage value activities, e.g. inventory control systems.
4. Information systems can optimize or co-ordinate activities across linkages e.g. CAD–CAM systems for computer integrated manufacturing.

Clearly these applications can be beyond the firm, in the wider value system interfacing with suppliers and customers, as well as internal. Such external possibilities include telemarketing, remote sensing of equipment breakdowns or stock-outs, and ATMs.

Just mapping the firm's operations and processes by the value chain technique has limited value. It provides no more than a high level check-list and possible prompt for IT applications. Nevertheless one service company which had successfully exploited IT in marketing discovered by value chain analysis that its main cost-base was in procurement and began to shift its focus of IS development accordingly. The key therefore is to ascertain the cost of each activity and analyse whether there is opportunity to reduce costs or add value through IT and IS. This may highlight principal areas for attention. Secondly, the linkages then can be analysed to see if there are problems of or opportunities for co-ordination, integration, or optimization.

Systems analysis frameworks therefore help in 'homing in' on opportunities. They direct the analyst towards areas of promise. They cannot prescribe what particular technologies have potential, and they do not delve into the specific possibilities of highlighted application areas. Thus detailed application ideas may have to be elicited from application users and specialists—or prompted by more specific frameworks such as those in the next sub-class.

Applications Search Tools

Applications search tools focus on a specific application area (and perhaps also on a specific technology) describing, analysing, and evaluating in detail the typical information processing requirements, attributes, or gaps. A useful example is the customer resource life cycle of Ives and Learmonth. This plots the life cycle of how a customer acquires a product or service and therefore focuses on the linkage between the supplying firm and its customers. The goal is to see where IS and IT can be harnessed to improve customer service, with benefits to each party. The supplier uses IT to solidify its business relationship with its customers, while the customer benefits from the added value of enhanced customer service. Incidentally, Ives and Learmonth claim that the potential value of such activities for building customer loyalty, defending market share, and creating competitive advantage often goes unnoticed. Their customer resource life cycle, reproduced in Table 2.2 is a development of earlier work by Burnstine (1980). Runge and Earl (1987) have taken the framework a small step further, in terms of telecommunications technology.

Table 2.2.   *Customer Resource Life Cycle (Ives and Learmonth)*

Requirements
Establish requirements—how much of the resource is required?
Specify requirements—what are the required resource's particular attributes?

Acquisition
Select source—from whom will the customer obtain the resource?
Order—how will the customer order the product?
Authorize and pay for—how will the customer pay for the product?
Acquire—how, where, and when will the customer take possession of the resource?
Test and accept—how does the customer ensure the resource conforms to specifications?

Stewardship
Integrate—how is the resource merged with inventory?
Monitor—in what ways can the customer monitor the resource?
Upgrade—how will the resource be enhanced if conditions change?
Maintain—how will the resource be repaired if it becomes necessary?

Retirement
Dispose of—how will the customer move, return, sell, or dispose of the resource when it is no longer needed?
Account for—how much is the customer spending on the resource?

The major phases of the life cycle are:

1. Requirements: determining the requirements of the resource
2. Acquisition: obtaining or developing the resource
3. Stewardship: managing the resource while in inventory
4. Retirement: disposing of the resource.

Using Ives and Learmonth's examples, Chevrolet's touch-screen micro-computer system which asks showroom customers about their driving habits and type of vehicle desired, and then recommends several models based on this analysis of needs, is an example of a competitive information system supporting the specify requirements step of the requirements phase of the life cycle. An estate agency provides brokers with access to an online mortgage search service. The system assists prospective home buyers in selecting among mortgage opportunities available through multiple sources. This is an example of a system supporting the select-a-source step of the acquisition phase. A case of a system supporting the maintain step of the stewardship phase is provided by a consumer appliance manufacturer. They provide toll-free telephone access to trained repair technicians who are backed up by computer-based assistance in trouble-shooting common problems. The disposal step of retirement is exemplified by the hotel chains who now use IT to permit guests to check out of rooms without the time-consuming process of dealing with a desk clerk. Many other examples are illustrated by Runge and Earl in Chapter 7 of this volume.

The way to use these application examination tools is to assemble an opportunity search team of line and staff managers from the application area, together with IS specialists. In the case of the customer resource life cycle framework, those responsible for product development, product management, sales and distribution would be included. Also, customers might be involved. The team is charged with generating ideas for prospective applications. Aided by the tool, the group then critically reviews current performance and practices, considers what competitors might be doing and aims to discover new and innovative opportunities presented by either development of new systems or enhancement of existing ones. We have adopted this approach in Oxford, using Feeny's marketing opportunities framework (summarized in Chapter 6 of this volume) in information systems workshops for sales and marketing personnel. Thus applications examination tools can be used in singular, targeted studies. However they are often given impetus by the prior use of business strategy frameworks.

Business Srategy Frameworks

Business strategy frameworks are required either to ascertain or to verify the firm's driving strategic assumptions or strategic posture. They also can begin to suggest where IT can bring advantage. Michael Porter's (1980) model of five competitive forces has its place here. Reproduced in Fig. 2.6, it helps executives at the level of the strategic business unit to clarify their business strategy and discuss where IT may potentially yield competitive advantage in terms of defending the firm against these forces or influencing them in its favour.

Porter's model helps analysis in the following ways:

1. It focuses on industry and competitive dynamics.

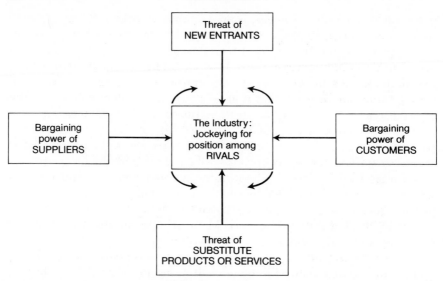

Fig. 2.6.   Porter's Five Forces of Industry Competition

2. It reminds us that competition is not just about the actions of rivals.
3. It provides a simple framework which facilitates discussion and yet is based on sound principles of industrial economics.
4. It usually suggests quickly which are the one or two dominant forces to consider.

However, detailed investigation is usually required subsequently to understand the sources and nature of the significant forces, what strategic actions are possible and what industry reactions are likely. There are generalizable rules, principles, and probabilities governing strategic actions on each force. One commonly finds some of the forces interact so that in reality iterative analyses are required, followed by mixed strategic actions.

McFarlan (1984) has suggested some of the IT options which can limit and enhance each force and Earl (forthcoming) has produced a general menu of IT potentials and mechanisms. However the Cash and Konsynski (1985) framework is reproduced in Table 2.3, focusing on inter-organizational systems. These are IT applications which link up two organizations, for example supplier and customer. Their framework is more a list of example uses of IT and is not exclusive, but it demonstrates many of the options.

Wiseman (1985) provides another business strategy framework which explicitly seeks strategic options. His strategic option generator is founded on the notion of strategic thrusts, based on earlier work of Chandler (1962) and Porter (1980) respectively. Five generic thrusts and

Table 2.3.   *Inter-organizational Systems (IOS) to Combat Competitive Forces (Cash and Konsynski)*

Competitive force	Implications	Uses of an IOS
New entrants	New capacity Need for substantial resources Reduced prices or inflated incumbents' costs	To provide: entry barriers, greater economies of scale, switching costs, product differentiation, limited access to distribution channels
Buyers	Lower prices Higher quality More services More competition	To influence buyers: differentiation switching costs
Suppliers	Higher prices Reduced quality and services	To reduce switching costs To encourage competition To threaten backward integration
Substitute products	Limited potential return A ceiling on prices	To improve price and performance To redefine products and services
Traditional	Competition on price Product, distribution and service	To improve cost effectiveness To control market access To differentiate product and company

three strategic targets are posited. His flowchart in Fig. 2.7 is self-explanatory. Its potential value is not only the conflation of previous frameworks for analysis, but the logical checklist of analytical questions it provides. Like Porter's model it therefore helps most in clarifying the firm's business strategy and suggesting the direction of the IT–strategy connection. It is less likely to pinpoint specific applications for development.

Opportunity frameworks generally aim to show where IT can be deployed for strategic advantage and to suggest application ideas. They vary in level of analysis and in specificity. It is likely that all three subclasses have their contribution to make. Additional systems analysis techniques may be required to bring other strategic perspectives than cost–value analysis. Certainly further application search tools are needed for different application areas and technologies. Most business strategy frameworks work reasonably well, if they help indicate the technology–strategy connection. Use of the awareness frameworks described earlier can help here.

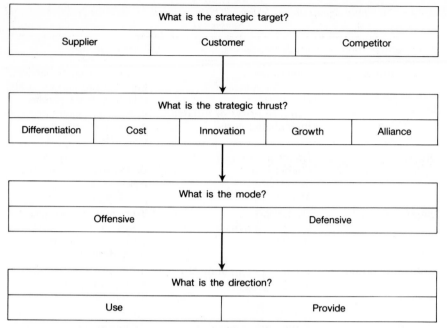

Fig. 2.7. Wiseman's Strategic Option Generator

Positioning Frameworks

Positioning frameworks are best seen as tools to help executives assess the strategic importance, the particular character, and the inherited situation of IT for their business. The aim is improve executives' understanding of how the information systems function and IT should be managed in their particular organization. Positioning frameworks therefore are concerned with assessing, developing, and improving IT capabilities in specific organizations. They are not very useful in searching for opportunities for strategic information systems but they can make some contribution in raising awareness of the strategic importance of IT for a firm. They thus have value in both education and practice.

Three subclasses of positioning frameworks make be identified:

1. Scaling frameworks which help indicate the scale of importance of IT to a business and the scale of the management challenges involved.
2. Spatial frameworks which help indicate the character of IT applications and IT management in different businesses or sectors.
3. Temporal frameworks which help assess the evolutionary position of an organization in using and managing IT.

Scaling Frameworks

A well known example of a scaling framework is McFarlan *et al*.'s (1983) strategic grid reproduced in Fig. 2.8. This aims to assess the past and future strategic impact of IT on the business, indicating one of four metaphors which suggest how the information systems function should be staffed, organized, and planned. For example, in support situations, IT budgets may be smaller, IS planning shorter-term, IS management lower profile, and IS managers lower status than in strategic contexts. Turnaround situations may require a revolution, with stepped increases in funding, education, and management support and involvement. Factory contexts are more likely to require consistent and steady management attention, with careful budgeting, sound project and operations controls, and emphasis on reliability and efficiency.

Strategic impact of
application development portfolio

		Low	High
Strategic impact of existing operating systems	Low	Support	Turnaround
	High	Factory	Strategic

Fig. 2.8. Strategic Grid (McFarlan *et al.*)

Typically this scaling assessment has to be done at divisional business unit level, since strategic contexts and IS histories differ within organizations. Indeed in managing IT in large organizations, it is important to recognize such differences, thinking of corporate IS management in a portfolio sense rather than as common and homogeneous in all constituent businesses. It is important to note, of course, that investment in just one strategic use of IT could quickly move a firm out of one management 'scenario' into another. Equally the activities of rivals, customers, suppliers, or new entrants could quickly move a firm from 'support' or 'factory' to 'turnaround' or 'strategic'. Indeed it is often sector pressures, perhaps compounded by capabilities of new technologies, which create the dynamic behind the strategic grid.

Thus, although McFarlan *et al*.'s grid is something of a tautology—the questions and answers are similar—and although it must be applied at the right level of analysis, it can help point out not only that firms are in different strategic IT contexts but emphasize that universal management prescriptions in this field rarely make sense.

Spatial Frameworks

An example of a spatial framework is Earl's (1987) sector model. This contrasts sectors from an IT perspective and leads to a more subtle framework emphasizing sector nuances in IS strategy formulation (see later in this volume). Earl posits from his work on IT strategy, that sectors are likely to differ in their attitude to and, belief in, using IT. As with McFarlan *et al*'s grid, management approaches therefore also are likely to differ.

In some sectors, for example financial services, airlines and, increasingly, retailing, IT has become the means of delivering the goods and services in the sector. Indeed the infrastructure of the sector is often IT itself and so each firm's IT infrastructure is a major plank of its asset base. This sector class is called 'delivery'. In others, for example automobile and textile manufacturing, business and functional strategies are increasingly dependent on IT for their implementation. Indeed critical success or survival factors in those industries are often reliant upon IT for their achievement. This is the 'dependent' class. In a third set of sectors, management believe that IT can yield some competitive advantage and that poor IS may prove to be a competitive disadvantage. However, the requirements and imperatives are by no means clear and managements need faith in IT and IS and have to drive continually for the next benefits. This set is called 'drive', and chemical and food companies seem to fit it. For the final group of sectors, the strategic importance of IT is either not yet apparent or is minimal. IT is never irrelevant but it is unlikely to make or break company performance in these sectors. This class is called 'delayed'—for technologies or competitive forces may prompt a reappraisal in the future.

This four way classification is reproduced in Table 2.4. Management differences might include the following: in delivery sectors, technology policies are important, investment in IT is continuous and business strategy and IT strategy are very closely inter-weaved. In dependent sectors, business-led direction is crucial, evaluation of IT can be against clear goals and strategies for IT and IS must be a function of business strategies. In drive sectors, users need to lead the use of IT as much as do IT managers, experiments and risks are to be encouraged, and spotting and recognizing winning applications is key. In delayed sectors, the profile of information managment need not be high, much activity can be left to the specialists, and investment in IT is limited.

Again, the condition of sectors can change over time. Cumulative dependence on IT can render a dependent sector firm eventually like a delivery sector firm and certainly a spectacular strategic strike by a firm in a drive sector may change the industry and thus its classification.

The main value of this framework is in thinking about sectors in an IT perspective rather than through more traditional lenses. Then the approach demanded of management can be explored. For example it becomes apparent that in firms in delivery sectors, managements are

Table 2.4.   *Sector Framework for IT (Earl)*

Strategic context	Characteristic	Metaphor
IT is the means of delivering goods and services in the sector	Computer-based transaction systems underpin business operations	Delivery
Business strategies increasingly depend on IT for their implementation	Business and functional strategies require a major automation, information or communications capability and are made possible by these technologies	Dependent
IT potentially provides new strategic opportunities	Specific applications or technologies are exploited for developing business and changing ways of managing	Drive
IT has no strategic impact in the sector	Opportunities or threats from IT are not yet apparent or perceived	Delayed

'stuck with IT'. If they thought 'it might go away soon', they have to revise their ideas! For managements in dependent sectors, who often worry that 'they are not like banks or airlines', they begin to see that whilst IT has an important place it is up to them to put it in its appropriate place—and not leave too much to the specialists.

Temporal Frameworks

Temporal frameworks are concerned with historiographies of IT. The classical model is Gibson and Nolan's (1974) stages of EDP growth which suggested that firms move through four stages of learning how to manage EDP. Learning was seen to be through experience and each set of management practices in a stage was a function of events in the last stage and anticipated needs in the next. This framework, which has been subjected to empirical testing, has become controversial in the literature, but it is by no means clear that the general trend is invalid and certainly most managers identify with it very readily. It may seem strange to include it in a paper on IT and strategic advantage. However some workers have developed or seen tools based on this framework as one set of IS strategy methodologies (Sullivan, 1985). More important, in our work with management teams in Oxford, we have found it instructive to assess a firm's IT management experience through this framework and then compare the agreed positioning with the metaphor chosen when McFarlan *et al.*'s strategic grid was applied. Some interesting tensions can emerge.

The most generalizable temporal framework is the technology

assimilation model of McFarlan and McKenney (1983) which can be applied to any particular information technology or perhaps to the average condition across IT as a whole. This is shown in Table 2.5. In stage one, the emphasis is on trying out a technology and management planning and control is thus relatively lax. In stage two, the emphasis is on expanding technology use so that management by exhortation and enthusiasm is likely. In stage three, concerns over cost, reliability and user satisfaction lead to introduction of management controls. In stage four, managements, users, and specialists begin to feel comfortable about the uses, supply, and implications of the technology and a more balanced management approach evolves.

Commonly, organizations place themselves in late stage three for data processing. This positioning can be disastrous for organizations who also place themselves in turnaround on the strategic grid—for heavy control will not lead to stepped changes in use, innovation, or adaptation through IT. Likewise telecommunications is often placed in stage two—but if communications networks are a core part of the IT infrastructure for companies in the strategic or turnaround quadrants of the strategic grid, some rapid management evolution along the stages curve will be necessary.

So the principal use of positioning frameworks is to help managements understand the importance of IT for their firm and examine the appropriate management approaches required. Each of the three sub-classes has its values—and their benefits tend to be enhanced, if they are used in conjunction with each other. Also it can be important to reassess the firm's position on these models from time to time—for technology, experience, and competitive forces render them dynamic over time.

Conclusion

I have referred occasionally to experience gained with these frameworks in management education. I and my colleagues have discovered that in management development events for executive management teams, we are often called upon to help them answer three questions:

1. Why is IT important and how important is it for our firm?
2. What strategic opportunities might we seek or gain from IT?
3. Given the answers to the above two questions, should we be managing IT differently?

We find this forms a progressive process which can be looked at through the lenses of organizational development (Lewin, 1951). The process behind question one is that of *unfreezing* current management attitudes and beliefs. The task is to open up new visions or horizons and exploit current issues and discontents, the objective being to generate a healthy

Table 2.5. *Stage Model of IT Management (after McFarlan, McKenney et al.)*

	Technology identification and investment	Technological learning and adaption	Rationalization/ management control	Maturity/widespread technology transfer
Gibson and Nolan stage	1: 'Initiation'	2: 'Contagion'	3: 'Control'	4: 'Maturity'
Challenge	Identify relevant technologies and fund a pilot	Encourage widespread user experimentation	Develop tools and techniques to manage use of technology	Adaption to and adoption of technology
Goals	Technical expertise early application	User interest Users discover applications	Value for money Reliability	Diffusion Integration
Management	Lax planning and control	Encouragement and observation	Technical standards Management controls	Balanced processes
Growth	Technological advance Application testing	Applications advance User learning	User advance Management learning	Management advance

mix of interest and discomfort. The process behind the second question is *changing* managers' thinking, perhaps by discovering new emphases, thrusts or opportunities. The task is to develop the new visions and examine the discomforts, facilitating the group to embrace new goals, consider relevant strategies and adopt changed thinking. Finally, question three is about reassessing management practices for this new thinking—about *freezing* again. The task here is to help the group agree what is required to put new ideas into action, provide realistic guidance and forge common language and frameworks which will underpin further activity. So the concluding view of the framework of frameworks is one of organizational development presented in Table 2.6. We find that several awareness frameworks are needed for unfreezing. The systems analysis, applications search, and business strategy versions of the opportunity frameworks are all required in the change phase, usually employed in workshop mode. The scaling, spatial, and temporal versions of the positioning frameworks are helpful individually and together in the freezing phase *but* also to derive an early collective view in the unfreezing phase.

Table 2.6.   *Framework of Frameworks: OD Perspective*

Question	Development process	Framework
IT importance	Unfreeze	Awareness
IT opportunities	Change	Opportunity
IT management	Freeze	Positioning

This organizational development view therefore is consistent with the general message of this paper. Many strategic IT frameworks are useful both in demonstrating that IT is becoming a strategic resource and in suggesting how IT can be exploited and managed strategically. It is important however to understand the comparative aims and advantages of each of these models and frameworks. The framework of frameworks in this paper seeks to help this understanding. Then users can select the framework to fit the purpose, but recognizing that several frameworks are probably required. What has been left unsaid until now, however, is that whilst all these frameworks—awareness, opportunity, and positioning—provide useful early guidance in their respective areas, they provide but a start. Nearly always much detailed analysis and reasoning has to follow both in discovering strategic information systems and in modifying current management approaches to be more strategic. However without the frameworks, managements may never understand the strategic era of IT or begin to contribute to its evolution.

References

Benjamin, R. I. *et al.* (1984), 'Information Technology: A Strategic Opportunity', *Sloan Management Review* **25**, **3**.

Burnstine, D. (1980), *BIATT: An Emerging Management Engineering Discipline*, BIAIT International Inc.

Cash, J. E., and Konsynski, B. R. (1985), 'IS Redraws Competitive Boundaries', *Harvard Business Review* March–April.

Chandler, A. D. jun. (1962), *Strategy and Structure: Chapters in the History of American Industrial Enterprise*, Harvard University Press, Cambridge, Mass.

Earl, M. J. (1987), 'Formulation of Information Systems Strategies: A Practical Framework' in *The Role of Information Management in Competitive Success*, Pergamon–Infotech Ltd., Maidenhead.

Gibson, C. F., and Nolan, R. L. (1974), 'Managing the Four Stages of EDP Growth', *Harvard Business Review*, January–February.

Ives, B., and Learmonth, G. P. (1984), 'The Information System As A Competitive Weapon', *Communications of the ACM* **27**, **12**.

Lewin, K. (1951), *Field Theory in Social Science: Selected Theoretical Papers*, Harper and Row.

McFarlan, F. W. (1984), 'Information Technology Changes the Way You Compete', *Harvard Business Review* May–June.

—— and McKenney, J. L. (1983), *Corporate Information Systems Management: The Issues Facing Senior Executives*, Irwin.

——, —— and Pyburn, P. (1983), 'The Information Archipelago—Plotting A Course', *Harvard Business Review* January–February.

Parsons, G. L. (1983), 'Information Technology: A New Competitive Weapon', *Sloan Management Review* **25**, **1**.

Porter, M. E. (1980), *Competitive Strategy*, The Free Press, New York.

—— and Millar, V. E. (1985), 'How Information Gives You Competitive Advantage', *Harvard Business Review* July–August.

Runge, D. A., and Earl, M. J. (1987), *Using Telecommunications-Based Information Systems for Competitive Advantage*, Oxford Institute of Information Management research paper **RDP 87/1**, Templeton College, Oxford.

Sullivan, C. H. jun. (1985), 'Systems Planning in the Information Age', *Sloan Management Review* **26**, **2**.

Wiseman, C. (1985), *Strategy and Computers*, Dow Jones–Irwin.

3

Strategy Formulation Methodologies and IT

MICHAEL SCOTT MORTON

Sloan School of Management, MIT

Premises

This topic is complex. Concepts that help with strategy formulation are continually evolving and information technology itself is changing, so the impact of one on the other is indeed complex. As such, it seems important to be clear about the underlying assumptions before beginning to address the substance of the question. There are some basic beliefs about the world and the way it operates which underlie the arguments developed in this paper. Four premises seem important.

The first premise is that information technology (IT) strategies are most effective when they are developed in the context of business and corporate strategies. Thus a critical first step is to know where the organization is headed before one begins to work on the question of what a sensible direction for the use of information technology should be.

Such an explicit statement of strategy assumes implicitly that the 'rational actor' model of the organization is the most effective one to use. This model has been espoused by a series of authors over the years; perhaps one of the earliest was Herbert Simon in his *New Science of Management Decision* published in 1960. In this view, decision making is thought of as falling into a series of phases. In Simon's terms, 'intelligence', 'design', and 'choice' being the three principal interactive phases. In light of the work since Simon's publication it seems useful to add a fourth step, namely 'action'. Thus in this model an organization, or an individual, first defines the problem, that is clarifies it, then creates alternatives that would solve that particular problem, then selects the best of these alternatives following which they go through implementation, that is, a set of actions are taken.

This 'rational actor' paradigm implicitly underlies much of the work that is going on in corporate strategy and strategy formulation. It dominates the writing and research, particularly in the area of methodologies and even more so as it relates to information technology since many who work in this area come out of an engineering and science background.

However, there are several alternative models which describe equally well the activity that takes place in organizations. For example, there is a large group of managers who seem successfully to follow a problem-solving process which basically acts first, based primarily on intuition, then examines the results in an intuitive way and senses if the results seem to be good. They then cycle back through to a next set of actions. In this view of management decision-making, the action comes first and the analysis comes second. Such a view turns the standard methodologies for strategy formulation upside down and there is little prescriptive or normative writing for managers or academics with this view of the world to act on. In the comments that follow, the rational actor model is dominant but is not in any way meant to be exclusive.

The second premise that underlies this paper is that the need for an explicit view of the organization's strategy is necessary because of an increasingly turbulent external environment. The premise is that the next decade is more likely to be one of 'economic war' than 'economic peace'. It seems that we are entering an era of discontinuities; over-capacity in industry, increasingly global competition, rising expectations both of the quality of products and services as well as expectations as to one's standard of living. If indeed we are entering a period of continuing economic change then the management systems and ways of doing business that will be successful in such a period of change will be different from those in the past. It is assumed that incremental 'business as usual' will not be adequate in the years ahead.

Although the pace of change is assumed to be higher in the coming years than it was in the 1960s and 70s, it is not assumed that most of these changes are IT-related. In fact quite the reverse; social, political, global economics, and technologies such as genetic engineering are driving organizations. Information technology enables the organization to facilitate and mediate these changes as they occur and have an impact on the organization. Indeed it is often argued that information technology facilitates a faster rate of change in general. For example, live television coverage in America on activities in South Africa has undoubtedly increased the awareness and added to the political pressure for America to intervene in some way. However, by and large, information technology seems to be facilitating change, or enabling it to happen, rather than driving it in a causal way.

A third premise is that information technology is merely one of several levers by which an organization adjusts to changes in the external world and in management practices. As is suggested in the second premise, there is no assumption of a technological imperative. Strategy to be effective has to be driven by ideas as they occur to informed, capable managers. On balance, it is unlikely that an effective strategy will be driven by the technology in a way that brooks no alternatives.

The fourth premise is that strategy formulation is more of an art than a science and to be effective it is the province of line management. Herein lies the built-in difficulty of IT strategy formulation. If corporate strategy formulation is an art practiced differently in different organizations by different managers and if the resulting strategy is articulated in some firms in great detail and others scarcely at all, then clearly there is no 'science' of strategy formulation! It is an observable empirical fact that good strategic management is all too rare. On top of this scarcity of good strategic management is the lack of the knowledge of IT capabilities among general managers. Line managers have traditionally not come out of the information technology field. Hence, those who know their corporate strategy are often ignorant of information technology and correspondingly those who understand the information technology are often uninformed of the corporate strategy. Hence to be effective there needs to be a shared process of strategy formulation and this is hard as both bodies of knowledge are changing rapidly and to some extent one is asking art and science to mix constructively!

Definitions and History

Terminology in a field such as management is woefully undefined and it turns out that many management terms have widely different meanings to different people. There are two terms which require definition for the purpose of this paper. The first of these is information technology (IT) itself. The most important point is that IT is *not* only computers. There is no clean way of categorizing IT but it consists of at least the following:

1. Computers—computers are of course a central component of information technology. There is a full smorgasbord of these ranging from large mainframe computers all the way through to the recently arrived personal computers and the even smaller, microcomputers, that exit in chip form. Together with this spectrum of computers from mainframes to micros exists the wealth of data and information that is available to an organization in an electronic form.

2. Telecoms—telecommunications has only recently begun to be recognized as a full partner with the computer itself as part of the main structure of information technology. The range of telecom options can be thought of as shown in Fig. 3.1. In addition to thse four cells which are part of the telecommunications world an organization must deal with, there is the additional complexity of having both public and private networks available to fill each of these cells. It is hard to capture the powerful difference between a computer that is isolated, and what the computer becomes in the hands of the user when it is linked into a network and has flexible access to information, other computers, and other organizations.

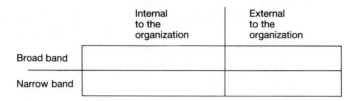

Fig. 3.1.   Telecommunications Options

3. White Collar Productivity Tools—these are commonly known as office automation and clerical support and could be thought of as partial robotics for clerical workers. Here routine well-structured tasks such as writing pay cheques and typing standard letters, are done with information technology tools such as a computer-based work station for the clerical worker. Similarly, there are work stations for managerial workers in the form of computer-based terminals that deal with management support systems in various forms. Typically in 1986, these take the form of decision support systems and executive support systems.

4. Blue Collar Productivity Tools—the most obvious case of blue collar productivity tools are robotics and related factory automation. However, it is interesting that a great many other professional work stations are now being installed where the prime purpose is for the production of the service itself. These work stations are used by humans, not by machine tools, and are closely related to the shop floor in terms of computer-aided design and computer-aided engineering. However there are other interesting examples such as loan officers in banks evaluating loan possibilities through the use of an interactive work station.

5. Smart Products—in addition to the above four categories of information technology there is also the inclusion of the technology into the product itself. Thus we have in a modern car several computers in the car to control fuel, anti-skid brakes, and so on, as well as information supposedly useful to the driver in terms of computed fuel consumption etc.

The important point to make in the context of this paper is that information technology is only partially computers. Equally important are the other four categories of information technology that must be thought of when one thinks about formulating strategies for IT in the context of a corporate strategic move.

The second definition that is important to make for the purpose of this paper is that of strategy itself. There are literally hundreds of books on strategy and strategic management in the literature. This article assumes the content of these kinds of books, such as Schendel and Hofer (1979) or Hax and Majluf (1984), is well understood to the reader. The central point is that strategy is not long-range planning, if by long-range planning we mean laying out the step-by-step path into the future, starting this from the present and assuming incremental progress of existing businesses and markets.

The original Greek word from which strategy comes means 'the art of the (military) General'. For the purposes here, this can be translated into strategy formulation as being about how to create an appropriate mission, and to position the organization to accomplish this mission in light of the reality of its internal strengths and weaknesses, its customers, and the external environment. Strategy formulation is concerned with the desired positioning of the firm and how to get there.

If one looks at business strategy historically one can see five phases of the development of the field up to the present time.

1. An early phase merely established for the first time the desirability of long-range planning. Steiner (1969) in his landmark book made a strong case for making explicit a functionally-based (marketing, production, finance, etc.) plan that covered several years into the future.

2. By the early 1970s the interest had shifted to a focus on business planning (Lorange and Vancil, 1977). To oversimplify this point of view it was basically one of executives giving top-down guidance to the organization and bottom-up plans then came from the division and functional levels. These were then put together for an overall corporate plan.

3. The third phase was that of portfolio planning, as espoused particularly by Henderson (1979). The essence of this approach was to see the corporation as a series of separate strategic business units (SBUs) which by and large had independent products, markets, and missions. These were looked at in terms of their cash needs and growth possibilities to identify an appropriate balance in the portfolio of SBUs, given the reality of the maximum sustainable growth for the corporation. Important to this point of view was the relative market position *vis-à-vis* the competition and the growth potential of the markets served.

4. Industry structure and generic strategies (Porter, 1980) was the next stage in the evolution of strategy formulation methodologies. Here the analysis was focused on the competitive position of the firm in the context of the infrastructure of its industry. The premise is that as industries have very different structures and dynamics it is important to understand these before identifying the possible generic strategy appropriate for the firm itself.

5. The fifth and most recent phase in the evolution of strategic planning is focused on a value chain (Porter, 1985) approach which turns the attention back to the inside of the organization. This technique analyses the internal steps by which an organization adds value to its product or service.

The point to note with all of these various approaches is that there has been a steady progression of ideas. There is no reason to suspect that we have reached any kind of end point in this progression and indeed in light of the turbulent environment, the purposes for which strategy formulation must be undertaken will change. This in turn will demand newer techniques and new concepts that will prove powerful in helping organizations to formulate their strategy in an effective way. Thus it can be seen that strategy formulation is a moving target, and this suggests that linking strategy formulation to changing information technology is going to require unusual effort and flexibility.

Conceptual Frameworks

If strategy is indeed a creative line management task then it follows that there is no formula or technique that will produce an answer. However it is possible to use frameworks and methodologies as ways of stimulating ideas, aiding consensus among management, and generally helping to maintain perspective. It is the last two of the frameworks mentioned above that appear to be particularly valuable as a way of stimulating powerful creative methods of linking IT use for the corporate strategic thrusts. There are a host of suggested ways of looking at the linkage that have come out of the major business schools of the last five years (Bacos and Treacy, 1986; Beaty and Ives, 1986; Cash and Konsynski, 1985; Ives and Learmonth, 1984; McFarlan, 1984) and many of these are discussed in other papers. Three streams of methods seem to be proving useful in some circumstances.

As an example of a framework being used to stimulate creativity it is possible to take Porter's (1980) framework of Competitive Strategy. Using Porter's basic diagram (Fig. 3.2) of the major categories of forces it is possible to go through each of the five areas and identify opportunities in each area. In some organizations this is done formally in small groups of line managers with an IT person, in others by different combinations of the line and staff. Focusing on the 'buyer' dimension of Porter's diagram, for example, one company came up with an idea for an electronic linkage between their buyers (ie. their customers) and themselves. The linkage gave the customer an ability to directly choose items that most nearly matched their needs, the process also markedly speeded up delivery of the product to the customer.

A second example of a conceptual framework that has proved to be

60 *Michael Scott Morton*

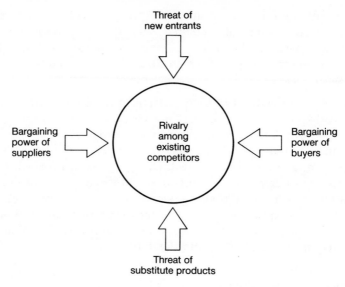

Fig. 3.2. Porter's Five Competitive Forces

very effective for understanding the strategic opportunities inherent in the internal aspects of the organization is the use of the 'value chain'. One of the first published references to its use occurred in 1980 as a result of some work that Strategic Planning Associates (SPA) (1981) did with some of their clients. In practical application, they found it effective to utilize both the analysis based on the 'value added chain' (based on cost of the value adding steps) and one based on 'value added leverage'. This latter analysis is management's judgement as to the most critical leverage points in the value chain. This early work by SPA was not followed up in the academic literature until Porter (1986) drew attention to the concept and expanded its application. The value chain is a pictorial representation of the sequence of activity the organization engages in to add value to its product or service as it moves from the initial stages of what it does through to the delivery of a product to the customer. Figure 3.3 shows the two classes of activity, those directly associated with the process of 'manufacturing' the goods and services and those that are necessary support to those direct steps. Organizing this 'value chain' as a percentage of cost leads to insights and provides a way of focusing on those steps that clearly account for a large proportion of the organization's cost structure. Such steps are very often the ones that offer the greatest potential for IT application. Such a view also makes it clear which steps might be linked to other organizations in joint ventures, or perhaps removing that piece of the value chain all together and having it contracted out to somebody else.

Management support:		Accounting	Legal	Personnel	Computer		
R&D	Purchasing	Manufacturing	Marketing	Distribution	Selling	Service

Fig. 3.3. The Value-added Chain

To repeat a point made above, the concepts are merely vehicles for management to discuss the potential of their businesses and hence where information technology might be used. The value added leverage step is one that is much less dependent on hard costs and much more dependent on management's informed judgement. Value added leverage refers to those steps in the 'value chain' where management feels the organization has a unique advantage or where there is the most powerful form of leverage. For example, an oil company arguably gets its greatest leverage from finding oil in the first place. It is relatively *unimportant* how efficiently it manages the manufacturing and delivery process if it is in fact sitting on huge supplies of low cost oil. In this case, the exploration stage in the 'value chain' is the one with the greatest leverage, although its costs may be proportionately very small.

These two frameworks (industry structure and value chain) are particularly useful because together they force the organization to think about how it does its business and ways in which that could be changed, as well as explicitly forcing attention on the external variables which impact the firm.

Both of these points of view, then, encourage thinking about 'electronic integration' which seems to be one of the major ways which information technology is having an impact on corporate strategy. However, beyond frameworks that suggest particularly powerful points at which technology may be utilized there has also been some useful work on the *process* of thinking through strategy formulation itself. The most well known of these is Rockart's (1979) Critical Success Factors methodology which was developed initially for use by managers in planning their information needs. Its initial success in the domain of information systems has been overshadowed by the use of the technique as a mechanism to get managers to think through what are the critical dimensions of their jobs to which they must pay undivided attention. Obviously, if an organization can agree on those things that must be done uniquely well for it to be successful it has gone a long way in identifying its strategic thrusts. Recent work by Henderson (1979) has built on the foundation that Rockart established by identifying the Critical Assumption Set that a group of managers share. He has shown it is important to get at the assumptions that underlie the critical success factors in order to get to the core of what really needs to be done to move the organization forward. These two conceptual frameworks are being used to stimulate thinking and creativity by managers. The Critical Success Factors methodology adds a definitive process that results in articulating and sharing the organization's direction. These have been shown in numerous organizations to be analytically useful and to result in changed behaviour (Bullen and Rockart, 1981).

There is another perspective which is being explored and seems to yield a different set of insights which are in many ways wider and more pervasive than those in the first two analytical frameworks. This framework arose out of two important streams of fundamental research that were done in the 1950s and 1960s. The first of these is the work done by Alfred Chandler (1962), a business historian. He developed the thesis that an organization's strategy changes over time and as it changes, the organization adjusts its structure to match the new strategy. Although this point is regarded as obvious today it is nonetheless a powerful point. At about the same time Leavitt (1965), working from an evaluation of the organizational behaviour literature and studies that had been done to that point, established a case that an organization could be thought of as consisting of four important sets of forces. These were the tasks the organization has to accomplish (in some ways its strategy), the organization structure it employs, the people in the organization and their skills, and the technology that is utilized. The technology in this case was not information technology so much as it was any of the technologies, telephone, materials, manufacturing process, etc. At the time this was a novel and powerful way of viewing organizations and it had the added advantage of being well grounded in fundamental research.

In addition to Chandler and Leavitt there was also at this period of time the development of the scenario school of corporate strategy (Wack, 1984). This school developed both methodologies and check lists but at the heart of their work was the idea that the external environment could most usefully be examined in context of its social, political, economic, and technical components. Their work had a big influence in the sixties but fell out of favour until its recent revival (Lorange *et al.*, 1986).

If these three streams of work are combined together one arrives at the model in Fig. 3.4. This diagram recognizes that organizations can usefully be thought of as a set of forces existing in a state of dynamic equilibrium. On the one hand you have its strategy, the mission it wishes to accomplish, and all the tasks that make up that mission. You also have its organization structure and, more importantly perhaps, the corporate culture that makes that structure become alive and vibrant. You also have the people, and not only the people themselves, but the roles they are being asked to play. For example, a person as head of marketing becomes a very different individual when he/she becomes the

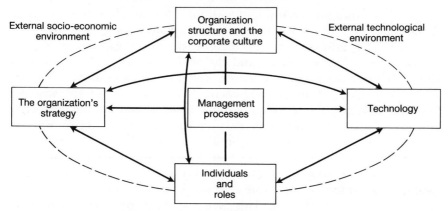

Fig. 3.4. Integration of Strategic Frameworks

head of manufacturing. The fourth major set of forces are the technologies that are available, particularly the information technologies as defined previously. Holding all these four forces together are the management processes; the planning, the budgeting, and the control systems as well as the informal processes that represent the way the organization does its business. All these sets of forces exist in an external environment which consists of the social, political, economic, and technical forces. These changes can have an impact on any one of the sets of forces although principally of course they are reflected in the strategy of the organization.

In the context of this diagram then, information technology can be seen to be a force in its own right and it certainly has a direct impact on the strategies that are available to an organization. American Hospital Supply (*Fortune*, 26 July 1982) demonstrated this when they had to look for some mechanism to give them sustainable competitive advantage in the market place. They took information technology, gave their customers a terminal, and allowed the customers to order directly from AHS. This gave the customer cost savings and quicker response and higher quality and gave AHS the ability to know more about their customers, their ordering patterns and their tastes. The combination was a situation where both parties gained. It was also true that AHS's competitors had a hard time breaking through the barrier of installed terminal systems to sell to these customers. There are many examples (Benjamin *et al.*, 1984) of similar IT uses for competitive advantage. However, as Fig. 3.4 suggests, the external environment is the major driving force for the strategy, the technology is merely enabling the strategy to be accomplished. In addition, there are three other sets of forces which clearly impact this technology strategy linkage. One can have the best idea in the world but if the organization structure and corporate culture are inconsistent with this idea then it is likely to come to nothing. Similarly, if the strategic vision of technology assumes a set of skills and attitudes of the people in the organization that is inconsistent with the culture and the reality of peoples' expectations then it is likely the whole experience will fail. Such an outcome is made even more likely if the management processes and reward schemes continue to reflect the old ways of doing business and not the new. Thus it can be seen that any attempt to formulate IT strategies without thinking very carefully about the implications that such a strategy would hold for the structure, the people, and the processes, is likely to fail.

An expanded version of this line of thinking was the conceptual origin of a project at MIT called 'Management in the 1990s' by John Rockart and Scott Morton. This is a five year research programme involving 15–20 faculty at the Sloan School together with ten corporate sponsors who are giving MIT five million dollars to conduct research on the impact of information technology. Our concern is not with information technology but the impact it will have on the processes, strategy, structure, people, and human resource practices in organizations. Our sponsors consist of three manufacting firms, British Petroleum, General Motors, and Eastman Kodak, three service firms, American Express, Arthur Young, and the Internal Revenue Service and four firms involved in information technology namely International Computers Ltd., Digital Equipment Corporation, Bell South, and MCI. Already it is clear that there has been a major impact on organizations as a result of IT and in many of the most successful cases this impact has gone straight to the core of the way they do their basic business.

The Future

The impacts of information technology, that the researchers in the 1990s program are finding, would not be of such major significance if it were not for the fact that there is no indication that changes are slowing down. That is, the external environment shows every sign of continuing to experience major changes over the next several years. These changes will in turn demand that organizations adapt to them. Such adaptation can be facilitated by the creative use of information technology. This technology is itself continuing to change. Recent technological breakthroughs suggest that the changes will affect some areas in major ways.

The first of these is in the hardware/software domain. The continuing drop in hardware costs plus developments in software architecture have resulted in machines that have now fallen below a cost threshold. For example in 1986 it is possible to buy a 'LISP' machine at around the $15,000 level which can deal with languages particularly suitable for qualitative knowledge and its manipulation. This can then be coupled with a knowledge base of usefully realistic size.

The second breakthrough is conceptual in nature. Herbert Simon in the 1950s first raised the idea of heuristics and their fit with the general background of Artificial Intelligence. Since then there has been a lot of work by many able researchers that have got us to the point (Scott Morton *et al.*, 1986) where it is possible to capture and work with judgemental qualitative knowledge of acknowledged experts. This has resulted in the so-called 'expert systems' which are an interesting development in the field. But to the extent they replace human judgement they can do so only in very limited domains and therefore are of marginal importance to corporate strategy over the next ten years. However, the concept of 'expert systems' and artificial intelligence can be used to build 'expert support systems'. These take the concepts of 'expert systems' but apply them to an interactive system that leaves a manager very much in the loop in a crucial part of the decision making process.

The conceptual breakthroughs that allows one to build the software for an 'expert support system' coupled with the enormous drop in cost of the hardware has resulted in an economically viable combination which for the first time give us the tools to attack directly the challenge of working with qualitative judgemental information (Davis, 1986; Bobrow *et al.*, 1986). This passage from data in the early 1960s to information in the 1970s to knowledge in the 1980s is of fundamental significance and opens up another class of problems for which an organization must have an effective strategy.

This 'knowledge era' matters since knowledge workers have scarcely been touched thus far. We have done much with computers over the last 25 years to help the very well-understood routine repetitive tasks that have to do with the transaction-processing activities of an organization. More recently we have begun to work on the physical manufacturing via robots. The advent of low cost viable telecommunications has allowed us to link remote sites together and capture transaction processing data closer to the source and integrate it more tightly with the organization. However, the tasks that have been affected have been largely clerical, such as payroll, order entry, inventory control, and keeping track of the day-to-day routine things. More judgemental areas such as assessing the credit risk of a possible loan candidate or configuring the components of a complicated customer order do not yield to the old concepts and 'sequential' hardware architecture that we have had to work with thus far. The new science of knowledge engineering, capturing heuristics, and the availability of 'parallel architectures' at reasonable prices offer the tools that will allow us to deal increasingly with these judgemental areas.

Given the continuous changes in the environment and in the

technology, the formulation of an IT strategy is tricky. It must involve line managers thinking creatively and it must invoke dealing effectively with the management of change. In addition, it involves the challenge of getting both the IT professionals and the line managers to engage in a constructive dialogue. From the evidence we have collected thus far in the 1990s program it would appear that the firms that have used IT successfully are the ones who have succeeded in starting such a dialogue. In order to get this effective dialogue it appears that one way to start *is to start*. It certainly seems clear that the business world is not waiting for those who are slow to begin this process. The 1990s, it appears, will continue to be a time of change.

References

Bacos, J. Y., and Treacy, M. E. (1986), 'Information Technology and Corporate Strategy: A Research Prospective', *MIS Quarterly* **10**, **2**.

Beaty, C. M., and Ives, B. (1986), 'Competitive Information Systems in Support of Pricing', *MIS Quarterly* **10**, **1**.

Benjamin, R. I., *et al.* (1984), 'Information Technology: A Strategic Opportunity', *Sloan Management Review* **25**, **3**.

Bobrow, D. G., Mittal, S., and Stefik, M. J. (1986), 'Expert Systems: Perils and Promise', *Communications of the ACM* **29**, **9**.

Bullen, C. V., and Rockart, J. F. (1981), 'A Primer on Critical Success Factors, *CISR Working Paper* **69**, MIT Center for Information Systems Research, Cambridge, Mass.

Cash, J. I., and Konsynski, B. R. (1985), 'IS Redraws Competitive Boundaries', *Harvard Business Review,* **63**, **2**.

Chandler, A. D. jun. (1962), *Strategy and Structure*, MIT Press, Cambridge, Mass.

Davis, R. (1986), 'Knowledge-based Systems' *Science* **231**, **4741**.

Fortune. (1982), 'The Hard-Selling Supplier to the Sick', 26 July 1982, pp. 56–61.

Hax, A. C., and Majluf, N. S. (1984), *Strategic Management: Integrative Perspective*, Prentice-Hall, Englewood Cliffs, NJ.

Henderson, B. D. (1979), *Henderson on Corporate Strategy*, Abt Books, Cambridge, Mass.

Henderson, J. C., Rockart, J. F., and Sifonis, J. J. (1984), 'A Planning Methodology for Integrating Management Support Systems', *CISR Working Paper* **116**, MIT Center for Information Systems Research, Cambridge, Mass.

Ives, B., and Learmonth, G. P. (1984), 'The Information System as a Competitive Weapon', *Communications of the ACM*, **12**, **12**.

Leavitt, H. J. (1963), 'Applied Organizational Change in Industry', in *Handbook of Organizations*, Rand–McNally, Chicago, Ill.

Lorange, P., and Vancil, R. F. (1977), *Strategic Planning Systems*, Prentic-Hall, Englewood Cliffs, NJ.

——, Scott Morton, M. S., and Ghoshal, S. (1986), *Strategic Control*, West Publishing, St. Paul, MN.

McFarlan, F. W. (1984), 'Information Technology Changes the Way You Compete', *Harvard Business Review,* **62**, **3**.

Porter, M. (1980), *Competitive Strategy*, Free Press, New York.

—— (1985) *Competitive Advantage*, Free Press, New York.

Rockart, J. F. (1979), 'Chief Executives Define Their Own Data Needs', *Harvard Business Review*, March–April, pp. 81–93.

——, and Treacy, M. E. (1982), 'The CEO Goes On-Line', *Harvard Business Review* **60, 1**.

——, and Scott Morton, M. S. (1984), 'Implications of Changes in Information Technology for Competitive Strategy', *Interfaces* **14, 1**.

Schendel, D., and Hofer, C. W. (1979), *Strategic Management: A New View of Business Policy and Planning*, Little Brown and Company, Boston, Mass.

Scott Morton, M. S. (1979), 'Decision Support Systems—Emerging Tools for Planning', TIMS–ORSA Conference Proceedings, New Orleans, May.

——, Malone, T. W., and Luconi, F. L. (1986), 'Expert Systems: The Challenge for Managers', *Sloan Management Review* **26, 4**.

Simon, H. A. (1960), *The New Science of Management Decision*, Harper and Row, New York.

Strategic Planning Associates, Inc. (1981), 'Beyond the Portfolio', *Commentaries*, Washington DC.

Steiner, G. W. (1969), *Top Management Planning*, MacMillan & Co.

Wack, P. A. (1984), 'Learning to Design Planning Scenarios: The Experience of Royal Dutch Shell', published manuscript, Harvard Business School, March.

Strategic Exploitation of Information Technology

Section One was essentially prescriptive and normative. The case that IT is strategic and can yield competitive advantage was either proposed or taken for granted. Section Two contains *empirical* papers. Such research and experiential evidence is required for many reasons. First, the concept that IT can be exploited for strategic advantage needs verification. It is too easy to be persuaded by rhetoric and to attribute the adjective 'strategic' to an IT application. Cross-sectional surveys, self-reported case studies, and sectoral or longitudinal field work all will help test the 'strategic advantage assertion'. These are presented here.

Behind this primary question lie several related curiosities. How has any strategic advantage been derived and are there any common principles, directions, or patterns? What methods or techniques have firms employed to seek strategic advantage and are any of them effective? How closely linked to business strategy analysis and strategic planning does the search for, and implementation of, strategic applications of IT have to be? These are important questions to establish the reality of strategic information systems and to test whether a new perspective is required. For as Earl implied in the previous section, most of the strategic information systems frameworks proposed to date are in many ways conceptualizations and/or rationalizations of observed cases of clever exploitation of IT. Futhermore most of the strategic information systems search methodologies, whilst seeming to be grounded in common sense and analytical logic, are but tentative or experimental approaches.

For the strategy theorist and, thus ultimately for long-term business practice, there are some deeper questions. Perhaps the dominant one is whether competitive advantage really is available. In other words can competitive edge or competitive weapons based on IT generate sustainable comparative advantage? Or are many of the apparent strategic strikes achieved through IT ephemeral, being soon copied or eroded by rivals and other competitive forces? Indeed it is likely that many strategic initiatives using IT actually are concerned with catching up with competition in the search for competitive *parity*. This seems to be common in sectors such as airlines, banking, and retailing.

The strategist therefore may see traditional questions at stake here, distinguishing for example between offensive and defensive strikes. From this follows a policy issue of whether in different circumstances it pays to be a first, second, or 'me too' mover. Likewise when are individual thrusts preferred to collaboration and alliances? Then many businessmen already claim that internal productivity generating or efficiency-oriented systems are 'just as strategic as external, market place systems'. The strategist might agree if they support a clear generic strategy—for example of low cost production—or create a distinctive competence which the market place appears to value.

Then there are the sector level effects which both Porter and Millar (1985) and Parsons (1983) claim arise from IT. For example, sectors which are essentially information-processing activities and networks can change in structure dramatically. A trite example is the virtual disappearance of the London Stock Exchange trading floor within two weeks of the Big Bang introduction of the TOPIC and SEAQ computer systems in October 1986. More markedly, questions are raised about the survival of agents, brokers, and knowledge processing professional firms in many service industries. At the detailed level therefore issues arise of whether IT erodes or creates barriers to entry and whether the technology homogenizes markets and sectors or enables more differentiation to unfold and more niches to be created. In other words, important areas for study are the dynamics of sectors once IT becomes strategic and the redefinition of sectors one IT is pervasive.

Also, there would seem to be some special strategic questions about IT and its use. For example can technology drive strategy or is the reverse more normal? Are techniques and methodologies for searching for strategic uses of IT the key or do the complexity and strangeness of IT mean that corporate cultures and management attitudes and skills need changing first? Is it important to be able to assess the strategic case for an IT investment or are visions and acts of faith equally necessary? Does IT bring special problems of timeframes and capital costs, as executives often explain?

Finally is it important to distinguish between information and technology from a strategic perspective? The distinction is often valuable in avoiding expensive mistakes in developing conventional information systems. Certainly in building networks and constructing inter-organizational information systems the important question seems often to be not who owns the terminal or network but who owns the data or information. Yet, as we have seen in the competition between building societies in the UK, for some societies sharing networks makes cost and marketing sense; conversely for at least one player, creating an independent network seems to capitalize on market strength. Equally in supplier and customer links, being first or most acceptable with a terminal may provide a preemptive strike. Yet in an information-based sector will it ultimately matter? These appear to be fundamental questions. As Cash and Konsynski (1985) suggest, in any inter-organizational information system or communications network, the key business decision is the degree of control or influence an actor or a facilitator has over access and participation.

It would be extravagant to claim that all these questions are answered in this section. However most of them are addressed explicitly or implicitly. King seeks to bring some clarity and rigour to the concept of information technology and competitive advantage. He confronts researchers and practitioners with a useful degree of reality based on a survey of how 84 US firms have been using IT for some kind of competitive advantage. He also reports on their experience with different approaches to strategic planning for IT.

Gooding provides a detailed case history of one firm's—Ford in Europe—exploitation of IT in business development. Driven by competitive pressures, and seeking to build on Ford's strengths, a five-year set of programmes to implement business visions of IT has been pursued. There are few cases documenting the scale and pace of IT adoption in manufacturing and Gooding's paper fills an important gap. There are even fewer accounts of how one company has evolved in connecting IT to strategy over time and the management experiences encountered. Gooding's account is equally valuable on this front.

One sector where IT has become the mechanism for delivering a service is the leisure travel sector. Here, in principle, telecommunications provide a pervasive distribution channel with the arrival of value added networks via which reservation systems can operate. Feeny has used the sector therefore as a laboratory in which to examine how the different players have exploited IT for competitive advantage or turned to it for competitive parity. He traces the success of the market leader's IT developments and draws conclusions on how competitive advantage opportunities in vertical markets can be analysed and then implemented effectively. Feeny's paper also provides a case study on the emerging effects of IT on one sector's structure and dynamics.

Readers should conclude from this section that IT *can* provide strategic advantage. At least one managerial implication is that firms in quite different sectors may find themselves strategically vulnerable if they are not investing in IT and IS, or if such investments are not connected to business strategy, or if the resultant information systems are poor in quality.

References

Cash, J. I., and Konsynski, B. R. (1985), 'IS Redraws Competitive Boundaries', *Harvard Business Review* March–April.

Parsons, G. L. (1983), 'Information Technology: A New Competitive Weapon', *Sloan Management Review* **25**, **1**.

Porter, M. E., and Millar, V. E. (1985), 'How Information Gives you Competitive Advantage', *Harvard Business Review* July–August.

4

Using Information Technology for Competitive Advantage

WILLIAM KING with ELLEN HUFNAGEL and VARUN GROVER

Graduate School of Business, University of Pittsburgh

Only a few years ago, computers and information processing were seen largely as service activities that facilitated, but did not importantly influence, the operations of most firms. With the exception of firms that are in the 'information business' and those in which computers represent the 'core technology' of the business, for example commercial database services and banks respectively, most firms treated computer operations as a necessary expense item. The computer budget was typically controlled as were other expense categories like heat, electricity, etc., in terms of year-to-year changes and the percentage relationship to sales revenues (or some other such ratio). Investments in computer systems were frequently justified on the basis of projected cost savings, with little attention being explicitly given to the potential for added revenues or other benefits.

Concurrent with the proliferation of personal computers and word processors throughout the organization came the realization that investments in information resources were growing rapidly. The great potential for these investments to produce substantial benefits, rather than to merely enhance efficiency, also gained increasing recognition. Anecdotes describing firms that had successfully achieved such benefits were widely cited and the notion of information and information technology as 'strategic resources' or sources of potential 'competitive advantage' became commonplace (King, 1981; 1983; 1984).

Unfortunately, while these notions are potentially both important and powerful, they are also imprecise and unstructured. Most of the literature in the area continues to be anecdotal, and the remainder is primarily prescriptive. There is little evidence of an accepted or evaluated theoretical framework or structure for the ideas (although a myriad of conceptual and analytic frameworks have been suggested to be useful in this context) and there is even less in the way of empirical evidence concerning the validity and utility of these notions.

In this paper an attempt is made to consider some of the fundamental issues surrounding the notion of information as a strategic resource as well as to report on some empirical evidence as to what is actually being done by US firms in making these concepts operational. In particular, the objectives are:

1. to distinguish between 'strategic' uses of information resources and uses for purposes of 'competitive advantage',[1]
2. to draw a distinction between the use of information and of information technology for these ends,
3. to report on the *specific ways* in which information resources are actually being used for these purposes by business firms,
4. to report on the planning and decision making *processes* that are being used to identify and select opportunities for these uses of information resources, and
5. to report on organizational factors that *facilitate or inhibit* these different uses of information resources.

Information resources: Information versus Information Technology

One of the most obvious things that can be inferred from the anecdotes that appear in the literature concerning the strategic uses of information resources is that information and information technology are often discussed interchangeably. 'Information technology' can be thought of as a resource that is fairly well defined and readily measurable—in terms of the number, memory capacity, transmission speed, processing capacity, etc. of computer-based systems. 'Information' is a quite different resource, one that is less well understood and much more difficult to measure (King and Epstein, 1976). Thus, it appears to be necessary to make the distinction between these resources as clearly and explicitly as possible if a useful conceptual framework is to be developed. This is particularly important since the potential strategic applications of information technology may be quite different from potential strategic uses of information.

To clarify this distinction, then, the following pragmatic definitions of these two varieties of *information resources* are suggested:

Information technology can be defined as the hardware and software that is used to collect, transmit, process, and disseminate data (symbols) in an organization.

Information, according to a traditional (non-operational) definition, is 'data that have been evaluated for some use'. In most organizations, there are a variety of 'evaluation' filters that are applied to data. Thus, there are a variety of levels of information. For example, there are those data that have been evaluated for, and

---

[1] The term 'strategic uses' will be taken to be all-encompassing for the moment. Subsequently, we shall distinguish between strategic uses and uses that are directed toward achieving competitive advantage.

thereby incorporated into, a database, those data that are further evaluated and are thereby routinely reported to division managers, and so on.

Clearly, the ways in which information technology can be used as a strategic resource may be quite different from the ways in which information can be so used. Possibly, the processes that may effectively be employed to identify such opportunities and the organizational factors that facilitate or inhibit these processes are also different.

Some companies have used information technology to achieve strategic objectives. Taking advantage of technological advances in computing, they provide new ways of relating to buyers or to suppliers to gain advantage over competitors. For example, Firm *A* determined that relations with its customers could be strengthened by placing terminals in each customer location to allow for easier order placement as well as providing a means of advance price and availability checking. While this information was previously made available to customers by phone on request, it is now provided instantly via communication links. Customers are thereby 'tied into' Firm *A* in a way that makes it more difficult and less attractive for them to change suppliers.

In the case of Firm *A*, it is *information technology*, and *not the information itself*, (since the same information was previously available), that was the key factor in achieving improved customer relations and/or competitive advantage.

Other companies are *using information itself*, rather than merely information technology, as a key resource to support overall business strategy and to strengthen their competitive position. For instance, Firm *B* is employing a strategy of expansion through acquisition of related businesses. Having identified criteria for evaluating potential acquisitions, the company now scans a commercial database to identify acquisition prospects that meet the criteria. In doing so, they are *using new data or using available data in new ways* to widen the range of firms that are considered and to make better strategic acquisition choices.

In Firm *B*, it is the *use of important new information or of available information in new ways* that is the key to success. Although computer technology facilitates the processing of this information, it is not the technology itself, as in the case of Firm *A*, that provides the advantage.

The primary distinction between these two approaches lies in the source of the value added. In the first example, the *introduction of technology* increased the value of existing information by providing easier access or speeding up transfer time. In the second, *the information itself* provides a strategic advantage through the new uses to which it is put.

Of course, in some situations, *both* information technology and information can be used to gain competitive advantage. Airline *C*, which has already pursued the use of *information technology* by putting computer reservation terminals into travel agencies and operating its reservation system to achieve competitive advantage in the marketplace (King, 1981), now begins to use the detailed *information* on supply and demand for various routes that it has thereby obtained to optimally manage the availability of discount-priced seats on each of its flights. This ensures that it will more effectively capture a greater proportion of business travellers' total demand for regular-priced unrestricted tickets and at the same time fill otherwise-empty seats via low-priced tickets that are sold with restrictions on timing, penalties for changing reservations, etc. Thus, Airline *C* has used *both information technology* (the terminals in the agents' offices and the associated software which give it advantages in terms of the way in which the system is operated) *and information* (the supply-demand data for various routes and the associated analytic software) to gain strategic advantage.

It may be argued that the strategic uses of information technology and information are interdependent. For instance, in the airline example, the strategic use of the technology was a necessary precursor to the strategic use of the information. However, if the same information had been available through some means other than the propietory reservation system, the same use could have been made of it. This situation actually exists since some airline reservation systems generate additional revenues through sales of such information to other airlines.[2] For the purchaser of this information, it is information, and not information technology, that may be used in ways that make it a strategic resource.

The important point is that, in our failure heretofore to draw careful distinctions between strategic uses of information technology and such uses of information, we have stifled efforts to develop frameworks and processes for guiding our thinking.

This is so because information technology is inherently different from information. It has a physical being; it is tangible; it is easy to assess and measure by counts, memory capacities, and processing speeds. Further, it undoubtedly obeys certain 'rules' that information does not.

Information, on the other hand, is intangible and hard to assess or measure. The literature on the 'value of information', for instance, is vast, yet no single agreed-upon measure of information value exists (King and Epstein, 1976). Moreover, information does not obey some important 'conservation' rules; if one uses a financial resource, it is no longer available for alternative uses; if one uses information, it is still available. If one uses a portion of a physical resource, the remainder invariably has less value than the original amount. The use of information may even add value to the information that 'remains'.

Since information technology and information are so different, it may be that the two entities should be considered and dealt with separately if

---

[2] This raises the interesting management questions of how to price such information, whether to 'cripple' it, etc.

the best results are to be achieved. When managers in a firm attempt to identify strategic uses of information resources, for instance, ideas that relate primarily to information technology will usually emerge first and most prolifically because it is easier to visualize and deal with these tangibles. The intangible information resource is likely to be pushed into the background when, in fact, it may have the greater potential to produce benefits. So, it is important to make the distinction, if only because it helps us to think in different terms, with different models and expectations, about the two varieties of information resources.

However, one problem with this neat dichotomy is the role of software. Clearly some software, such as operating systems, compilers and computer languages, adds value in very much the same way as does hardware. Therefore these types of software can probably be assessed very much in the same terms as we use to value hardware, for example, processing speed, reliability, etc. On the other hand, applications software is different. This needs to be assessed primarily in terms of the *use* to which it is put, or the task that it performs, or the benefit that accrues from it in the task-context. Valuation here is similar to that required for information.

In the case of the previously-mentioned airline that uses both information and information technology strategically, the reservation system software that is used to collect and process data is very much part of the information technology. The software used to analyse the supply-demand data has attributes that are much like that of information.

The dividing line between information technology and information is therefore not completely clear, particularly at a time when even the distinction between hardware and software is itself becoming nebulous. Nonetheless, the distinction is useful to guide one's thinking about the strategic opportunities that may be provided by information technology and information.

The Strategic Use of Information Resources

Whichever variety of information resource is being dealt with, the literature has not clearly distinguished between *strategic* uses of information resources and those *applications that are aimed at using information resources as 'competitive weapons'*. A strategic use is one that is aimed at achieving a sustainable comparative advantage; a 'competitive weapon' is anything that is useful in competing in the marketplace.

Because the literature has been so imprecise, it is not surprising that managers tend to discuss specific opportunities or accomplishments in the 'strategic' domain in terms that do not really apply. How, for example, can a new inventory control system be used to achieve a sustainable comparative advantage? While many such 'organizational support' systems are discussed in the literature, they are generally designed to create greater organizational efficiency. They are seldom strategic, in the sense that they are not a key element of the organization's strategy and they do not importantly influence its ability to achieve a *sustained comparative advantage*—which is the objective of all strategy.

That is not to say that an inventory control system *cannot* be strategic or important to the achievement of comparative advantage; it merely suggests that most such descriptions in the literature are justified not on these grounds but on grounds that they represent complex and expensive applications of information technology. The implication is that they 'must' be strategic! However, it just isn't so! For an inventory control system to be strategic, it must play a direct role in the implementation of the business strategy and the achievement of a sustainable comparative advantage. This might be the case if product availability were a critical success factor for the business and/or if inventory costs were a major cost element for a firm seeking to compete as a low-cost producer.

In most other cases, an inventory control system, however complex, sophisticated, and costly it may be, is neither strategic in terms of importance to the organization's goals nor more than a secondary element in its seeking of comparative advantage. Such systems perform traditional support roles much as the heat and light systems perform support roles. They may be 'competitive weapons' in the sense that they help in the competitive struggle, or even because they can be 'pointed to with pride' to impress customers or to help close sales, but they are seldom really strategic in nature.

To be a strategic use of information resources, the information resource application must be a significant element of the business strategy—the way in which the firm seeks to gain a sustainable comparative advantage in the marketplace. Although the term is defined only imprecisely, the anecdotes in the literature suggest that a system can be a 'competitive weapon' on the basis of much less potential impact.

The Empirical Study

Having conceptualized the dinstinction between information technology and information, and having defined 'truly strategic' applications of information resources, we set out to identify the ways in which these resources were actually being used by business firms. We also wished to identify the business processes which provide the framework for such decision-making and any organizational characteristics that might serve to facilitate or inhibit these processes. The data were gathered using a mail survey of information executives (members of the Society for Information Management).

A variety of frameworks has been prescribed to aid manages in identifying potential strategic uses of information resources. The most fundamental of these appears to be Porter's (1980) well-known model which describes the competitive business environment in terms of five primary competitive 'forces'.

Because of the great face validity and widespread awareness of these notions, an adaptation of this model was used as a basis for collecting data concerning the specific strategic applications that firms had made of information and information technology. Consistent with this approach, we asked respondents whether or not their firms had made strategic use of both information technology of information in the areas of:

1. supplier relations,
2. customer service,
3. product/service differentiation,
4. new product planning,
5. cost competitiveness,
6. market segmentation.

In each question, we gave an example of what each application might be expected to do and then asked respondents to provide their own specific examples to substantiate any positive responses that they gave. Because of the potential importance of the use of information technology in the area of environmental scanning we also asked similar questions in that domain (Fahey and King, 1977).

Respondents were further asked to judge the *relative importance* of each of these areas, both currently and in the future, by selecting and putting in order of priority the three most significant areas.

We were also interested in the organizational processes and systems that might be used to address these important issues. Therefore, we asked whether the value-added chain (Grant and King, 1982) was used as a basis for identifying such opportunities. Additional questions focused on the frequency and nature of the process used now and three years ago by each firm and whether any formal processes exist for:

1. soliciting ideas,
2. funding the exploration of ideas,
3. providing administrative support, or
4. measuring the benefits that are expected to result, or which do result, from uses of information or information technology to gain comparative advantage.

From the literature on implementation, we identified organizational factors that have been studied as facilitators and inhibitors in various contexts. These were reviewed for overlap and redundancy and modified to apply more specifically to the information and information technology enviroment. On a five-point scale ranging from 'greatly inhibiting' to 'not an inhibiting factor' and 'greatly facilitating' to 'not a facilitating factor', respondents were asked to judge the degree to which each of these factors had in fact been an inhibiting or facilitating agent. Ten inhibitors were tested and nine facilitators were tested.

Results of the Study

Table 4.1 shows the industry distribution of the 84 responses, representing 84 different firms, that were received. Manufacturers are represented somewhat more heavily in these responses than in the sample to which the survey was mailed, indicating a possible bias. This should be kept in mind when interpreting these results.

Table 4.2 shows the summary of yes–no responses of 84 respondents to the six areas of potential strategic application for *information technology*. Over 64% of respondents claimed to have installed applications in the area of customer service and more than 66% claimed applications in cost competitiveness. Surprisingly, only slightly more than 28% claimed applications in supplier relations.

Table 4.1. *Respondents by Line of Business (n = 84)*

Manufacturer	38.10
Finance/Insurance/Real Estate	11.90
Medicine/Law/Education	2.38
Wholesale/Retail Trade	8.33
Bus Services	7.14
Government	2.38
Public Utility/Communications/Transport	13.10
Mining/Construction/Agriculture	14.29
Publisher	1.19

Table 4.2. *Areas of Application for* Information Technology *as a Strategic Resource (n = 84)*

Area of Strategic Application	No (%)	Yes (%)	No response (%)
Customer Service	34.52	64.29	1.19
Supplier Relations	71.43	28.57	—
Product/Service Differentiation	54.76	45.24	
New Product Planning	64.29	32.14	3.57
Market Segmentation	58.33	41.67	—
Cost Competitiveness	30.95	66.67	2.38
Other	71.43	26.19	2.38

Table 4.3 shows the same summary with respect to strategic *information-based* applications. While the largest proportion is also in the area of customer relations, the profile is quite different. Only 39.29% claim applications of information in the area of cost competitiveness (compared with almost 67% for such applications of information technology) and over 52% had applied information to market segmentation.

So, while the primary application of both information technology and information is to customer service, the overall profile of areas of such applications is different for the two varieties of information resources.

With regard to the processes used in the organization to identify opportunities for the application of information technology and/or information for competitive advantage, only 15.48% of respondents indicated that they used the value-added chain framework.

When asked to describe the frequency of the process employed as either continuous, regular, or irregular (Fahey and King, 1977) the responses given are as shown in Table 4.4. Nearly 55% reported either 'irregular' or 'no formal process', suggesting that *analyses dealing with information technology and information as a strategic resource have not yet become a routine and regular part of the planning process.* This is confirmed by the responses to a question of whether these analyses were made as a regular element of the IS planning process, the business planning process or 'no formal' process. While 28.57% indicated 'IS planning', 15.48% indicated 'business planning' and 51.19% indicated 'no formal process'.[3]

Table 4.3. *Areas of Application for* Information *as a Strategic Resource (n — 84)*

Area of Strategic Application	No (%)	Yes (%)	No response (%)
Customer Service	33.33	64.29	2.38
Supplier Relations	57.14	40.48	2.38
Product/Service Differentiation	61.90	36.90	1.19
New Product Planning	64.29	34.52	1.19
Market Segmentation	46.63	52.38	1.19
Cost Competitiveness	60.71	39.29	—
Other	79.76	15.48	4.76

Table 4.4. *Frequency of Process for Dealing with Strategic Information (n — 84)*

Continuous	Regular	Irregular	No Formal
22.62%	19.05%	34.52%	22.62%

[3] Note that the 'no formal' option was provided as a rough consistency check in two different questions dealing with the 'frequency' and 'nature' of the process. Given the imperfect distinction between the 'irregular' and 'no formal' responses to the frequency item, the responses seem to be quite consistent.

As to whether formal approaches exist for idea generation, funding, administration, and result measurement, only administrative support and result measurement stand out at all—35.71% and 32.14% respectively, compared to less than 30% for the other two areas.

These overall results suggest that formal processes have not yet been widely developed for identifying and supporting the development of ideas for using information technology and information as strategic resources.

Table 4.5 shows the areas of opportunity as they were ranked in terms of *relative importance* by the respondents. As expected, 57.14% ranked customer service first and only 10.71% omitted it from their top three choices. Surprisingly, supplier relations and new product planning, two of the areas commonly suggested in the literature as particularly fertile ones, were omitted from the top three by more than 80% of the respondents. It was also surprising to note that market segmentation, which was second in terms of frequency of application for information, was not ranked in the top three by nearly 68% of respondents. This suggests that this area may be perceived as having already been 'milked' for its primary benefits.

Table 4.5.   *Relative Importance of Areas of Application (n = 84)*

	First	Second	Third	Other
Customer Service	57.14	21.43	9.52	10.71
Supplier Relations	0.00	9.52	7.14	82.14
Product/Service Differentiation	9.52	23.81	16.67	48.81
New Product Planning	3.57	5.95	3.57	85.71
Market Segmentation	5.95	10.71	14.29	67.86
Cost Competitiveness	17.86	22.62	25.00	33.33

Thirteen possible inhibitors that may have 'actually prevented or inhibited your company's efforts to utilize information or information technology for strategic purposes' were identified and respondents were asked to rate each of them on a five-point scale. Table 4.6 shows the results.

The relative importance of information resources as a strategic priority for the organization, the lack of appropriate planning, the lack of top management support, and the difficulty in assessing tangible contributions stand out as major inhibitors. These results strongly suggest that information resource-based areas of opportunity still have not received adequate attention from top management, through priorities that have been set, through integration into the planning process, or through the development of measurement paradigms. Thus, while the area is much discussed, it seems obvious that more remains to

Table 4.6. *Organizational Inhibitors, Mean and standard deviation; 1 = Not Inhibiting; 2 = Greatly Inhibiting.*

	Mean	Standard deviation
Lack of appropriate planning	3.310	1.270
Low perceived importance of concept	3.096	1.2555
Lack of appropriate technical support staff	2.298	1.240
Budgetary constraints	3.036	1.156
Difficulty in assessing tangible contribution	3.429	1.021
Complexity of the concept	2.855	1.095
High potential start-up difficulties	2.786	1.042
Lack of organizational/top management support	3.250	1.334
Power and politics in the firm	2.952	1.496
Nature of external environment or industry	2.750	1.260
Ill-defined management objectives	2.893	1.193
Other priorities (are more important)	3.590	1.082
Other (please specify)	4.75	0.463

Table 4.7. *Organizational Facilitators. Mean and standard deviation; 1 = Not facilitating 2 = Greatly facilitating.*

	Mean	Standard deviation
Strong market position of the firm	2.951	1.396
Existing information technology leadership position	1.171	1.284
Strong planning capability of the firm	2.378	1.118
Extensive computer facilities within the firm	3.220	1.2470
Strong organizational/top managment	2.598	1.294
Pressure from competition	3.146	1.228
Strong technical support/expertise within the firm	3.395	1.069
Strong financial position of the Firm	3.134	1.284
Need for uniqueness of innovation	2.671	1.218
Other (please specify)	4.250	0.957

be done in integrating strategic information-based considerations into the strategic milieu of the organization.

With respect to facilitators, the ten items on the left of Table 4.7 were identified. The primary facilitators were, as expected, strong technical support and expertise, the leadership position in information technology, competitive pressure, financial position, and computer facilities. Thus, the existence of appropriate resources and competitive pressures appear to be the strongest facilitators of effective performance in this area.

Summary

The distinction between 'information' and 'information technology' as well as the distinction between 'strategic' applications and those that merely constitute the use of information resources as 'competitive weapons' are posited as being important to the further development of rigorous frameworks, processes, and research in the area of the strategic employment of information resources.

Preliminary analysis of an empirical survey suggests that:

1. the areas in which information technology and information have found most frequent strategic application are, in fact, different.
2. Different importance profiles exist for areas of opportunity for the two varieties of information resources.
3. Most organizations have not yet instituted formal processes for assessing and implementing business strategies that are based on information resources.
4. The factors that are most important in respectively facilitating and inhibiting such uses of information and information technology can be identified.

References

Fahey, L., and King, W. R. (1977), 'Environmental Scanning in Corporate Planning', *Business Horizons* **20**, **4**, pp. 61–71.

Grant, J., and King, W. R. (1982), *The Logic of Strategic Planning*, Little, Brown, and Company.

King, W. R. (1981), *Information as a Strategic Resource*, **WP 504**, Graduate School of Business, University of Pittsburgh, Pa.

—— (1982), 'New Strategic Business Resource: Information', *Proceedings of the National Seminar on Strategic Planning*, New Delhi, India, 14–15 December 1982.

—— (1983), 'Information as a Strategic Resource', editor's comment, *Management Information Systems Quarterly* **7**, **3**.

—— (1984), 'Exploiting Information as a Strategic Resource', *International Journal of Policy and Information* **8**, **1**, pp. 1–8.

—— and Cleland, D. I. (1974), 'Environmental Information Systems for Strategic Marketing Planning', *Journal of Marketing* **38**, **4**, pp. 35–40.

—— and Epstein, B. (1976), 'Assessing the Value of Information', *Management Datamatics* **5**, **4**, pp. 171–80.

Porter, M. E. (1980), *Competitive Strategy*, Free Press, New York.

5

Exploiting IT in Business Development: Ford in Europe

GRAHAM GOODING

Ford in Europe

Ford of Europe

Ford of Europe Incorporated was formed in 1967 to co-ordinate the various Ford activities in Europe. There are two product design and engineering centres, one in Essex and the other at Cologne. There are manufacturing facilities in five countries. Car assembly operations are located in Britain, Germany, Belgium, and Spain, and facilities for manufacturing light vans and heavy trucks are sited in Britain and Belgium. Fifth is France with a powertrain facility. These vehicle assembly plants are, in turn, supported by some twenty-five feeder plants, most machining and assembling power train components such as Engines, Transaxles, Transmissions, and Rear Axles. The large car body and assembly operations each employ between 6,000 and 8,000 people and the powertrain plants 1,000 to 2,000 people.

Ford has Vehicle and Parts Sales Operations in fifteen European countries selling through some 2,500 independent dealers. These dealers are also supported by a Parts Distribution system with depots in most countries.

Ford's Business Environment

The fundamental challenge facing Ford in Europe is to carve out a viable, profitable business in the changed conditions of the late eighties and nineties. Little or no significant growth in the European economies is forecast. The Japanese have taken the Export markets and made inroads into the European domestic scene. This has been achieved with vehicles built in Japan and imported into Europe, despite constraints on imports in some national markets. The more immediate threat is from Nissan's manufacturing facilities at Washington, England, now coming on stream. This will give Nissan the status of a European manufacturer with a significant cost advantage over local manufacturers.

Faced, then, with significant over-capacity, Ford cannot look to volume growth or sales revenue for a strategy for survival. Instead, we have developed strategies that will drive down our costs. Also the Japanese have taught us that quality is the key to productivity.

Our key survival strategies are, therefore, concentrated on five broad areas:

1. Improved quality, as the key to customer satisfaction and loyalty.
2. Quality of share, that is, improving margins by more cost-efficient products while maintaining market share.
3. Improved productivity, by reducing fixed costs in all areas of the business.
4. Investment in human resource management by encouraging increased employee involvement and instituting major retraining programmes as our numbers of personnel decrease and the skill requirements increase.
5. Joint Ventures, pursuing profitable business opportunities with other automobile manufacturers.

All these strategies are focused on the cost side of the equation. They are all rooted in 1985 actual performance, a profitable year which gives us confidence in the strategic direction we are pursuing.

The Role of Information Technology

The importance of computing and telecommunications in our business has long been recognized. Over the last 15 years, for example, the US aircraft and automotive industries have led the way with the development of computer-aided design (CAD) concentrating on body surface geometry. More recently, we in Europe have seen an exploding population of robots on the shop floor. At the end of 1980, we had a robot count of 106. By the end of 1985, this had increased to 1,350 and is forecast to increase significantly in the years ahead.

As a large engineering and manufacturing organization, all the computing and telecommunications technologies have application somewhere in Ford's business. We are involved in basic vehicle and engine research, product engineering techniques, manufacturing automation, as well as the full range of business computing that reaches out to our dealers and suppliers. Our computing growth statistics follow industry trends.

If all this is true, what, then, is new? I will borrow the stage concept (Gibson and Nolan, 1974) and suggest three 'stages' which illustrate significant change.

Stage One—Cost Efficiency: old history which saw extensive use of computing, which was always cost-justified and employed as a contributor to efficiency. Growth was largely technology-constrained.

Stage Two—Business Linkage: in the last five years, a period of massive growth in the use of computing. Still the emphasis has been on cost effective use to support efficiencies. However, there has been, on the part of senior operating management, an increasing awareness that computing and telecommunications technologies were major factors in determining the competitive edge. Essentially, it was important to establish linkage of systems initiatives to corporate business objectives in order to give coherence and purpose to the large investments in hardware and people. By stressing, for example, the savings in time, quality and productivity being gained by the Japanese we were able to accelerate our investment in CAD/CAM, as part of our response to that competitive threat. The key word is 'linkage'.

Stage Three—Strategic Investment: now establishing linkages to corporate business objectives is no longer enough. The language has changed. The talk today is of the next battleground which will be fought over the competitive deployment of computer and telecommunications resources. This means, in our industry that, say, decisions to invest in Computer Integrated Manufacturing (CIM) will rank alongside mainstream product decisions.

While this transition is most usually thought of in computing terms, the change has been greater for the Telecommunications fraternity. In Stages One and Two they were judged as wire-providers of cost effective services. In Stage Three, they too, must come out on to the battlefield and into the front line. Only recently have I been able to establish a Telecommunications Business Planning activity, where the key word is Business.

In short, Ford in Europe recognizes the role that Information Technology is playing in responding to the competitive challenges of the late 1980s and 1990s. This awareness has been reflected in the evolution of our Systems Business Planning in recent years.

Systems Business Planning

Ford in Europe uses a three-stage corporate planning process. In the First Quarter of the year we complete a Strategic Review which is focused on the tough survival issues. This is followed in the Second Quarter by a Corporate Business Plan which is supported by a five-year run-out of profits, cash flow returns, etc. In the Third Quarter, we produce the following year's Budget.

We first produced a Systems Business Plan in 1982. The Plan is structured in two parts: The outward facing section or demand section embraces our users' demands, and builds into the Applications Portfolio. The inward facing, or supply section, reviews the Enabling Technologies, feeding new opportunities back in to the Applications Portfolio to be expressed as new business opportunities.

In the initial years the Systems Business planning process coexisted with the corporate planning process. In 1985, the Corporate Business Plan included an Information Technology Plan. In 1986, computing and telecommunications are an integral part of the Strategic Review. Our senior operating management have acknowledged that we 'own' one of the resources that will ensure competitive advantage or survival.

We introduced the concept of business visions to give coherence and a sense of purpose to our work and to provide those working with the Information Technologies with mission statements. Four such statements were derived.

1. To bring quality products to market faster. Along with the rest of the automobile industry we have recognized the Strategic importance of CAD/CAM. We are committed to the day when all design work will be enacted through the screen.
2. Manufacture high quality low cost products. Here, the key is computer integrated manufacturing as we seek to integrate CAD/CAM, Machine Process Control, and the Production material scheduling systems.
3. Get close to the customer. Here, the key is telecommunications as we seek to be more responsive to our customer demands.
4. Merge computing and telecommunications resources. We see this as crucial in supporting the other three statements. We seek a seamless weld but do not think it will be achieved without friction. The opportunities are immense, as is the task.

On a visit to Japan in 1981, we had concluded that the Japanese were ahead of Ford in Europe in the exploitation of CAD/CAM. We recognized that the CAD/CAM lead gave the Japanese potential competitive advantages in time, quality and productivity. Therefore in 1982, we defined three key elements in our CAD/CAM strategy for Ford in Europe. We believed, that in Product Development, CAD already had achieved critical mass. By this we meant the coming together of the technology, economics, and an invested base of expertise. From this base, the first element of our strategy was to accelerate penetration of the technology in product development, firmly targeted at the Scorpio and following models. Next we had to achieve critical mass with CAD/CAM in Manufacturing. Finally we had to prepare for the day when our suppliers, with their own CAD/CAM systems, would be an integral part of our automated design and manufacturing processes.

Achievements To Date

I can now report our achievements to date through four business cameos. In product development compared with 28 CAD workstations in 1981, we now have 168 workstations installed. We expect to install a total of 300 workstations by 1990. Always we focus CAD penetration on our new products. The Sierra launched in 1982 had 8% of the design work carried out by CAD. We trebled this to 25% for the launch of the Scorpio. New models being engineered now have to percent the design work carried out by CAD, and we target 90% penetration in 3 to 5 year's time.

Program leadtime in Product Development has been shortened by 2 months for the body tooling of a new model launch. Even more impressive time savings have been made in specific areas, like prototype model manufacture. Futhermore, with compatible CAD/CAM strategies across Ford affiliates worldwide, we have been able to exchange design geometry in joint exercises with Ford US and Ford Australia. We also have started the same process with the most advanced of our suppliers.

We now decree that all designs started on CAD are maintained on CAD for life, to guarantee the integrity of the CAD data for the growing number of downstream CAD/CAM processes. We call this commitment 'Once-on-CAD, Always-on-CAD', an essential stage in the progression towards a totally CAD environment.

To date the focus on our efforts therefore has been within our Product Development activity, and between it and our Manfacturing activities. For us, that involves moving large volumes of CAD data between Britain and Germany. These traffic flows of CAD data are projected to increase rapidly, especially when communicating with our Suppliers gathers momentum. Indeed, we see CAD data as the future driver of traffic growth requiring high speed data links across Europe. Accordingly, one of our prime objectives is to get ahead of the traffic growth curve and implement wide bandwidth networks so that we continue to support rather than constrain our business.

In manufacturing, our objective was to achieve critical mass. In fact, the groundrules were changed as the acronym became not CAD/CAM but CIM. And, even before this acronym settles down, our management has begun to think of it as the integration of *all* computers in Manufacturing, as depicted in Fig. 5.1.

From a base of one workstation in 1981, there are now 57 graphics workstations installed in Manufacturing. We are projecting a five-fold increase over the next five years as the technology moves out into the manufacturing plants. At our Body and Assembly Operations, the emphasis is on sheet metal die design, die model manufacturing, and die manufacturing. Automation in these areas is taking 4 months out of the

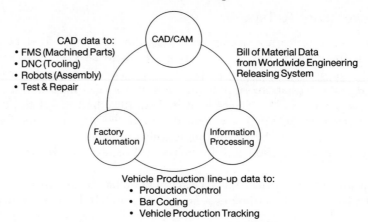

Fig. 5.1. Computer Integrated Manufacturing Data Flows for Integration

design cycle. We can now flow CAD data right through from design to 5-Axis DNC metal cutting of the dies without the need for wood models.

Our manufacturing engineeers in Power Train are also doing exciting things, including numerical control tool machining of gearboxes driven by CAD data from Product Development. Additionally, CAD/CAM is being used for tolerance charting, process layouts, in-process sketches, robot cell design, and tool design. We are into our second explosion of CAD workstations as these applications start to flow out into our Plants.

Ford's interpretation of CIM is the integration of those elements of CAD/CAM, shop-floor process control and business systems used to manage a manufacturing plant. For vehicle production, we have implemented a CIM architecture through five levels of the production hierarchy (Fig. 5.2). These are

1. European production programming, covering our total vehicle manufacturing base.
2. Production scheduling of an operation or manufacturing site which has, say, body construction, paint, and vehicle assembly facilities.
3. Production tracking at the operations level.
4. Plant monitoring of production, quality and maintenance in, for example, a body construction plant.
5. At the lowest level, computer-controlled manufacturing cells, for example, the body weld robots.

Through this computer integration, we can now pass electronic images of vehicle orders submitted by Sales through the manufacturing process right down to the control of body weld robots on the factory floor.

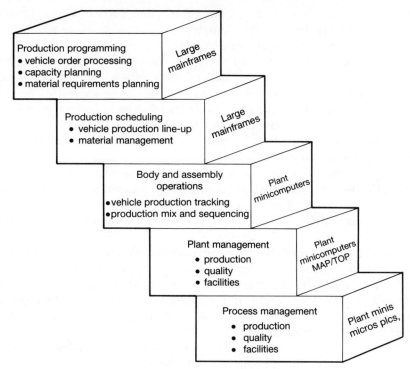

Fig. 5.2. CIM Architecture

Increasingly effective telecommunications will be of critical import-ance here. In addition to CAD traffic growth, we are experiencing a major growth in data transfer between our manufacturing plants and predicting major growth in information exchange with our suppliers. For some time we have been piloting electronic transmission of the weekly releases of our six month production schedules, daily advice of our ten-day production line-ups and, of course, just-in-time deliveries.

All this activity is poised to move forward at speed. For Ford, it is a European project playing to our multi-national strength.

In Sales and contributing to 'Getting close to the customer', we have made several initiatives. Ford has a Europe-wide parts distribution system. In moving into the electronic era, it is absolutely vital that we maintain and enhance the competitiveness of these networks. We must reach out and build customer loyalty.

Indeed Ford is the only automotive manufacturer in Europe that recommends a particular in-dealership computing system to its dealers. This system provides point-of-sale, inventory management, and manage-ment services. There are dial-up batch communication links to Ford. We now have 830 dealers in 10 countries on the system. We are targeting

1,000 dealers who handle 50% of the Vehicle and Parts business. That is quite an achievement in the complex European market, when you recognize that our dealers are independent businessman.

In parallel, we have been developing dial-up interactive enquiry services using Videotex. At the end of 1985, 30% of our dealers used these services to locate vehicles or enquire of the order status. 70% of our dealers have interactive Parts Rush Order capability. Our plan is to implement these services in all dealerships.

The scene is set therefore for automating the vehicle order process. We are presently piloting in Britain a plain-language, menu-driven ordering process. That process will be common across Europe, regardless of the media employed. We are adding a low-cost personal computer to our product line to give us extended coverage of the market. The customer will be able to define and check his order, and Ford will edit it before it leaves the dealership.

Once the orders have been captured electronically we can eliminate paper orders and in-desk order banks. Order bank management will be greatly improved with the creation of a Euro-order bank, which, in turn, will stabilize the scheduling of our manufacturing plants. Our plans extend that inter-activity to our supply base and so take significant time out of the vehicle ordering process.

All this is an important step in building customer loyalty. A motor trade magazine in Britain recently voted Ford dealerships as having the best computing and telecommunications capability. We aim to keep it that way and earn that accolade in the other countries in which we operate.

Again, our sales initiatives boost traffic growth. We have long experience of exchanging data electronically with our dealers. In capturing vehicle orders electronically, and managing Euro-order banks, we greatly increase the criticality of telecommunications to our business.

A fourth cameo is in the administrative area. The Finance community is committed to a staff reduction objective of 50% with a FINEFIM or Finance Efficiency Improvement Program. This program reflects employee involvement concepts with a series of workgroups seeking to write the charter for finance for the nineties.

One of these groups has been exploring information architectures or, as I would prefer, information sharing concepts. As we embark on a major program of 'core' systems renewals, we are seeking to establish whether we can provide the Decision Support Systems long advocated by leading thinkers. Can we provide a 'Finance database' or architecture of information stores that will permit Finance to support business decisions far more effectively than today, in terms of both accuracy and cost?

More specifically, can we, for example, provide on-line the economic profits of vehicles sold in, say, Switzerland? Can we call up the revenues of Escorts sold in Switzerland and compare those revenues with the variable costs of production in Spain? To enable us to answer that question requires common product definitions—an unbelievably complex issue—and single stores or sources of volumes, prices, costs, exchange rates, etc. And, to provide all that on the desk will require major cultural change, for we will be at the seventh layer of telecommunication with all the lower levels defined and in place.

The final achievement has been in teleconferencing. In order to demonstrate one competitive opportunity that telecommunications can offer, we have installed full motion videoconferencing between Essex and Colgone using the latest compressed transmission techniques. In May 1983, British Telecom demonstrated 2 megabit compressed videoconferencing to us in the laboratories. All the European PTTs had just adopted the 2 megabit protocol as standard. We were pursuaded that compressed video technology was available and cost-effective. We were interested in using videoconferencing in a problem-solving environment. Our video facilities would allow Product and Manufacturing Engineering staff to stimulate the 'see-and-touch' of problem solving without the need to travel between locations. In October 1983, we said we would provide, in May 1984, satellite videoconferencing facilities to support the Scorpio launch. At the time, the European Communications Satellite— ESC I—was still on test

The videoconferencing facilities were commissioned on schedule in May 1984. It was just 12 months on from seeing the system demonstrated in the laboratories. We had designed, built, and equipped the studios. We had established the satellite links in Britain and Germany, requiring microwave and landline connections to the PTT earthstations. We had trained our users, and, by means of a questionnaire determined how we would evaluate what, at that time, was a trial. We were the first commercial, non-media user of the European Satellite.

The trial was successful and the service has since been institutionalized. We have added a third studio in Germany, and have, on an experimental basis, linked up with public networks in the US and Japan. We are still the only commercial, non-media user of the European Satellite.

Lessons and Issues

What then are the lessons learnt and the outstanding issues that we must address? Five areas emerge.

1. I remember all those years ago being apprehensive of having to rule on technical choices. 'Do not worry', said the consultants, 'have your people express the technical options in terms of business choices'. For

the most part this has worked but it is a painful process. We came to videoconferencing by way of wanting to make a contribution at the heart of our business—reducing the time it takes to bring quality products to market. The classic route of a technical solution looking for a problem, in this case, reducing travel costs, would have failed.

Today, we look at our voice-dominated networks and electro-mechanical telephone exchanges, and people plead for new 'phones. Voice modernization is not a winning strategy. If we, however, focus the business case on the need for efficient, wide-bandwidth networks to transport CAD geometry as the springboard to CIM, a critical survival factor for us, we are likely, as an economy of innovation to achieve that modernization of the voice exchanges.

2. As recently as two years ago when we looked at the issues involved in investing in digital networks namely the mix of technical, regulatory, 'ownership', and human resource issues, we focused on the technical issues. Today, the issues are the same but human resource issues dominate.

3. We have worked hard at customer support using the Systems Business Planning process. We have our users (customers) involved, and reasonably satisfied, an essential platform from which to involve senior management.

4. The Systems Planning Process has increased Operating Manage-ment involvement. I would mislead if I implied that our management is as familiar with the economics of telecommunications as, say, profit and loss accounts and balance sheets. But, we are set for the next stage when our senior operating management not only acknowledge that IT is strategic to our business, but as a consequence, acknowledge that they must manage the resource.

5. There is nothing in the career progression of programmer, systems analyst, project manager, or IT manager that equips our people to deal with the management issues of today or tomorrow. I am privileged to lead a splendid group of people. I would like to think that as part of their career development they could take time out and qualify as MBAs in Information Technology.

In conclusion, I offer two reflections from nearly five years experience of striving to exploit IT in business development. First, we are no longer constrained by technology. Indeed, there is merit in being at the leading edge as we have demonstrated with videoconferencing, and as we are now doing with Expert Systems. It is a time for boldness, a time for encouraging innovation, a time for rewarding creativity. Second, we are constrained by company culture, organization, and people issues. Our ability to respond to technological change is moving at a much slower rate than the technology itself. Systems directors are required to be battlefield commanders, advancing on all fronts. The idea that Systems resources can be prioritized is irrelevant and misleading. Tomorrow's winners will have encouraged innovation and creativity in exploiting technology, but to be winners they will also have found new and inventive ways to deliver these technologies.

References

Gibson, C. F., and Nolan, R. L. (1974), 'Managing the Four Stages of EDP Growth', *Harvard Business Review*, January–February.

6

Creating and Sustaining Competitive Advantage with IT

DAVID FEENY

Oxford Institute of Information Management, Templeton College, Oxford

The Promised Opportunity

The emerging importance of Information Technology (IT) as a tool for supporting or facilitating the achievement of competitive advantage has been widely recognized during the past few years. An often quoted exemplar is the American Hospital Supply Company, who established direct IT links with their customers. In the period 1978–83, AHS revenues grew at 17% per annum (versus an overall decline in the size of the industry sector) and AHS achieved a return on sales which was four times the industry average. Authors such as Benjamin *et al.* (1984), McFarlan (1984), Parsons (1983), and Wiseman (1985) have cited other firms who have achieved competitive advantage through IT in many industry sectors.

The AHS exemplar (and many others, as Runge (1985) has stressed) depends upon the communications element of IT to establish applications which operate between companies. Broadly speaking, these Inter-Organizational Systems (IOS) can be divided into two types: one variety operates like an enhanced postal system, on a store-and-forward basis, and is used to improve the timeliness, and reduce the cost of information flows between the organizations concerned. Other benefits, such as reduced inventories and faster reaction to changing market conditions, can flow from the improved information cycle. The participants then bargain on how to share the results. A further dimension is added in the second variety when, as in the AHS case, the IOS operates on a truly interactive basis. The immediate access which, for example, the buyer can get to information such as price and availability can be instrumental in determining where he places the business. In other words, the system can affect the *level* of business which flows between the organizations it links, as well as the cost of servicing such business. While Cash and Konsynski (1985) caution that IOS may also insidiously alter the balance of power between buyer and supplier (by increasing switching costs), this can be interpreted as further underlining the importance of telecommunications as a new competitive variable. Indeed Clemons and

McFarlan (1986) have written that 'The new technologies of communications have the power to change the competitive game for almost all companies of all sizes'.

In Europe, the scope for IOS has historically been limited by the monopoly supply position of PTTs. However in the UK the Telecommunications liberalization legislation of 1981 fundamentally changed the position by allowing non-PTT organizations to develop and market so-called Value Added Network Services (VANS) built onto the basic transmission facilities provided by licensed common carriers. While the precise definition of VANS has consistently eluded commentators and even legislators, the concept is clear enough: a VANS provides some or all of the elements needed to move from transmission facilities to end-user systems. We can think of these additional elements as falling into three broad categories:

1. Enabling services which are concerned with surmounting hardware constraints, and are transparent to the end-user. Examples are protocol and/or speed conversion between disparate terminal devices; or packet-switching to allow large numbers of users to make simultaneous use of a single physical network.
2. Services which provide enhanced business communications. These may be general purpose services such as electronic mail or teleconferencing; or specific services such as Tradanet which links retailers and their suppliers to exchange orders, invoices etc. in industry standard format.
3. Full application services provided across a network. These services equate to our second category of IOS. Instead of just forwarding an order to a supplier as in Tradanet, the retailer actually enters the order onto the supplier's system, probably after displaying price and availability information from the supplier's system files.

Now consider the effect of the 1981 legislation on a business which is seeking competitive advantage from IT. Suppose the intention is to provide some desirable IT-based service to its customers who are situated up and down the country. The company no longer needs to negotiate with British Telecom whether such a scheme is allowable; it no longer needs to possess the scarce and expensive staff who understand how to implement telecommunications-based applications successfully; it no longer needs to invest large sums of money building a network which inevitably will have low utilization unless/until the system's success can be established. It can reasonably expect to find a third party VANS supplier who will provide an established shared network facility, and charge for it on the basis of utilization. A relatively low-cost, low-risk opportunity is opening up for organizations to invest in IOS in search of competitive advantage.

The Research Question

In this environment it seems important to consider the impact of IOS at the level of an Industry Sector. Sectors, or 'Vertical Markets', such as Insurance, Automotive, and Retail are the early targets of the major VANS suppliers—IBM, ICL, ISTEL, and British Telecom. Ideas for the applications enshrined in IOS are coming from existing exemplars and from the prescriptive frameworks offered by authors like Ives and Learmonth (1984) and Porter and Miller (1985). But what enables a particular company to succeed with IOS while others in the sector fail? And what, if anything, prevents competitors from quickly following the first successful company and cancelling out any advantage—particularly if the same networks are available to all?

This paper tries to find some answers by examining the experience of one sector where IOS have been in widespread use for several years. It describes the results of field research[1] carried out in the UK Leisure Travel Sector. The extent to which the lessons of Travel may be applicable to other sectors, is then examined concluding with presentation of a framework which I believe provides a focus on the critical factors involved.

Overview of the UK Leisure Travel Sector

The Market for Packaged Holidays

The number of foreign holidays (of 4+ nights) taken by UK residents has grown from 8.5 million in 1972 to 15.5 million in 1984. Air-packaged holidays, which were the focus of the research fieldwork, represent around half of all such holidays. They comprised a market of 8.5 million holidays in 1984, worth £2 billions.

The companies supplying this market achieve relatively modest returns on sales (3–5% overall for the top 30 companies during the first half of the 1980s). However leading companies achieve better margins on sales (10–12%) and an attractive 30%+ return on capital employed. Even weak profit performers produce a strong positive cash flow for much of the year. In recent years, profitability has been declining as fierce price competition has developed. Industry opinion seems divided on whether consumers will continue to buy on the basis of price, or will be prepared to trade up in return for more sophisticated and adventurous packages.

Air-packaged Holiday Operators

The market is served by around 700 companies, of which a large majority are small specialist operators. The top 30 companies taken

---

[1] This research was carried out by the author and Chris Brownlee of PACTEL.

more than 70% of the market, and in volume terms the industry is dominated by six or seven. Figures for individual market shares are hard to find, and those which do appear are frequently contradictory. Table 6.1 shows one set of estimates for four leading companies. The Intasun group figure increased to 16–17% with its acquisition of Global; British Airtours, the BA subsidiary, takes around 7% of the market; Rank Travel about 6%. Thus six companies hold around two thirds of the total market by volume.

Table 6.1.   *Tour Operators' market Shares (% volume air holidays)*

	1981 (%)	1982 (%)	1983 (%)	1984 (%)
Thomson	18	18	19	20
Intasun	10.5	11	12	14
Horizon	7.5	9	8	9
Cosmos	9	8	6	7

Source: James Capel (Stockbrokers)

For the past ten years there has been a clear market leader in Thomson Travel, whose share has been as high as 25%. Thomson own much the biggest single brand in Thomson Holidays, which is roughly twice as big as its nearest competitor. The Intasun group has grown very quickly from a share of only 5% in 1980 into a clear second place. This has been achieved partly by aggressive price competition, partly by acquisition. Below Thomson and Intasun, the fortunes of the other four ebb and flow and their positioning is always open to change. A major recent feature was the initiation by Thomson of a price war for the summer 1986 season, which many interpreted as a warning to Intasun that Thomson would not allow its leadership to be threatened further.

The cost structure of a major operator is typically assessed to be:

	% of Sale Price
Air flight	35%
Accommodation	35%
Travel Agent Commission	10%
Salaries, Marketing, Overheads	10–15%
Profit	5–10%

Sources: Jordans Survey of British Tour Operators and Travel Agents 1984 and Keynote Report on Travel Agents and Overseas Tour Operators 1985.

The industry operates largely under the auspices of ABTA (Association of British Travel Agents) whose membership includes all the major (and most of the minor) operators and the majority of Travel Agents who

retail the holidays to the Consumer. ABTA operates a closed shop—
ABTA operator members sell holidays only through ABTA agents, who
in turn sell only ABTA operators' holidays. ABTA also continues to
achieve resale price maintenance, at least to the point that there is no
direct discounting to the public.

Travel Agents

There are approximately 12,000 retail travel outlets in the UK, including
a large number of so-called 'bucket shops' who focus on the sale of
discounted air tickets. More than 6,000 outlets are operated by ABTA
members, and these derive most of their income from commission on
the sale of package holidays. Historically, the business of retailing
package holidays has been very fragmented but in recent years the
ownership of ABTA member outlets has begun to concentrate. Table 6.2
shows the approximate strength of the ten largest retailing chains
(known in the industry as 'multiples') at the end of 1985.

Table 6.2.   *Leading Travel Retail Chains*

Name	Parent Organization	Approximate Number of outlets
Thomas Cook	Midland Bank Group	415
Pickfords	National Freight Corporation	280
	Hogg Robinson	215
A. T. Mays	35% owned by Low & Bonar	215
Lunn Poly	Thomson Travel	200
National Travelworld	National Bus Company	135
	W H Smith	100
Co-op	C. W. S.	60
	Automobile Association	60
	American Express	55

These ten chains therefore account for nearly 1,750 outlets, up from
600 in 1980 and now around 30% of the ABTA total. Since the outlets of
the multiples tend to be larger than those operated by independents, it
is likely that the top ten already handle more than 40% of all ABTA Tour
Operator sales.

Every travel agent sells the holidays offered by numerous operators.
Under the ABTA specified resale price maintenance, competing agents
offer the same holidays from the same operators at the same prices.

Competition between agents is therefore on the basis of service,
broadly defined. Elements of service include the convenience and
attractiveness of the outlet's location, the perceived quality of the agent's
advice to customers on holiday and operator selection, and the efficiency of the agent's dealings with the customer. The agent's prime
motivation in advising a customer is obviously to conclude a sale, but

customer satisfaction with the outcome is a major consideration since that same customer and his contacts are likely to be seen as the source of next year's revenue.

The Evolution of IT Use by Travel Agents

When Prestel[2] was launched in 1978 by what was then the Post Office, the Travel Industry was an early target for the technology. It was already recognized that this was an information-intensive industry sector, and it was calculated that Viewdata technology would enable information to be distributed to the travel agent at a price he could afford. The initial emphasis was placed on the provision of a wide range of background information such as country/resort characteristics, visa requirements etc.

In 1979, a group of companies from within the Operator and Agent ranks came together to form the Holiday Systems Group. The group's purpose was to develop a blueprint for linking Travel Agents to the reservation systems of Tour Operators. The first to implement such a system, in October 1980, was Olympic Holidays. Olympic was and is a relatively large specialist operator—providing 80,000 holidays p.a. to Greece—but a minnow in the sector as a whole with less than 1% market share. The Olympic move was followed by Thomson with a pilot project in March 1981, and by Thomas Cook for their own-brand holidays in June 1981. The next major development came in October 1982 when Thomson launched a new system on a national basis. Horizon responded with a system launch in June 1983. Within a further twelve months, all the leading companies except Cosmos had a system available.

By the time our research fieldwork started in October 1985, Viewdata was established in widespread use in the industry. Five of the six largest Tour Operators had had a reservation systems link available to travel agents for eighteen months or more. According to the annual MORI survey of the industry (conducted in October 1985) 92% of all ABTA agent outlets had one or more Viewdata sets installed. 81% of these outlets used the sets more than five times per day; 42% used them more than 20 times a day. Reference to Tour Operator reservation systems was the dominant use of the technology. The industry had apparently moved through a cycle of innovation and competitive response and was rapidly achieving maturity in its acceptance of viewdata based systems.

---

[2] PRESTEL is an information service operated by the Post Office Telecommunications Division, now British Telecom. A central database of information from independent Information Providers is made available via a network. Users must be equipped with a viewdata terminal, typically a modified television set; they gain access by dialling over the public switched telephone network; information is located through the user's responses to a tree-structure of menus, and is then presented as a series of pages. A subsequent enhancement called the Gateway facility allows the user to be switched across out of PRESTEL into alternative information and transaction processing services.

Research Methodology

The objectives of the fieldwork were to identify:

1. what if any competitive advantage had been achieved through the provision to Travel Agents of links into Tour Operator reservation systems,
2. who had achieved such competitive advantage, and
3. what factors had enabled any competitive advantage to be achieved.

The prime focus of the fieldwork was therefore the Travel Agent outlet, using a methodology designed to learn through interviews with counter staff what role the use of viewdata links to Tour Operators played in the servicing of customers. Subsequent interviews took place with management representatives of leading Tour Operators to elicit the role they saw for systems links to travel agents, and how it related to their overall strategy for competing in the industry.

Travel Agent Interview Design

Agent representatives interviewed were presented with a standard customer set and asked to explain how they would respond to each customer type. Seven types made up the set, and their definitions can be summarized as follows:

'*The Late Booker*'; dominant concern is that he/she must find a holiday which fits in with a specified departure date window not more than 6–8 weeks hence.

'*The Preliminary Searcher*'; does not expect to make a decision on this visit to the agent.

'*Something New*'; the adventurous consumer who wants the stimulation of some significant new element in this year's holiday.

'*Something like last year*'; had a good previous experience, and wants to keep hold of its best features while adding in a bit of 'new' excitement.

'*Budget-conscious*'; thinking dominated by the need to keep within a strict budget ceiling.

'*Which Operator?*'; knows exactly what he/she wants; the question is which Operator or Operators can meet the specification.

'*Product Specific*'; already made his/her choice and can quote the Operator and reference number; the agent is expected to turn the choice into a firm booking, or to find an acceptable alternative if the chosen product is not available.

The transaction set was initially tested for credibility and completeness through visits to two Oxford travel agents. Agents were also asked at subsequent interviews for comments on the representative nature of the chosen set.

Travel Agent Outlet Sample

The interview sample was constructed to allow analysis of potential contrasts between the responses of outlets belonging to Multiples versus outlets owned by independent Travel Agents; and between the responses of outlets in inner London versus outlets in the Provinces. The 'Provinces' were largely represented by Oxford. Table 6.3 shows a breakdown of fieldwork interviews between these categories.

Table 6.3.   *Travel Agent Outlet Sample*

	Multiples	Independents
London	8	6
Provinces	7	5
TOTAL	15	11

Travel Agent Outlet Interviews—Issues of Validity

There are three aspects of the interview programme that from the outset place some limits on the acceptance of the information collected as fully representative of actual practice.

1. The information describes what Agent staff *say* they would do in response to customer situations; it does not necessarily describe what they actually do.
2. The travel industry is subject to very pronounced peaks of activity, with intense activity in certain months of the year. There is no such thing as an average working pattern for the year as a whole. Most of our interviews took place in October/November (1985) which are traditionally months of low activity. This made access easier and allowed thoughtful agent response, but it may have led to an information base which describes how agents would *like* to handle customer situations rather than how they actually behave in more stressful months.
3. Our sample is biased roughly 60:40 in favour of Multiples versus Independents, whereas the market split is more like 40:60.

Interviews with Tour Operator Management

The prime purpose of these interviews was to determine whether or not the senior management regarded the provision of Viewdata system links to Travel Agents as part of their competitive strategy. Therefore companies were approached through a letter to the Chief Executive (in all cases except one, where only the name of the Marketing Director was available from the switchboard!). The letter explained the objectives and nature of the research and requested an interview. The six largest companies were approached (Thomson, Intasun, Horizon, Cosmos, British Airtours, Rank) plus Olympic Holidays as they had taken an early lead in the implementation of systems.

Research Findings

As described above, Travel Agent outlets were presented with a standard customer set and asked how they would respond to each customer type. Apart from their own travel industry knowledge, the agents have a set of tools available to use in their response, with the objective of arriving at a choice of holiday which is available and acceptable to the customer. A Tour Operator Reservation System (TORS) is one such tool; the overall list we identified from the interviews was:

1. Brochures, issued by Tour Operators, describing the holidays they have designed with price and departure data information.
2. Telephone contact with the Tour Operator.
3. General information systems, increasingly implemented on Viewdata, which give background information on countries, weather, visa requirements, etc.
4. Guides aimed at specific needs, such as the *Holiday Guide* which allows the agent to look up a particular resort or hotel and find out which tour operators provide holidays there.
5. *Late Availability Sheets*, hard copy issued by Tour Operators approximately weekly which gives information on which of their holidays are still available for departure in the near future.
6. *Late Availability Systems* which set out to provide the same type of information as above, but via viewdata systems. Data is obtained from the major operators on a regular basis to update the system. There are now a number of competing offerings, some from independent sources. Of the eight Multiples represented in our sample, four had such a system of their own available.
7. *TORS* At the time of our fieldwork, five of the six largest Tour Operators had such systems available, as did Thomas Cook, Olympic Holidays, and a number of other Operators.

The interview data was analysed to determine, for each customer type, what was the *sequence* in which the agents use these various tools and therefore which tool or tools play a part in determining choice between Operators. This allowed us to examine the role of TORS in terms of:

1. influencing choice between Operators, therefore giving direct competitive advantage

2. assisting the agent to turn a provisional choice into a firm booking
3. providing a communications link between Agent and Operator, as an alternative to the telephone.

Role of TORS in determining holiday selection

In the 'Late Booker' category, we found that one particular TORS—Thomson's system, known as TOP—played a major role in determining the choice of holiday and Operator. Responses of Travel Agent staff indicated that they look to one of four tools as the first line of assistance in handling this customer type, as shown in Table 6.4.

Table 6.4. *Servicing the 'Late Booker'*

1st Choice Action	%age of Agent Responses
Access Late Availability System	38
Refer to Late Availability Sheets	8
Access Thomson's TORS	50
'Telephone an appropriate Operator'	4

Thus fully half of the agents interviewed immediately biased customer choice towards Thomson Holidays; no other Operator was favoured in this way. The value to Thomson is hard to determine but may be substantial including:

1. the percentage of customers who fall into the Late Booker category varies from year to year. However, one major retailer (Hogg Robinson) took more than 30% of its bookings for Summer 1985 holidays after June 1st.
2. with travel and accommodation capacity already firmly committed by the Operator, every late booking makes a contribution to profit of more than 80% of revenue.

This unique positioning of Thomson's TOP system, which is seen as still contributing to competitive advantage for that company more than three years after going live, seems to be due to a number of factors; namely:

1. The Late Availability Systems, which are in theory the most appropriate first reference for the Agent, still have a number of shortcomings. They have to be individually and periodically updated with information from the Operators; the information they display on holidays available cannot be relied upon as accurate. Secondly, they are information-only systems; to make a booking the Agent must subsequently connect to the Operator of the holiday selected, via telephone or TORS.
2. With their overall volume due to their clear market leadership

position, Thomson are regarded as at least as likely as anyone else to have holidays available. With their reputation for quality, they are regarded as a safe choice of Operator for the Agent to recommend to the customer.

3. Thomson's TOP system is easily the best liked TORS among Travel Agents. This was continually apparent from our fieldwork, and is formally recorded by the aforementioned MORI survey (87% of respondents placed TOP as the 'best system available'). I shall discuss later the probable reasons for this phenomenon.

In customer categories other than 'Late Booker', TORS did not feature significantly as a tool for determining customer choice. One agent proposed the use of TORS search facilities for a 'Budget Conscious' customer; two said they would use such facilities for the customer seeking 'Something like last year'. But in these and two other customer categories, 90% or more of the agents said they would guide choice using Brochures. They felt these customers needed to see photographs of resorts and hotels, something which cannot be achieved on Viewdata-based TORS. In the 'Which Operator' category where the customer had already chosen a destination, more than 90% of agents said they would turn first to the Holiday Guide publication which provided exactly the required information.

In the final category, 'Product Specific' where the customer has already made his choice, all agents indicated that they would attempt to book the declared choice unless they had very strong reasons for advising reconsideration. However, in the event that the first choice holiday was not available, 52% would try to find an alternative holiday (different dates or resort) with the original Operator. This was straight-forward if they had been using the telephone to request the original choice. The use of TORS however, would put the Operator at a dis-advantage unless the system could display such alternatives, because a substitute sale might be lost.

The use of TORS as Sales Aids

While overt competitive advantage was restricted to the 'Late Booker' category, there was consistent evidence from agents that the concept of TORS was well liked and considered superior to the use of the tele-phone. At some point during their interview, more than 30% of agents volunteered that a good TORS is a sales aid, helping them to translate the watching customer's choice into a firm booking. Adding in the responses of agents who didn't volunteer the point, but agreed it when asked, more than 80% believe it. Some agents wondered aloud whether they tended to select the brochures of particular Operators for discus-sion because they wanted to have such sales aids available when the right moment came. Secondly, 88% of those expressing an opinion believed that TORS provided a significantly faster way than the telephone of contacting an Operator. For both these reasons, there is a real possibility that covert bias exists among agents, guiding customers towards Operators whose TORS are successfully established. Our interview with Cosmos Holidays, who did not have a TORS available, established that Cosmos paid an additional 1% commission to agents primarily to counteract such bias.

TORS and Operator Productivity

When we interviewed the Operator companies who did have a TORS available, we found a wide variation in system acceptance, as measured by the percentage of bookings made through the system rather than by telephone. Table 6.5 shows the figures reported by company representatives.

Table 6.5. *Percentage of Bookings on TORS*

Olympic Holidays SPARTA	10%
Thomas Cooks HOLIDAYMAKER	10–15%
Thomson Holidays TOP	>80%
Horizon Holidays VISTA	10%
HORIZON	80%
British Airtours ARCHIE	<20%
Rank Group POWER	<20%
Intasun Group INTA	<20%

Two figures are shown for Horizon Holidays; in October 1985, they withdrew their original TORS called VISTA which had been carrying approximately 10% of bookings, and introduced a new system called HORIZON. Within two months the new system was carrying 80% of their bookings.

Prior to this event, Thomson's TOP had stood supreme for three years. Since 80% of their bookings were made directly by travel agents, Thomson had effectively transferred a significant proportion of their clerical costs out of the distribution channels. In fact Thomson claim that their productivity, measured as sales per employee, doubled between 1982 and 1985. Far from matching this, the other companies had incurred the cost of developing and operating TORS, while still having to maintain almost the same number of telephone reservation staff.

Company representatives suggested several possible reasons for this situation. These include:

1. inadequate network facilities which resulted in many agents having to make long distance rather than local calls to access their TORS,

2. inability of their TORS to handle late bookings, and
3. different user interface of their TORS compared to TOP.

Since Rank's POWER, for example, was exempt from the first two criti-cisms, our attention was focused on the lack of compatibility with TOP. Horizon provided confirmation of this diagnosis with the success of their new system. It was designed to have the same user interface as TOP and this feature was aggressively promoted at launch time; its acceptance was immediate. Since then Intasun and Thomas Cook have launched replacement systems, both of them more like but not the same as TOP. We have no firm data on their acceptance.

Before analysing further the reasons for Thomson's success, let us summarize the achievements. Our evidence is that Thomson's TOP has provided overt competitive advantage in biasing holiday selection for the late booker; it has probably covertly biased holiday selection for other customer categories; it has significantly improved Thomson's productivity; finally it has enabled large numbers of bookings to be taken very quickly, possibly inhibiting competitive reaction—in one single day at the start of the Summer 1986 holiday sales campaign, 105,000 holidays were booked on TOP. All this has been achieved des-pite the fact that two small rivals (Olympic and Thomas Cook) implemented TORS ahead of TOP; and has been sustained until the end of 1985 although larger rivals followed TOP within months.

Analysis of Research Findings

I believe there are six reasons why TOP succeeded in creating and sustaining competitive advantage despite the efforts of other companies. They would seem to have considerable relevance to other industry sectors, as I shall go on to discuss.

'User-Friendliness'

It is obviously conventional wisdom to stress that systems should be 'user-friendly', but Thomson were unique in the sector in conducting a significant pilot scheme—code-named CARS—to establish user needs in detail. They discovered that user-friendly does not mean ultra-simple; users react against what they see as too much prompting. As a result of the CARS pilot, TOP was launched with a modified user interface and a completely different technical architecture to achieve the response times users required.

User Training

Again conventional wisdom stresses the importance of user training, but most industry participants faltered when confronted by the staff of 5,000 travel agents. Thomsons devised a package which enabled them to train

9,000 such staff in a six week period in September/October 1982. Travel agent branch managers had to pass an end of training test before their outlet was allowed onto the system.

Potential for Frequent Use

TOP always had the potential for frequent use because of Thomson's 20% market share. Agents who had been trained could remember how to use TOP through regular experience. The small Operators who preceded Thomson had very little chance of establishing their systems based on 1–3% market share, even if they offered good systems and training.

Establishment of Switching Costs

Once the TOP system was successfully established, it became a *de facto* industry standard. Although agents could use their Viewdata sets without difficulty to link into the systems subsequently introduced by other companies, they were unwilling (and perhaps unable) to learn and remember the different procedures required to operate them. They may also have been inhibited because of the visibility their mistakes would have to customers.

Withdrawal of Substitute Service

When it was clear that a large number of users were happy with TOP, Thomson consolidated its position by rapidly reducing the staffing of the telephone reservation service to the point that travel agents found telephone booking very unattractive. TOP became entrenched as the dominant means of communication with Thomson, and the system which *all* agents knew. It is not clear whether Thomson management realized that they were actively strengthening the position of TOP in doing this, or whether they were simply pursuing the cost savings. Nevertheless it was a tough decision which resulted in both these benefits.

Senior Management Involvement

It is clear that, once the CARS pilot showed promising results, Thomson's executive management became both committed and involved. The TOP project became a central feature of Thomson's approach to the market, aggressively promoted, properly funded and professionally implemented, with decisions being taken by business managers. By contrast, when we analyse the first three years of competitive response to TOP, we have the impression that most management teams said to the Information Systems function of their company 'We want a system too; here's the budget'. In that sense, they were committed but not involved. Information Systems Departments typically focused on producing a 'good' system in a technical sense; even when they succeeded on their own criteria (not all did), they found that this was not what users wanted.

This situation may still persist. I have described the way in which seven Operator Companies were approached for interview, with a letter to the Chief Executive. In two companies, the Chief Executive responded directly—in the case of Thomson Holidays declining to participate because of the competitive sensitivity surrounding the subject of the research! The other Chief Executive to respond directly was from Cosmos, the only company in the sample who do not currently have a TORS. Each of the other five companies passed our request to the Manager in charge of Information Systems, and the interviews were conducted at this level. It could be interpreted that five of the companies still regard the specification, development and implementation of TORS as the preserve of specialist management.

The Network as a Competitive Variable

Nowhere in the above analysis is there mention of networks; while the Telecommunications liberalization legislation allowed the emergence of TORS in their present form, the network has to date appeared to be a largely neutral facilitating mechanism. The Tour Operator companies we have been considering have adopted a number of different technical implementation strategies in terms of computer hardware, network provision, and application code development. Thomson opted for in-house systems development, large mainframes, and a private network; others used application packages, mini-computers, and third party VANS. At the end of 1985 the seven companies studied were using four different networks between them. All this was transparent to the user/travel agent who tended to have little concept of networks but a pragmatic approach—they knew which menu line to select on the screen to initiate automatic dialling to the required operator. Thus the main competitive effect of VANS to date had been to allow Thomson's competitors to respond more quickly with full geographic coverage, and at lower initial financial outlay. However, these potential advantages were not realized because of the poor user reaction to systems that were not the same as TOP.

One can speculate that the network might become more significant as a variable. If most companies follow the example of Horizon and introduce TOP-like systems, the user could differentiate on a new basis which could be network oriented: the first call might be made to the VANS which carries the highest composite market share, discriminating against Thomson's private network; Operator companies would increasingly choose their network supplier on the basis of market pull rather than technical function or price. Alternatively Thomsons, having had three years to think about it, may be able to stay ahead by building on TOP in ways that the user finds attractive.

Understanding the Lessons for Other Industry Sectors

At first level the findings from this industry sector have many parallels with earlier experience elsewhere. The IT application, extending order enquiry/order entry facilities into the distribution channel, is essentially the one made famous by American Hospital Supply and subsequently copied in many sectors. The establishment of switching costs through user learning is also mentioned in at least one account of the AHS story (Jackson, 1985), and of course it finds consistent echoes in the short history of computing with the fierce loyalty of software staff to whatever programming system represented their baptism. The importance of linking functional strategies, including IS strategy, to business strategy through general management involvement is likewise a familiar theme.

However, there are also limits to the transferability of ideas and lessons. We would not expect a manufacturer of nuclear power plant to win orders for new stations by providing order entry terminals to the utility companies; I doubt that the AHS system could increase orders for CT scanners rather than bandages. And why haven't powerful retailers in the travel sector long since imposed their own multi-Operator systems on the travel companies? I shall conclude by examining the extent of and limits to transferability under three headings: generation and evaluation of application ideas, system implementation, and the evolution of competition.

Generation and Evaluation of Ideas

I approached the research fieldwork with the hypothesis that six product-market characteristics were crucial determinants of the successful application of IT to support marketing. This framework succeeded in providing insights into the workings of the travel sector, and also highlighted key sector-specific factors in subsequent fieldwork in the Insurance industry. I believe it is a good basis for examining the real opportunities in any product-market situation. The six determinants which the framework identifies are:

   Perceived Product Differentiation
   Sector Channel Structure
   Relationship between Need and Product
   Frequency of Purchase Decision
   Frequency of Delivery within Contract
   Buyer's Access to IT Resources

A full explanation and discussion of the framework is contained in

Feeny and Brownlee (1986). In the context of the travel sector, the important determinants were:

1. Frequency of Purchase: the first movers—Olympic and Thomas Cook could not establish their systems because of low usage potential, resulting from small market share. Such companies could only succeed by allying with others to offer a common, higher usage potential, system.
2. Perceived Product Differentiation: even TOP only succeeds in biasing choice for the 'Late Booker'; these consumers believe that any distinction between the products of alternative suppliers is unimportant compared to the need to secure a definite booking for the required dates. Other consumers perceive their holiday to be a high value/ differentiated purchase, and insist on considering many options using brochures.
3. Buyer's Access to IT Resources: If a supplier offers a buyer a benefit based on some IT application, the buyer will generally consider providing it for himself if he can, to avoid increased dependence on that supplier. Travel agents now have good access to IT skills and facilities through VANS suppliers, but they lack the crucial third element—access to availability data. By contrast in the Insurance sector, brokers have the information they need to make buying decisions for personal consumer insurance, because the Rate tables of Insurance companies are available to them. While operator-specific systems led by TOP dominate the travel sector, independent systems developed by VANS suppliers are being adopted by large personal insurance agents such as the Halifax Building Society.

It is my contention that a business in another industry sector can successfully apply the ideas of the travel sector provided that it is equivalently positioned with respect to the six determinants.

Systems Implementation

To return now to some of my earlier terminology, there seem to be two factors which differ at least in degree when implementing an Inter-Organizational System (IOS) rather than an in-house system. They both arise from the fact that the users of the system are not employees of the company introducing the system. The system provider cannot therefore specify or directly control the attributes or skills which users must bring to the system; he must understand their existing attributes and design accordingly. Second, the provider cannot demand or instruct that the user accepts his system; he must persuade. The travel sector experience illustrates both points and suggests ways to proceed:

1. Thomsons used the CARS pilot to establish a detailed understanding of user capabilities and needs. As a result the user-interface of

TOP was neither as complex (and fast) as that for the professional users of the in-house reservation system, nor as simple (and slow) as CARS. In addition the CARS project allowed Thomsons to assess accurately training needs.

2. The motivation problem was complex. At the macro level Thomsons claimed that TOP was giving agents a good deal by reducing their telephone charges. (Thomsons recently claimed that the first three years of TOP operation had saved agents £1.5 millions.) However, such savings apply only to some agents, and rarely accrue to the person at the desk who is using the system. Direct benefits to the user compared to the substitute telephone reservations service were probably rather marginal: they depended on the agent's belief that TOP was a sales aid, and his/her assessment that TOP was faster than the telephone. Thus aggressive promotion of the image-building qualities of TOP were helpful; degradation of the parallel telephone service was probably decisive.

Evolution of Competition

What we have seen in the travel sector is that one company gained competitive advantage from an IT-based system for a substantial period. Although the emergence of third party VANS gave competitors the ability to respond quickly, they did not understand what response was required. Ironically if they had been less ambitious, and chosen to copy TOP rather than produce a 'better' system, the evidence is that they would have been much more successful.

But the tentative conclusion, that TOP-like success may not be achievable in other sectors because of rapid competitive response, is not necessarily correct. In travel, each company's TORS represents a relatively simple front end, using the limited Viewdata technology, to an in-house reservations system. In other sectors, a company may have to substantially rework the equivalent in-house transaction processing system to provide the desired external user interface—making rapid response very difficult.

Further evolution, in travel and other sectors, may be expected to take one of three broad patterns:

1. One or more companies will start to extend the scope of TORS, offering additional services to the agent over the network. The objective of such moves is to renew differentiation and build more switching costs. This is the route taken by American Hospital Supply, building on its successful order entry service by providing inventory control, costing and other, services for the management of the customer's in-house operations.
2. One company, or a third party, will produce a definitive reservations

system which links agents to all Tour Operators via a single connection and interface. The system is then a tool for biasing choice at the agent level, as well as a source of market data; advantage flows to the system provider at the expense of all others. American Airlines and United Airlines succeeded in achieving this position for large segments of the US air travel market.

3. The sector will standardize, formally or informally, and each participant will individually provide a system which conforms. The tendency then will be for the consumer and agent to indulge in electronic shopping comparisons, resulting in sharpened competition between suppliers and reduced margins. The eventual winners will be those who can achieve and sustain cost leadership or niche positions; likely losers will be middle rank companies.

The prognosis for travel is not clear. Thomson is currently improving the holiday search facilities available (see my third determinant of opportunity), which might indicate the first scenario. However, it seems unlikely that the majority of consumers (non 'Late Bookers') will accept the results of a single company search unless their perception of the market changes. In this context Thomson's dramatic change of pricing policy for the 1986 season, bidding to achieve the 'never undersold' image, suggests they may be preparing for the third, electronic shopping, scenario.

Summary

In summary, the liberalization of telecommunications and the emergence of VANS is indeed enabling fast implementation of new ideas for using IT for competitive advantage—and fast response to those ideas. Senior managers with insight into the dynamics of their sector will find real opportunities; IS departments alone will not. If Thomson's largest rival, Intasun, had linked IS strategy to their business strategy of low-cost/follower, they would have introduced a TOP-like system in 1983. There would have been much less to write about.

References

Benjamin, R. I., *et al.* (1984), 'Information Technology: A Strategic Opportunity' *Sloan Management Review* **25, 3**.

Cash, J. I., and Konsynski, B. R. (1985), 'IS Redraws Competitive Boundaries' *Harvard Business Review* March–April.

Clemons, E. K., and McFarlan, F. W. (1986), 'Telecom: hook up or lose out' *Harvard Business Review* July–August.

Feeny, D. F., and Brownlee, C. G. (1986), *Competition in the era of Interactive Network Services*, Oxford Institute of Information Management research paper **RDP 86/17**, Templeton College, Oxford.

Ives, G. B., and Learmonth, G. P. (1984), 'The Information System as a Competitive Weapon' *Communications of the ACM* **27, 12**.

Jackson, B. B. (1985), *Winning and Keeping Industrial Customers*, Lexington Books.

McFarlan, F. W. (1984), 'Information Technology Changes the way you Compete' *Harvard Business Review*, May–June.

Parsons, G. L. (1983), 'Information Technology: Competitive Weapon' *Sloan Management Review* **25, 1**.

Porter, M. E., and Millar, V. E. (1985), 'How Information Gives you Competitive Advantage' *Harvard Business Review* July–August.

Runge, D. A. (1985), *Using Telecommunications for Competitive Advantage*, unpublished D.Phil. thesis, University of Oxford, 1985.

Wiseman, C. (1985), *Strategy and Computers: Information Systems as Competitive Weapons*, Dow Jones–Irwin.

Formulating IT Strategies

FOREWORD

If IT is a strategic resource in that it can create or support business strategy, a number of propositions follow:

1. No business or corporate strategy is complete if there is no information systems strategy. For most firms it is the *business strategy* that increasingly is dependent on, or made possible by, investment in appropriate information systems. For some, however, the *corporate strategy* may be linked closely to information systems, especially if information technology provides the infrastructure through which the firm positions itself in its sector or plans to diversify or integrate into another sector.
2. Planning for strategic information systems should be an important and integral part of the firm's competitive strategy development process. This point has been emphasized by Wiseman (1985) as more and more cases have been documented of businesses exploiting IT for competitive advantage and building their competitive strategy upon information systems which limit or enhance the competitive forces operating in their market place.
3. Planning for information systems can no longer be treated as either a budgetary exercise or a longer range resource allocation process. Information systems planning becomes a strategic exercise concerned with alignment of IT with business needs, identifying strategic opportunities from IT and ensuring appropriate levels of investment in IT and information systems are made.
4. Information systems strategic planning can no longer be left to the DP.IT professionals. Certainly they have a vital role to play in advising on information systems matters, recommending strategy formulation methods and often driving the IS strategy formulation process. However, those who influence business strategy by formal planning or ongoing actions must be involved, whilst top management has to support, commit to and often steer information systems strategy formulation.

It is realizations such as these that have made IS strategic planning the dominant concern of IT directors and many chief executives (Earl, 1983; Dickson *et al.*, 1984). Indeed in the second half of the 1980s, IS strategy formulation may be enjoying more exposure and debate than business strategy itself. Perhaps this is understandable as the former may be youthful, if not primitive, and the latter mature and established. Indeed, business strategy formulation has evolved through at least three different eras. In the 1960s it was perhaps characterized as to do with leadership and bold strokes, all in the hands of top management. In the 1970s an apparent sophistication developed as consultants and academics introduced portfolio models, for example those of the Boston Consulting Group or Shell Chemicals, and statistical relationships between policies and results such as those investigated in the PIMS studies. By the 1980s, a more complex picture of business strategy formulation has emerged, seeking to balance planning with opportunism, internal growth with partnerships and joint ventures, and implementation with analysis. In other words, in concept or in practice, business strategy formulation is not as simple as it seems and despite nearly three decades of thought and experimentation the evidence is still inconclusive on what are appropriate methodologies and approaches.

Unfortunately, formulating information systems strategies may be more complex still. After all we are trying to connect the exploitation of IT, which itself is complex, rapidly changing, and often not well-understood by managers, to development of business strategies, where neither the principles nor methods are yet agreed. Paradoxically in seeking to bridge these two problematic and somewhat unstructured streams, the desire seems to be to find a structured methodology; managements seek a concrete approach even if, or because, the task is complex, the context uncertain, and the linkages many. Indeed the levels of strategy that have to be handled and linked together include at least those in the diagram below.

Of course planning for information systems is not new. Three different eras might be identified here also. In the late 1960s a blueprint

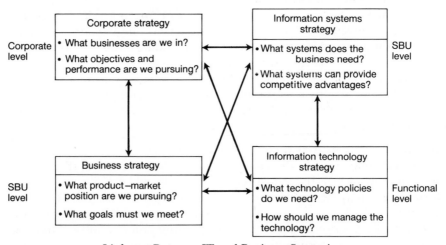

Linkages Between IT and Business Strategies

approach was often advocated. Typified by Blumenthal's (1969) work, blueprint planning was concerned with systems integration, logical hardware, software, and development paths, and essentially a bottom-up, ordered procedure. In the mid 1970s, long range planning approaches were suggested, emphasizing directional allocation of scarce resources, alignment with business needs and formal planning procedures. Often the debate was about top-down versus bottom-up methods, sometimes mirroring the business long-range planning developments at large. This era spawned procedures such as IBM's Business Systems Planning, Nolan's Stage Assessment methods, and derivatives of Priority-Based Budgeting techniques. In the 1980s strategic planning of IS arrived, not only trying to raise the level of linkage between systems planning and business planning, but gradually recognizing that IT was a strategic resource which could be exploited for competitive advantage. This strategic planning era has spawned softer methodologies, perhaps because of the business and organizational complexities involved.

So the detailed questions which arise about formulating IT strategies include; how can the various linkages be made, who should be involved, what methodologies are available and which approaches are effective in what circumstances? More generally can we learn anything about IT strategy formulation from business strategic planning; indeed are there general principles which can be borrowed? More specifically, are there useful techniques of environmental assessment, technological forecasting, creativity, and innovation, and competitive analysis? and more particularly, is there any evidence that strategic planning for IT can yield IS that product competitive advantage?

In the first paper by Runge and Earl, the results of an investigation into 35 telecommunications-based systems which produced competitive advantage for their companies are reported. Two key questions were asked: how did the idea originate and what were the factors that contributed to successful implementation of the idea? The findings suggest that some of the conventional wisdoms of IT strategy formulation are inadequate if competitive advantage is one objective of the systems planners.

Seddon describes the experience of ICI in reorganizing the IT function in pursuit of strategic advantage from IT. He describes their encounters with different IT strategy formulation methodologies and discusses the consequent organizational tensions that have to be managed in a giant, multidivisional company. Since ICI has provided the teaching and consulting communities with exemplars of using IT for competitive advantage, it is instructive to learn from ICI's recent experience.

Finally Earl describes and evaluates IT strategy formulation methods and modes. He advocates a multiple methodology and suggests that the emphasis of approach depends on the business sector and the historical development of IS planning in the company. These suggestions are based on casework and action research in European companies.

References

Blumenthal, S. C. (1969), *Management Information Systems: A Framework for Planning and Development*, Prentice Hall.

Dickson, G. W., Leitheiser, R. L., and Wetherbe, J. L. (1984), 'Key Information Systems Issues for the 1980s' *MIS Quarterly* September.

Earl, M. J. (1983), 'Emerging Trends in the Management of New Information Technologies', in Piercy, N. (ed.), *The Management Implications of New Information Technologies*, Croon Helm.

Nolan, R. L. (1979), 'Managing the Crises in Data Processing', *Harvard Business Review*, March–April.

Wiseman, C. (1985), *Strategy and Computers: Information Systems As Competitive Weapons*, Dow Jones–Irwin.

7

Gaining Competitive Advantage from Telecommunications

DAVID A. RUNGE and MICHAEL J. EARL

Oxford Institute of Information Management, Templeton College, Oxford

Telecommunications and Business Strategy

According to Bell (1979), telecommunications forms the central infra-structure of an information society in which information becomes the strategic resource. For businessmen, the economic implications of tele-communications are becoming ever clearer through the 1980s; telecom-munications eliminates barriers of geography and time on service and co-ordination (Keen, 1986). Telecommunications networks provide the information highways over which new products and services can be offered, thereby redefining concepts of customer service, opening up new arenas of innovation, and altering the economics of distribution. It is for these reasons that telecommunications becomes a strategic resource, capable of fundamentally altering firms' competitive positions and reshaping entire industries, as Keen, and, earlier, Cash and Konsynski (1985) have noted.

Investment in telecommunications equipment by industrialized nations already represents as much as 9% of their total GDP (*Business Week*, 24 October 1983), fuelled by the growth of digital mechanisms. With the continuous improvement in the cost–performance curves and the convergence with computing, current telecommunications market growth rates of about 9% (Lloyd, 1985) seem likely to accelerate. This may be partly facilitated by the trend towards deregulation of the tele-communications sector itself. The divestiture and reconfiguration of AT&T in the USA, and the privatization of British Telecom accom-panied by gradual licensing of new entrants in the UK, illustrate the newly liberalized telecommunications environment of the 1980s. In the UK, one outcome of this has been licensing of private suppliers wishing to offer value added network services (VANS) over BT's network. In principle, this further enables firms to exploit telecommunications for competitive advantage.

Telecommunications-based information systems (TBIS) will typically comprise input/output terminals or workstations transmitting data to and from a host computer or network of computers. They can support a broad spectrum of business activities, either improving and changing *internal* operations and management through better co-ordination or more effective forms of communication or transforming *external* relationships by linking together different organizations or introducing new services and products via new distribution channels. Many of the exemplar cases of the use of information technology for competitive advantage have required telecommunications for their delivery; for example the American Hospital Supply order entry and stock control systems and American Airlines' reservation system (as documented by Lucas, 1982; McFarlan, 1984; Wiseman and MacMillan, 1984; and Benjamin *et al.*, 1984 amongst others). Indeed it is probably the telecommunications technology, rather than advances in computing, automation, or software that has so far released most of the strategic gains claimed of IT in the 1980s.

The research which this paper describes and reports therefore was concerned to understand how competitive advantage opportunities afforded by TBIS can be recognized, and to discover what factors seem to enable their successful implementation. As King (1986) observes, terminology in this new field of study can be loose. He distinguishes between strategic applications of IT which create sustainable comparative advantage and use of IT as a competitive weapon in the market place. Both phenomena were of interest in this study and no distinction was drawn. (Indeed an anticipated competitive weapon actually may turn out to provide unanticipated comparative advantage). Referring to Benjamin *et al.*'s strategic opportunities matrix, nor did the investigation distinguish between traditional and radical exploitation of telecommunications. However, borrowing from the other dimension of their matrix, the focus was entirely on use of TBIS in the competitive market place. Using Porter's (1980) concept of competitive advantage, we were concerned with the use of IT to change competitive forces, particularly the relationship between the firm and its customers. As implied by Porter and further argued by both Parsons (1983) and McFarlan, the potential of IT in this relationship includes the ability to differentiate from other suppliers and to create switching costs for the customer. For example, American Hospital Supply grew their sales by 17% p.a., 'locking in' hospital purchasing officers having provided them with order entry terminals. American Airlines improved their payload, earned substantial revenues from reserving seats for other airlines and built their Advantage Program customer database on the back of their reservation system which had terminals in over 40% of US travel agents.

Recognizing opportunities for exploiting IT for competitive advantage is not easy, as Clemons *et al.* (1984) observe. Indeed many organizations are desperately searching for opportunities as they hear of others' avowed successes or feel the impact of competitors' actions (Earl, 1986*c*).

Most of the opportunity frameworks in the literature are more effective for raising awareness than seeking specific applications (Earl, 1986*b*), although some such as Porter and Millar's (1985) value chain analysis, are approaching a more relevant level of analysis.

Implementing opportunities also is likely to be a non-trivial matter, as past information systems experience shows (Lucas, 1975), the history of innovation suggests (Quinn, 1980), and the ability of some firms to jump ahead of many of their competitors demonstrates. By field study investigation of such companies who have deployed TBIS to customers, the two research questions in this study therefore were:

1. How did these companies recognize the opportunity to use tele-communications for competitive advantage?
2. What structures or processes enabled them to respond readily to the opportunity seen?

Research Methodology

Examination of the literatures on information systems, management science, competitive strategy, marketing, and organizational behaviour provided an early set of 'hypotheses' for more detailed study. A taxonomy was derived of factors that might enable a firm to recognize and exploit opportunities to use TBIS links to customers for competitive advantage. The four sets shown in Fig. 7.1 were constructed, being heavily influenced by prior work of Clemons *et al.* (1984). The factors within the sets are reproduced in Appendix 1. The application opportunities set refers to product-market characteristics generally emphasized by workers in strategy (Porter, 1980; 1985), marketing (Ives and Learmonth, 1984; Leavitt, 1965; Kotler, 1980), and innovation (Maidique and Zirger, 1984; SPRU, 1972). General policy variables refer to the planning, organization, control, and technical principles found in the information management literature. Significant here are ideas such as risk management (McFarlan, 1981), systems planning (McLean and Soden, 1977; Pyburn, 1983; Earl, 1984), data processing management (Gibson and Nolan, 1974; McFarlan and McKenney, 1983) and technology policies (Keen and Mills, 1984; Earl, 1986*b*).

Operational and design constraints include outside factors which may

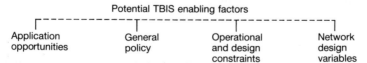

Fig. 7.1. The Outline Taxonomy

affect the design and use of a communications system. These include the availability of the technology (Keen, 1986), regulation (Cash and Konsynski, 1985), industry practices in the use of technology (Parsons, 1983), and organizational capability such as structure, skills and power (Burns and Stalker, 1961; Hull and Hage, 1982). The inherent technology factors were termed network design variables and include factors such as capability or range of services (Fitzgerald, 1984), adaptability to deliver new services (Clemons *et al.*, 1984), flexibility to handle growth (Keen, 1986), and quality of service (Clemons *et al.*, 1984).

It is important to mention what the three pilot case studies added to the literature review in deriving this taxonomy. In recounting the history of two TBIS which had competitive impact in the case study companies, it was clear that the application, identification, and opportunity had been facilitated, if not driven, by processes rarely described in the information systems literature. Rather, the facilitating factors were reminiscent of lessons learnt from industrial innovation. Hence factors such as marketing, awareness of customer needs and the role of product champions were added to the more structured, formal, and technical variables suggested by the literature review.

Having constructed the taxonomy, field studies were then conducted to validate the taxonomy. Thirty-five cases of TBIS which linked firms to customers were identified for study. These were located in 16 companies in different sectors and investigation was by semi-structured interviews of IT, general and line executives associated with each system. For reasons of competitiveness, some of the firms and systems have to remain anonymous, but firms involved were located in the automobile, banking, chemical, computer, insurance, oil, stockbroking, and travel businesses.

Investigation of IT and strategy is relatively new, especially in the tele-communications field, as Scott Morton (1984) and Clemons *et al.* (1984) report. This research therefore was essentially exploratory and descriptive, for which the field study method is well suited (Van Horn, 1973). The use of a taxonomy of enabling factors became both the means and the end; it provided the structure for exploration and highlighted the significant conclusions. Interpretation of the field evidence was both quantitative and qualitative. The outcome was a framework for seeking TBIS opportunities to link a firm with its customers, and the discovery of five recurring factors which seem to help organizations both identify and implement such opportunities.

Identifying Opportunities

Thirty-five systems were studied and examples are listed against their sectors in Table 7.1. To help answer the first research question, the

Table 7.1.   *Sectors Studied and Example TBIS*

Automobile	Links to dealerships
Banking	Homebanking
	ATM services
Chemicals	Product information enquiry service
	Advisory expert systems
Computer	Support services and Helpline
	Product information enquiry service
Insurance	Brokers administration services
	Insurance quotation service
Oil	Links to petrol stations
Stockbroking	Market and portfolio information services
Travel	Travel reservation system
	Links to corporate clients

application, objective, and impact of each system were analysed to see if patterns emerged. Both interpreting the competitive strategy (following Porter, 1980 and Parsons, 1983) the TBIS seemed to support the observing the marketing activity addressed failed to produce any pattern or classification. However matching the applications against customer resource life cycle models was more productive. These models describe the stages that a company's products or services go through in the interaction between supplier and customer. IBM (1981), Burnstine (1980), and Ives and Learmonth (1984) all have developed and tried to operationalize such models.

This study of 35 TBIS and other cases in the literature suggests that 12 functional linkages between supplier and customer—close but not identical to those in previous life cycle models—provide opportunities for development of TBIS which differentiate the supplier from his rivals or create switching costs for the customer. These interactions are listed and described in Table 7.2. Some of the systems studied support more than one of the interactions and often integrating across the interactions was particularly powerful. Exemplar cases from the field studies and the literature are presented below. Only cases T1 and T11 are borrowed from the literature, the remainder being examples from the 35 cases studied.

T1. GTE have provided sales representatives of their commercial lighting division with portable computer terminals. These access an information system which performs a detailed analysis of prospective customers' lighting requirements and prepares sales proposals on the spot. By helping *to establish customer requirements* this may have increased sales by 10% (Notowidigdo, 1984). Such systems which help determine what resources, or how much, are required may help establish early or new links with potential customers.

Table 7.2. *IS Interactions between Customer and Supplier*

Stage	Linkage	Description
Requirements	Establish requirements	To determine how much of a resource is required
	Acquire information	To acquire information regarding alternative choices
Acquisition	Specify	To specify the attributes of the desired resource
	Select a source	To provide alternative sources for the desired resource
	Order	To place orders with a supplier
	Authorize and pay for	To transfer funds or extend credit
Stewardship	Monitor	To provide information regarding services which have been contracted for
	Manage	To effect changes in the level or type of resource held in inventory
	Support	To service a resource if necessary
Retirement	Terminate use	To return or dispose of a resource
	Account for	To monitor where and how much was spent on a resource

T2. ICI's Plant Protection Division developed 'Counsellor', an expert system for advising farmers via viewdata terminals on disease control. It analyses input on wheat varieties grown, soil type, disease history, etc. and recommends fungicides. The farmer thereby *acquires information* on ICI's product range and other alternatives. Such systems which provide information on alternative choices seem to provide added value and service and thus indirectly may attract and keep customers.

T3. Friends Provident, the Insurance Company, introduced FRENTEL an on-line quotation service to brokers. The objective was to increase broker loyalty in an intensively competitive marketplace. This videotex-based system allows brokers to obtain quotations and surrender values directly from the insurer's central computer, as well as perform policy maintenance functions. Brokers improve their service to clients and are attracted to the on-line facilities of the system to make *specific enquiries about the service*. Being first in the field, Friends Provident increased market share. Such systems which specify the attributes of a desired resource clearly suit selling of services where some search is required. Often they also provide selection and ordering facilities.

T4. Thomas Cook, travel agents, offer a network service which links the many separate airline, tour operator, car rental, hotel, ferry, and cruise reservations networks. Called Travinet, this product is designed to allow the travel retailer to *select a source* from the wide range of services available with ease and at low cost. TBIS for selecting from alternative sources seem well suited for distribution channels which involve middlemen.

T5. A UK Chemical Company recognized that 70% of all orders come from the top 15 customers in each division. The company developed electronic data exchange with these customers so that they can *order* directly and exchange all documents, such as invoices, statements, and remittance advices. The benefits include reduced order processing costs, increased accuracy, and decreased ordering time. The scope for order entry by TBIS is well recognized now, as demonstrated by American Hospital Supply and others. It seems to be an obvious opportunity for many, with early advantages to both parties.

T6. Clydesdale Bank operate a system whereby bank cards normally accepted by ATMs can be used at terminals in retail outlets and petrol stations. Called 'Counterplus' this is a form of EFTPOS whereby customers can *authorize and pay for* transactions by direct debit (and also withdraw cash). In one pilot scheme involving 26 outlets, there has been a reduction of 30% in cheque processing and an increase in both customers' loyalty and value of their transactions. 'Counterplus' demonstrates where funds transfer or credit extension by TBIS can be beneficial not only in providing customer and distributor convenience but in creating switching costs for end user customers.

T7. Scrimgeour, Kemp-Gee through their DOGFOX system offer real-time information on equities, gilts, stocks, foreign exchange, and money market rates, from both London and New York. Information products such as analyses, trends, and company data can also be *acquired* by their investment customers over this dedicated, high speed communications link. This case suggests how products with high information content can be directly delivered by suppliers and acquired by customers.

T8. Sedgwick, the UK insurance company, provides on-line information to clients through their LIAISE system. This enables clients to *monitor* exposures and claims and systematically evaluate their risks by type of business, event, etc. The insurer claims that LIAISE has been instrumental in winning and keeping important accounts. This case is an example of monitoring services and resources which have been contracted for. The key seems to be in finding out what information on the resources being managed seems most valuable to the customer and indirectly to the supplier.

T9. Midland Bank's Advisory and Payment Services (MAPS) is a comprehensive electronic banking service incorporating cash management, automated payment and advisory capabilities. MAPS provides information on cash balances, transactions and uncleared effects to help customers better *manage* their overall cash positions. Through links to other systems such as CHAPS and SWIFT, same-day payments can be made electronically worldwide. Information on the clients foreign exchange exposures and hedging, together with forecasting routines are also provided. This case is an example of managing the resource transacted between customer and supplier. Often the resource will be an inventory held in transit or reservation.

T10. IBM offers Personal Computer Support Service, PCSS, to dealers to assist them in performing repairs on PCs. Dealers send queries to IBM electronically, and if the question or problem has been addressed before, anywhere in the world, an answer is sent back immediately. If it is a query which the data base is unable to answer, the problem is automatically referred to an IBM service team which goes to work on it. The answer is made available as soon as the problem is solved, and in the meantime information on the status of the query is available to dealers through PCSS. IBM also uses PCSS as a means of disseminating new product details, promotional information, and educational programs to dealers. Also dealers can communicate with each other through the system. PCSS is an example of customer *support* and demonstrates that for after-sales service TBIS can both automate some of the relationship and provide added value information facilities.

T11. TBIS can be used to automate *termination* of a customer relationship, by returning or disposing of the resource. SAS, the Scandinavian airline, now provide flight check-in facilities at terminals in their hotels so that customers can settle their hotel accounts, receive flight boarding passes and check in baggage at their convenience. Here the TBIS automates purchase closure, consummates another purchase, and influences future buyer behaviour (Keen, 1986).

T12. A reinsurance company once it has underwritten an insurer's risk then transmits detailed accounting records underpinning the transactions. The customer's business is *accounted for* by the supplier, reducing costs for both parties and increasing accuracy and reliability. The aim is to account for where and how much was spent on a resource.

Ten of the above TBIS were studied in the field. The remaining 25 case studies can all be placed in the twelve types of interaction between customer and supplier reproduced in Table 7.2. They are drawn from several industries suggesting that the TBIS opportunities framework has general applicability. Admittedly, many of the case TBIS are from the service sector, particularly financial services, probably because the information content of both channel and product tends to be high. However manufacturing examples also were studied and fit the framework.

One important aspect in which these TBIS differed, however, was the degree of strength as a competitive weapon. 'Strength' here is defined as the degree to which the TBIS allows the supplier firm to reach into and control its customers. In the research this aspect was assessed interpretatively. However what emerged was another important dimension to the opportunities framework which converts it from a list to a matrix (Fig. 7.2). This dimension is further reinforced by results from the second focus of the study. Three levels of strength are suggested:

1. 'internal support' where TBIS replace either internal mechanisms supporting the customer interaction life cycle or other routines in internal operations which have indirect customer consequences;
2. 'link up' where the supplier's value chain is electronically linked up to those of the customers, but where switching costs for customers are still relatively low;
3. 'lock in' where the TBIS achieves a degree of operational dependency by the customers on the supplier. Here the TBIS has introduced switching costs for the customer.

A significant finding from the field studies, discussed again in the next section, was that the majority of the systems studied (77%) were basically

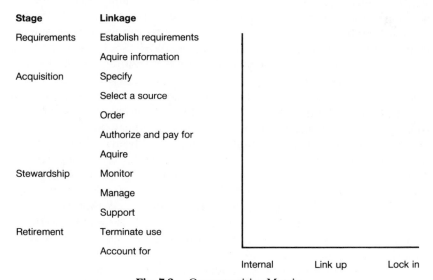

Fig. 7.2.   Opportunities Matrix

extensions across organizational boundaries of existing internal information systems. The TBIS allowed customers direct access to what previously had been a system for internal use only. For example the automobile manufacturer's TBIS which located vehicles in the distributors' and producer's stocks when dealers made sales enquiries was previously available in 'intermediate' form. Formerly a dealer telephoned the manufacturer's sales clerks who then queried, via terminals, the company's computerized stock and distribution system. Likewise the steel manufacturer's major customers now have direct access to its unallocated stock system, which previously was used only by the company's internal sales force. Also, the reinsurer gave a major client a terminal to the company's internal insurance and claim's data system, and kept a customer which they were in danger of losing.

Thus an internal support TBIS may possess latent competitive advantage which can be realised if further extended into the customer's or distributor's premises. All 35 cases studied had reached at least link-up stage. However in the link-up condition, whilst the TBIS often provide valuable information, service, or support for the customer in exchange for passing on some responsibility or costs, they do not create significant switching costs or operational dependencies. FRENTEL (Case T3) and DOGFOX (Case T7) exemplify link-up systems in that customers and middlemen value them but they can still quite easily move or place their business elsewhere.

Link-up TBIS become lock-in when the firm has effectively integrated itself into the value chains of its customers through (to quote McFarlan, 1984) 'a series of increasingly complex and useful procedures that insinuate themselves into customers' routines'. Lock-in TBIS offer mutual benefit but introduce switching costs by prompting customers to change their own systems to conform, or allow the TBIS to take over their own routines, or invest in interfaces and training to use the TBIS, or use the TBIS in preference to other channels. Of the systems described earlier, LIAISE (Case T8) is a good example; to utilize fully this system's risk management capabilities, customers must place all their insurance business through Sedgwicks. Otherwise the analysis of exposures and claims is inevitably incomplete. Thomas Cook's 'Chequemate' TBIS which performs administrative activities for selling agents of Thomas Cook travellers cheques (the accounting for customer interaction) has had a similar effect. The provision of sales advice documentation and management information reports has motivated agents to alter their procedures and conform to Chequemate, thereby becoming more dependent upon Thomas Cook. From the literature, American Hospital Supply is *the* exemplar case of 'lock-in'.

To achieve lock-in, the supplier often has to add value to the information or service provided by the TBIS. Once a TBIS link up is in place, the key seems to be to add function. As the infrastructure is already in place, the marginal cost may be low. Thus just as 77% of the systems investigated were link-up outgrowths of internal support systems, so we might expect many to evolve into lock-in over time. One example of this evolutionary path was a supplier who gave their salesmen portable terminals with on-line access to its product database. Then customers were connected to this internal support with viewdata terminal access, creating link-up. The planned next step is for the business to download a digest of constantly updated product information to customers who can directly access the product database through personal computers; the intention is to achieve lock-in.

Thus the TBIS opportunities framework for customer interactions in Fig. 7.2 describes the evolutionary path suggested by the research. (Firms with either internal support systems or link-up TBIS in different customer interactions might profitably examine whether they can be developed further down the evolutionary path to release and secure latent competitive advantage.) However 'leapfrogging' directly from internal support to lock-in should also be possible. There were insufficient examples discovered to suggest authoritatively what conditions are required to achieve this. Likewise there are opportunities for exploitation of TBIS in more than one of the twelve interactions with customers. For example Midland Bank's MAPS (Case T9) provides both 'monitor' and 'manage' capabilities. Thus firms also might search for vertical migration through the customer interactions to achieve competitive advantage.

Derivation of this opportunities framework has been interpretative and indicative. It applies only to TBIS which connect suppliers to customers and thus is not a universal tool for discovering competitive advantage. However, as Earl (1986b) has suggested, it is likely to be such focused tools, addressing operational levels of analysis, rather than sectoral or broad, descriptive models, that will help practitioners identify strategic applications. The findings from the second research question about exploitation and implementation of TBIS links to customers are likely to be more generalizable.

Implementation Enablers

Analysis of the 35 cases investigated suggested only three recurring factors from the many in the original taxonomy were conducive to successful implementation of TBIS linking customers to suppliers. These were:

1. the role of a product champion,
2. customer involvement in the development process,
3. marketing efforts for the system.

In addition two factors frequently emerged from one of the open-ended questions asked during interviews. In response to 'in what ways was the planning or development of this system unique?', two further enablers were identified:

4. the TBIS was an interorganizational extension of an information system which already existed internally,
5. normal information systems planning and approval processes were either ignored or purposely circumvented.

Each factor is now discussed in turn.

'Product Champion'

Development of TBIS for competitive advantage 'depends almost entirely on the will of individuals' who are often 'prophets in the wilderness' according to one marketing manager interviewed. Indeed, in 83% of the systems studied, a particular individual was deemed to have played a vital role in the implementation process. Further, the rate of customer acceptance of the TBIS was also found to be correlated with the presence of such a 'product champion' during implementation, as shown in Table 7.3. Interviewees generally believed that without the interest and support of product champions, the TBIS would not have been implemented.

Table 7.3. *Rate of customer acceptance with and without product champion. (Spearman Correlation Coefficient = 0.244; 5% Significance level = 0.359*

	Slow	Moderate	Rapid
With product champion	3	3	13
Without product champion	1	1	1

Here a product champion is defined as any individual who made a decisive contribution to the innovation by actively and enthusiastically promoting its progress through critical stages (SPRU, 1971). In this survey, the product champions were characterized by a high level of authority and responsibility. 64% were at or above director level. 72% were located in the department which would make primary use of the TBIS. Often they had only a low level of awareness or experience of IT, but clearly sufficient to recognize that TBIS had a role in customer interactions in the market place.

The label 'product champion' is given to these promoters of TBIS because they tend to have four general characteristics. Importantly, they possess or acquire a vision both of how the company's markets are developing, changing, or under threat, and of the potential role of IT in meeting customer needs. In a chemical business the general manager saw that his customers needed enormous amounts of product data to select the right product and so TBIS could become marketing tools. In a travel business the board, including the IS Director, believed their sector was but a network where the winners would be those with effective electronic delivery systems. In an insurance company, the Chief General Manager had a similar vision and saw IT as strategic ten years ago.

Second, the product champions had to secure the necessary resources to implement the system, often 'against the odds'. Either the IT function or top management, and sometimes both, would be concerned at the level of financial and personnel resources required. The champion therefore had to 'power through the approval', often avoiding formal organizational processes and procedures for securing IT resources. Also, the product champions had to overcome resistance to the TBIS initiation or development. This could come from the IS group, the users, or top management and was broken by persistence and/or demonstrating the benefits of the early stages of the TBIS migration towards lock-in.

Finally, the product champion actively promoted the system during implementation, by, for example, seeking to change attitudes amongst users, promoting the system in marketing brochures and working closely with customers. Similar personal support from system champions was found by Curley and Gremillion (1983) to be important in implementing decision support systems. Indeed there is considerable prior research support for the concept of the product champions and the ways they have to work. However it largely is found in the literature of industrial innovation, not information systems administration. Schon (1963) identified similar themes for the implementation of any radical innovation. Quinn saw the need for 'fanatically committed' champions to overcome organizational conservatism and technical and market obstacles. Maidique and Zirger (1984), Rothwell *et al.* (1974) and the SAPPHO project (SPRU, 1971) all have emphasized the key role of product champions in innovation and the power they have to muster.

Thus this study suggests that for developing TBIS for competitive advantage, product champions must be found. Typically the field studies suggest they are likely to have business rather than technical management experience and positions, possess power and status, know how to exploit the informal networks within organizations, and interact with those who might help influence their vision—customers, suppliers, and IS managers.

Customer Involvement

Twenty-four of the TBIS studied had been in operation long enough for interviewees to comment on their success. Success was indicated by the rate of customer acceptance which was found to be associated with the level of customer involvement in the system development process. As

Table 7.4 suggests, the higher the level of customer involvement in TBIS development the greater the likelihood of rapid acceptance of customer links.

Table 7.4. *Rate of customer acceptance at different levels of customer involvement. Spearman Correlation Coefficient = 0.712; 5% level of significance = 0.343; 10% level of significance = 0.485*

Level of customer involvement	Slow	Moderate	Rapid
None	5	3	2
Some	0	0	2
High	0	1	11

It is often claimed, of course, that user involvement is crucial to development and implement of any information system (Lucas, 1975; McCosh *et al.*, 1981) although Olson and Ives (1981) queried the empirical support. Innovation research is much stronger on this principle. Maidique and Zirger (1984) and SPRU (1972) both found a high degree of customer involvement was associated with success in industrial innovations. Von Hippel (1982) has found the same pattern in his research and, like Keen (1986), notes that many good ideas are generated by customers. Further, from this study it seems that customer involvement reduces the need for modifications. When customer involvement was high, in 75% of the cases modifications found to be needed were identified early in development. Conversely, in 80% of the cases with no customer involvement, necessary modifications were not identified until after the TBIS was implemented.

The means of acquiring customer involvement varied and probably reflects industry structure and distribution channels as well as the supplier's initiative and drive. In one case, a joint working party was set up with distributors to study how TBIS could serve joint needs. A brain-storming session identified one of the cases described earlier. Pilot projects involving small groups of customers were used in 14 of the 35 cases. IBM assessed needs of dealers in several countries before developing its PCSS (T10) system. The company in case T5 had lengthy discussions with key customers in developing its electronic data exchange services. Whatever approach was adopted in the 24 cases with high customer involvement, often the product champion participated.

Finally, to emphasize the importance of this factor, some of the companies which did not achieve immediate success with their TBIS subsequently recognized that this was due to lack of customer involvement in the development phase. In one case non-involvement was deliberate to avoid premature disclosure of a TBIS product; however 'the customers are ahead ... and now all development is customer led'. In one of the successful cases quoted earlier, two earlier attempts failed through lack of distributor involvement; now enhancements are based on the distributors' suggestions.

So customer involvement may be a special case of the user participation rule; however if 'the customer is King', he presumably has to be involved. However, the King customer often will need some incentive, especially if lock-in is the ultimate objective.

Marketing Effort

Eighteen of the TBIS had been in operation long enough for interviewees to assess the effect of marketing activities Table 7.5 shows the perceived association between degree of marketing effort and rate of customer acceptance. Indeed in 78% of the cases overall, marketing efforts were considered to be important to the successful exploitation of TBIS linking customers.

Table 7.5. *Rate of customer acceptance at different levels of marketing effort. Spearman Correlation Coefficient = 0.200; 5% level of significance = 0.399*

Level of marketing effort	Slow	Moderate	Rapid
None	1	1	1
Some	1	2	3
High	2	1	6

Four methods of marketing were discovered:

1. Market research was conducted in 8 cases, six of which achieved rapid customer acceptance. Rapid acceptance also occurred in 7 cases where no market research was done, but 5 of these were marked by high customer involvement. In one case of high market research with only moderate acceptance, no customer involvement occurred. Market research and customer involvement thus seem a good policy.
2. Focused promotion, rather than general publicity or advertising, characterized many of the TBIS studied. Example methods include holding seminars for customers, customer and conference demonstrations and advertising in targeted journals.
3. Customer education was deemed to be important in almost 70% of the cases. Table 7.6 suggests an association between customer education and customer acceptance. Methods included 'hands-on' education for customers, full time help and training support staff and after sale education for TBIS products.
4. Alignment between the TBIS offered and the supplier's marketing policies and practices also seemed to be associated with customer acceptance. In 15 of the TBIS considered to have close alignment, 10 achieved rapid customer acceptance and three achieved moderate take-up.

Table 7.6. *Rate of customer acceptance with and without customer education. Spearman Correlation Coefficient = 0.529; 5% level of significance = 0.377; 1% level of significance = 0.534*

	Slow	Moderate	Rapid
With customer education	2	4	11
Without customer education	2	0	0

Marketing of systems is rarely mentioned in the IS literature. However marketing effort has been found to be crucial in studies of innovation (Rothwell, 1976; Myers and Marquis, 1969). Indeed Cooper (1979) found well targeted sales efforts strongly correlated with innovation success, Maidique and Zirger (1984) stressed the importance of new products being built on the firm's present marketing strengths and Rothwell (1976) and SPRU (1972) both stressed the importance of customer education.

Marketing effort is probably essential when providing a system to any external user. Furthermore many marketing executives probably see a TBIS customer link as no different from any product or service. It needs to be marketed. No doubt the same cast of mind prompted the common encouragement of customer involvement.

Extension of Internal Systems

Seventy-seven per cent of the TBIS studied were inter-organizational extensions of information systems which already existed internally. Usually no or few changes had to be made to existing infrastructure and the external link-up was not generally seen to be the driver for the system being telecommunications-based. In the pattern of the previous enabling factors, an association was detected between those TBIS created by extending internal customer support systems and the rate of customer acceptance. Table 7.7 produces a Spearman Correlation Coefficient of 0.330 with 5% level of significance of 0.343 for this association.

Table 7.7. *Rate of customer acceptance with or without extensions of internal systems*

	Slow	Moderate	Rapid
Extension of internal systems	3	2	12
No extension of internal systems	2	2	2

Again the evolutionary pattern, discussed earlier, of migrating from internal support through link-up to lock-in receives support from innovation studies. Cooper found that 'technical and product synergy' with a firm's existing capabilities characterized new products. Likewise, innovations which 'build on present technological strengths' were found to be correlated with success by Maidique and Zirger. Quinn has stressed the importance of incrementalism in technological innovation and Abernathy and Utterback (1978) noted that within industries most process and product innovation is limited to incremental improvements.

In discussing the opportunities framework earlier, we emphasized this enabling factor; indeed the evolutionary migration path formed the columns of the matrix. It is clear that as well as examining whether an application or technology can fit the 12 linkages of customer inter-actions (the rows) or be extended down or up them, it is equally important to seek link up and lock in opportunities in existing internal support systems.

Information Systems Planning

In 80% of the TBIS studied, existing IS planning and project selection procedures were either purposely circumvented or simply ignored. Yet most companies have established formal procedures for planning and justifying investments in new information systems. These usually com-bined detailed investigation of a project proposal, typical of the feasi-bility stage of the systems development cycle, with longer range assess-ment of IS needs and prioritization of applications proposals. Also IS projects sometimes had to be assessed on a multiple criteria basis before receiving management approval.

However such formal planning mechanisms were often subverted. In one company, two of the TBIS never were examined against the laid down criteria; competitive parity and customer pressure were the arguments used. In a manufacturing company, a TBIS providing information to customers was 'an act of faith' and justified as essential to keeping and growing market share. In several cases the product champions powered their way around formal procedures. A chief executive circumvented the DP function and secured approval of a TBIS direct from the Board. In another case the product champion received no support from his IS group and so he went to an external bureau. In another case, the cash flow benefits from one customer system were siphoned off to fund a second TBIS. In yet another case, the business development team classified the proposed TBIS as low risk and thereby avoid any rigorous appraisal.

The reasons for 'bucking the planning procedures' vary. Satisfaction of customer needs, gaining experience with a new capability, and long-term market positioning were all quoted as needs for developing customer-oriented TBIS but also as factors the formal appraisal and planning procedures resisted. It seems that the control-oriented planning proce-dures typical of the early 1970s (McKinsey, 1968; McFarlan, 1971) and the strategic planning focus of later years (McLean and Soden, 1977) are too detailed, bureaucratic, and traditional for exploitation of IT for competitive advantage. Keen refers to 'analysis paralysis' in many of these procedures and it is perhaps becoming apparent that innovative, competitive information systems based on fast-moving technologies in rapidly changing market places will arise by other means. Again, innovation studies have something to say. Utterback *et al.* (1976) found 'formal planning was conspicuous by its absence' in successful innovations. Burns and Stalker (1961), of course, advocated organismic rather than mechanistic management of innovation. Indeed in IS planning, Pyburn found informal planning processes suited volatile business environments.

So what planning prescriptions emerge? Keen (1986) has recently advocated radically new approaches to appraisal of information systems, often relying on business vision and argument rather than cost benefit calculus. McFarlan (1984) advises separation of competitive advantage applications from other IS in appraising the prioritizing system proposals. Earl (1986a) has proposed that three 'legs' are necessary in IS strategic planning: top down to align IS with business needs, bottom up to build on and extend the inherited system base and inside out to exploit technological opportunities outside the apparatus of formal planning and control. Much of what Earl describes in the inside out leg relates to the environments in which the 35 TBIS were proposed and implemented. That 80% of them were prosecuted outside the formal planning procedures seems to suggest that plans must be kept in their appropriate place and planning takes on many forms.

Conclusions

We have presented an opportunities framework for identifying and developing TBIS which link customers to suppliers. Such systems are perhaps the most frequently quoted examples of using IT for competitive advantage. In addition, five factors have been discovered which seem to enable the identification, and particularly the implementation, of TBIS which link up customers for competitive advantage. We suspect that these five factors may apply to the development of IT applications for competitive advantage at large. At least three implications arise.

In information systems research, there is much to be learnt from studies of innovation. The processes of recognizing, developing, and implementing information systems are similar to the processes of any industrial innovation, whether targeted internally or externally.

In information systems practice, there would seem to be limitations in investing heavily in formal IS strategic planning mechanisms to seek IT applications which may yield competitive advantage. A more appropriate route may lie in what Earl (1986a, 1986c) termed the 'inside out' approach—a necessary informal and processual complement to 'top down' and 'bottom up' methods.

In information systems theory, the development of strategic IS (systems which are strategic weapons and/or inherent to strategic initiatives) seem to be somewhat different to those described by the classic models of MIS. They do not relate closely to the traditional decision-oriented MIS frameworks derived from Anthony (1965) and from Simon (1960). Often they are closer to the 'ordinary' transaction processing systems of everyday life. Their creation and implementation however require a new perspective. Wiseman (1985) calls this the 'strategic perspective'. The research reported here suggests, not for the first time, that it is practitioners '*innovating*' in the continuous arena of competitive forces who are sketching out the new Theory.

References

Abernathy, W. J., and Utterback, J. M. (1978), *The Evolution Innovation*, MIT Alumni Association.

Anthony, R. N. (1965), *Planning and Control Systems: A Framework for Analysis*, Harvard University Press, Cambridge, Mass.

Bell, D. (1979), 'Thinking Ahead: Communications Technology—for Better or for Worse', *Harvard Business Review*, May–June, pp. 20–42.

Benjamin, R. I., *et al.* (1984), 'Information Technology: A Strategic Opportunity', *Sloan Management Review* **25, 3**, pp. 3–10.

Burns, T., and Stalker, G. M. (1961), *The Management of Innovation*, Tavistock, London.

Burnstine, D. C. (1980), *BIAIT: An Emerging Management Engineering Discipline*, BIAIT International Inc. Working Paper, Petersburg, NY.

Cash, J. I., and Konsynski, B. R. (1985), 'IS Redraws Competitive Boundaries', *Harvard Business Review*, March–April, pp. 134–42.

Clemons, E. K., *et al.* (1984), 'Telecommunications and Business Strategy: The Basic Design Variables', In Nolan, Norton, and Company. *Managing Telecommunications for Strategic Advantage in Europe*, unpublished multi-company study, London.

Cooper, R. G. (1979), 'The Dimensions of Industrial New Product Success and Failure', *Journal of Marketing* **43, 3**, pp. 93–103.

Curley, K., and Gremillion, L. L. (1983), 'The Role of the Champion in DSS Implementation', *Information & Management* **6**, pp. 203–9.

Earl, M. J. (1984), 'Emerging Trends in Managing New Information Technologies', In Piercy, N. (ed.), *The Management Implications of New Information Technology*, Croon Helm, London, pp. 189–215.

—— (1986*a*), 'Formulating Information Technology Strategies', In Piercy, N. (ed.), *Managing New Information Technologies*, Croon Helm, London.

—— (1986*b*), 'Information Systems Strategy Formulation', In Boland, R. J., and Hirscheim, R. (eds.), *Critical Issues in Information Systems Research*, John Wiley and Sons, London.

—— (1986*c*), *Information Systems Strategy Formulation: A Practical Framework*, Infotech State of Art Review of IT for Strategic Advantage, Pergamon.

Fitzgerald, J. (1984), *Business Data Communications*, John Wiley and Sons, New York.

Frohman, A. L. (1982), 'Technology as a Competitive Weapon', *Harvard Business Review—The Management of Technological Innovation*, Harvard University Printing Office, Boston, Mass. pp. 23–30.

Gibson, C. F., and Nolan, R. L. (1974), 'Managing the Four Stages of ED Growth', *Harvard Business Review,* January–February, pp. 76–88.

Hull, F., and Hage, J. (1982), 'Organizing for Innovation: Beyond Burns and Stalker's Organic Type', *Sociology* **16, 4**, pp. 564–77.

Ives, B., and Learmonth, G. P. (1984), 'The Information System as a Competitive Weapon', *Communications of the ACM* **27, 12**, pp. 1193–1201.

IBM Corporation (1981), *Business Systems Planning: Information Systems Planning Guide*, IBM Document GE200527–3, White Plains, NY.

Keen, P. G. W. (1986), *Competing in Time: Using Telecommunications for Competitive Advantage*, Ballinger, Cambridge, Mass.

—— and Mills, R. D. (1984), 'Stages in Managing Telecommunications', In Noland, Norton, and Company, *Managing Telecommunications for Strategic Advantage in Europe*, unpublished multi-company study, London.

King, W. R. (1978), 'Strategic Planning for Management Information Systems', *MIS Quarterly* **2, 1**, pp. 27–37.

—— (1986), 'Using Information Technology for Competitive Advantage', In Earl, M. J. (ed.), *Formulating Information Technology Strategies*, Oxford University Press.

Kotler, P. (1980), *Marketing Management* (4th edn.), Prentice Hall, London.

Leavitt, T. (1965), 'Exploit the Producer Life Cycle', *Harvard Business Review*, November–December.

Lloyd, A. (1985), 'Telecommunications: Stormy Passage Ahead', *Newsweek*, 15 April 1985, special section on High Technology.

Lucas, H. C. (1982), *Information Systems Concepts for Management,*McGraw-Hill, New York.

—— (1975), *Why Information Systems Fail*, Columbia University Press, New York.

McCosh, A. M., Rahman, M., and Earl, M. J. (1981), *Developing Managerial Information Systems*, MacMillan, London.

McFarlan, F. W. (1971), 'Problems in Planning the Information System', *Harvard Business Review*, March–April, pp. 75–89.

—— (1981), 'Portfolio Approach to Information Systems', *Harvard Business Review*, September–October.

—— (1984), 'Information Technology Changes the Way You Complete', *Harvard Business Review*, May–June, pp. 98–103.

—— and McKenney, J. L. (1983), *Corporate Information System Management*, Richard D. Irwin, Homewood, Ill.

McKinsey & Co. (1968), *Unlocking the Computer's Profit Potential*, New York.

McLean, E. R., and Soden, J. V. (1977), *Strategic Planning for MIS*, John Wiley and Sons, New York.

Maidique, M. A. (1980), 'Entrepreneurs, Champions, and Technological Innovation', *Sloan Management Review* **22, 2**, pp. 59–76.

—— and Zirger, B. J. (1984), 'A Study of Success and Failure in Product Innovation: The Case of the US Electronics Industry', *IEEE Transactions on Engineering Management* (November 1984), pp. 192–203.

Myers, S., and Marquis, D. G. (1969), *Successful Industrial Innovations*. National Science Foundation Report NSF 69–17.

Notowidigdo, M. H. (1984), 'Information Systems: Weapons to Gain the Competitive Edge', *Financial Executive*, February, pp. 20–5.

Olson, M., and Ives, B. (1981), 'User Involvement in System Design; an Empirical Test of Alternative Approaches', *Information and Management* **4**, pp. 183–95.

Parsons, G. L. (1983), 'Information Technology: A New Competitive Weapon', *Sloan Management Review* **25, 1**, pp. 3–14.

Porter, M. E. (1980), *Competitive Strategy*, Free Press, Glenwood, Ill.

—— and Millar, V. E. (1985), 'How Information Gives you Competitive Advantage', *Harvard Business Review*, July–August, pp. 149–60.

Pyburn, P. (1983), 'Linking the MIS Plan with Corporate Strategy: An Exploratory Study', *MIS Quarterly* **7, 2**, pp. 1–14.

Quinn, J. B. (1980), 'Managing Strategic Change', *Sloan Management Review*, Summer, pp. 3–11.

Rothwell, R. (1976), 'Marketing—A Success Factor in Industrial Innovation', *Management Decision* **14, 1**, pp. 43–53.

Rothwell, R., *et al.* (1974), 'SAPPHO Updated—Project SAPPHO Phase II', *Research Policy* **14, 1**, pp. 258–91.

Schon, D. A. (1963), 'Champions for Radical New Inventions', *Harvard Business Review*, March–April, pp. 77–86.

Science Policy Research Unit (1971), *Success and Failure in Industrial Innovation*, Center for the Study of Industrial Innovation, University of Sussex.

Scott Morton, M. S. (1984), 'The State of the Art of Research', In McFarlan, F. W. (ed.), *The Information Systems Research Challenge*, Harvard Business School Press, Boston, Mass., pp. 13–41.

Sells, S. B. (1964), 'Toward a Taxonomy of Organisations', In Cooper, W. W., Leavitt, H. J., and Shelly, M. W. (eds.), *New Perspectives in Organisation Research*, John Wiley and Sons, New York, pp. 13–41.

Simon, H. A. (1960), *The New Science of Management Decision*, Harper & Row, New York.

Utterback, J. M., *et al.* (1976), 'The Process of Innovation in Five Industries in Europe and Japan', *IEEE Transactions on Engineering Management*, February, pp. 3–9.

Van Horn, R. (1973), 'Empirical Studies in Management Information Systems', *Data Base* **14**, pp. 172–80.

Von Hippel, E. (1982), 'Get New Products from Customers', *Harvard Business Review*, March–April, pp. 117–22.

Wiseman, C. (1985), *Strategy and Computers*, Dow Jones-Irwin, Homewood, Ill.

—— and MacMillan, I. (1984), 'Creating Competitive Weapons from Information Systems', *Journal of Business Strategy* **5, 2**.

Appendix 7.1. A Taxonomy of Potential TBIS Enabling Factors

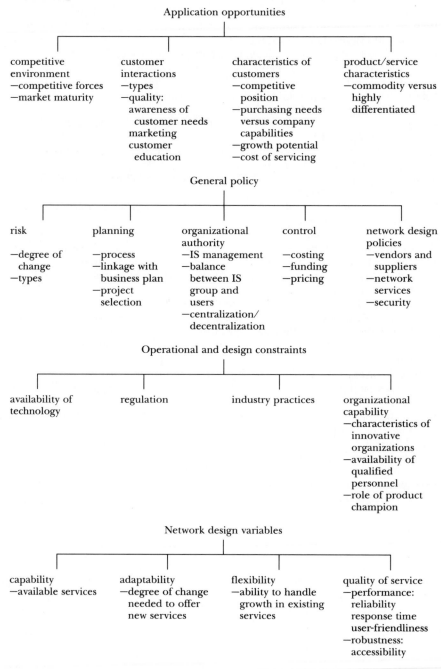

Application opportunities

competitive environment	customer interactions	characteristics of customers	product/service characteristics
—competitive forces	—types	—competitive position	—commodity versus highly differentiated
—market maturity	—quality: awareness of customer needs marketing customer education	—purchasing needs versus company capabilities	
		—growth potential	
		—cost of servicing	

General policy

risk	planning	organizational authority	control	network design policies
—degree of change	—process	—IS management	—costing	—vendors and suppliers
—types	—linkage with business plan	—balance between IS group and users	—funding	—network services
	—project selection	—centralization/ decentralization	—pricing	—security

Operational and design constraints

availability of technology	regulation	industry practices	organizational capability
			—characteristics of innovative organizations
			—availability of qualified personnel
			—role of product champion

Network design variables

capability	adaptability	flexibility	quality of service
—available services	—degree of change needed to offer new services	—ability to handle growth in existing services	—performance: reliability response time user-friendliness
			—robustness: accessibility

8

Experiences in IT Strategy Formulation: Imperial Chemical Industries PLC

DEREK SEDDON

Imperial Chemical Industries plc

IT Strategy vs. Strategic IT

In discussing ICI's development of competitive IT it will become evident that I differentiate very strongly between the two concepts of formulating an IT Strategy and identifying and applying Strategic IT. I suggest that:

1. IT Strategy is concerned with the deployment of total IT resource,
2. Strategic IT is concerned with applying IT aimed at effecting markets.

As will be evident, the two are not always interdependent but sometimes significantly in tension. The Management Services Function is normally responsible for formulating an IT Strategy, whereas I believe Strategic IT must always be business-led.

The ICI Group and Its Economic Environment

The ICI Group consists of Imperial Chemical Industries plc (with eight operating Divisions) and over 400 subsidiaries. ICI is one of the world's major manufacturing organizations and one of the top six chemical companies. Its products range from oil and basic inorganics such as lime and salt to complex and specialized chemical derivatives including pharmaceuticals and agrochemicals. Its types of business extend from commodity chemicals to consumer products. Key figures in 1985 were:

Sales	£10,725m
Trading profit	£ 1,408m
Employees	120,200

The geographic diversity of the Group, with manufacturing in more than forty countries and substantial sales in over sixty, is the widest of all the chemical majors.

The economic recession triggered by the OPEC oil price increase led to very poor profit performance for ICI in 1980, when for the first time in our history we made a loss in one quarter. This caused the Executive

Directors of ICI to undertake a fundamental reappraisal of our business strategy and the organization required to support it. That reappraisal was necessary because of the scale and scope of the socio-economic changes affecting us. These included:

1. An increasing differentiation and specialization of markets. Over perhaps the past 200 years, social and economic activity has been characterized by growing integration and standardization—whether in the development of nation states or mass industrial production. Now there is a demand for more diversity and choice. At the same time that demand is less predictable, and more changeable.
2. The arrival of the global economy; companies and governments no longer operate in a purely national context. We are shifting rapidly from self-sufficient national economies to an *interdependent* global economy. Competition is *international* and economic trends and influences *transnational*. Production and marketing must be efficient in world and not merely national terms.

At the same time, ICI was moving from being a company supplying *products*, to a company supplying *services.* More particularly, we aim to be a company supplying services about scientific *knowledge.* Our strength lies not in what we have, but what we know.

Therefore the organizational context in which ICI's IT Strategies have to be formulated is that of a large, diverse, and developed organization reshaping its business strategies and changing its organizational boundaries.

ICI Group IT Strategy

The formulation of ICI's Group IT strategy is based upon the following principles and procedures:

1. The ICI Executive Team determine Business Strategies.
2. From the portfolio of Business Strategies the Director of IT identifies Group IT needs.
3. The Group IT Strategy influences and is influenced by individual business IT strategies.

The Group Business objectives which have been set by the Executive Team require ICI to become:

1. more international which requires business regrouping.
2. more market oriented which requires customer service.
3. more knowledge-intensive which depends on human networking.

My vision of how IT can facilitate these business objectives is the provision of an IT infrastructure which enables knowledge to be shared electronically within the ICI Group worldwide. In order to realize this vision the Group IT Strategy centralizes control of infrastructional *technology*, thereby creating an 'information utility' and devolves even further the specific *application* of IT to individual business units.

Before this strategy was adopted the main difficulty within a decentralized organization was getting agreement and implementation of the IT standards necessary for the vision to work.

IT Strategy Lessons

In attempting to draw out the lessons to date in developing a corporate IT strategy, it is necessary to describe the history and evolution of the Management Services Function of ICI plc, which serves eight European divisions. In the 1970s every Division had an autonomous Management Services Department. Note that an ICI Division is a very large business in its own right. The individual Management Services Departments were highly professional and responsible for very large applications portfolios. Each regarded itself as the 'corporate' MIS Department of its Division. Organizationally they were separately responsible for:

1. Business Analysis
2. Application Development.
3. Programming and Maintenance
4. Technical Support
5. Computer Operations
6. Data Communications.

Most MIS practitioners will remember the abortive attempts in the early 1970s to create 'corporate integrated databases'—whereby a user could ask innumerable questions and be provided with an instant perfect answer! In reality application systems continued to be organizationally bounded, often within a function of a division. Even where integration within a division was possible its systems would be totally dissimilar from related systems in other divisions.

It was from the shared problems of such experiences that the Management Services Departments within the various Divisions identified the need to agree ICI plc company standards. The will to co-operate was evidenced in the establishment of expert teams reporting to a federation of Management Services Managers, with the central (Head Office) Department acting as secretariat and identifying those areas where standardization would be beneficial. Standards agreed during this period were:

1. An Applications Development Standard—LBMS
2. A Data Base Management Standard—ADABAS
3. IBM Applications Security—ACF2

The motivation at this point was largely concerned with the economics of avoiding re-inventing wheels and of efficient purchasing. There was no conscious awareness of the potential for IT services fundamentally to change the way ICI did its business, nor that there would be business-driven changes necessitating revision of our whole approach to managing IT.

In 1981 the review of ICI's organization described earlier included a study of the Management Services (MS) organization. This study was led by a divisional Chief Executive. The team recommended the appointment of a Functional Head responsible for Corporate IT strategy and the formation of a Management Services Board comprising divisional MS directors. The Board's role was to provide policy guidance to the Function and to aid the implementation of Corporate IT strategies. These recommendations were put into effect during 1982 when I was 'promoted' from a business general manager to become the Head of Corporate Management Services.

My aims in this job have been to:

1. Establish an IT vision for ICI
2. Communicate this vision, both to business managers and functional experts
3. Integrate IT and business planning
4. Develop an IT infrastructure to support networking within the ICI group worldwide.

Although I had little knowledge of IT it did not take long, with the help of the professionals in the Function, to produce an IT vision. Realizing this vision has taken somewhat longer!

Coincident with my appointment, a panel of divisional and central management services experts produced a report recommending a corporate standard for wordprocessing. The MS Departments within the various Divisions had identified that this was a generic service, with the potential to lead to electronic mail and information retrieval—provided there was agreement to work in a co-ordinated and cohesive way. There followed a series of 'expert panel' led standards on hardware and software, in particular:

1. word-processing equipment—Wordplex
2. managerial workstations—IBM PC
3. 'integrated office'—DEC All-in-one

In retrospect, these decisions on standards now look as if they were taken in isolation of other existing or later standards and optimal only at a moment in history. To be fair, this reflected the state of the supplying industry rather than stupidity on the part of ICI. The standards adopted were seen to be sufficiently generic, and of such a

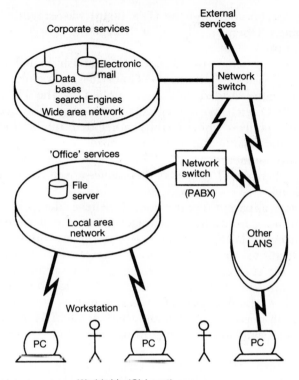

Corporate services

External services

Network switch

Electronic mail

Data bases

search Engines

Wide area network

'Office' services

Network switch

(PABX)

File server

Local area network

Other LANS

Workstation

PC

PC

PC

Worldwide ICI Locations

Fig. 8.1. IT Infrastructure Vision

scale as to warrant the 'counter-cultural' behaviour of 'imposition'. Had we been aware that the elapsed time before the electronic office would become effective was eight and not three years, it was doubtful whether office technology would have been the catalyst it was for organizational co-operation.

Whilst the early development of a corporate IT strategy was primarily driven by professionalism within the IT function, it became increasingly evident that economics and ease of management of the technology must take second place to the rapidly changing needs of a very dynamic business. The MS function belief that each Department could exist in isolation was blown apart by a double explosion: the demands of business reorganization and the increasing complexity of technology. Viewed corporately it became clear that the incremental technical decisions still being taken by Divisions were inevitably frustrating the IT vision. The best way forward was seen to be to centralize the management of multi-user computing and telecommunications (the IT infrastructure).

This occurred in 1984 when I was appointed ICI Group Director of

Information Technology and the CMS Board was expanded to include major overseas Operating Units. It brings the story on IT strategy development up-to-date.

We are now conscious of the need to establish an ICI IT Technical Architecture (Policies, Standards and Guidelines) at a global level and to develop the Value Added Networks implied by the IT vision (mail, messaging, SPSO, etc.). We are equally conscious of the need to adopt infra-structure policies which enable, rather than inhibit, organizational change and business flexibility. We recognize that too rapid imposition of immature standards will frustrate sensible experimentation, particularly when the IT products themselves are in the early phases of their life cycles.

Despite the apparent contraction, I believe that the very act of imposing some constraints encourages greater experimentation and variation. It has certainly freed up scarce resources within each business for IT applications, rather than the ten times over pursuit of the *best* technology. Yet several industry observers have commented that ICI's move to centralize technology runs counter to the trend in most organizations to decentralize IT. My response is that our history of autonomous IS departments pursuing independent IT strategies shows there is a significant price to be paid in the loss of corporate direction and synergy.

For the future, even more challenging and not yet solved, is the increasing need for a corporate Applications Architecture. The data processing systems inherited from the 1960s and 1970s, with their high maintenance cost and inflexibility, represent an enormous millstone limiting the Company's desire to achieve organizational flexibility and

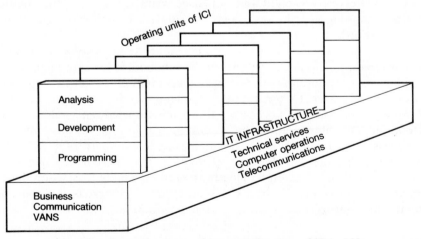

Fig. 8.2. Centralization and Decentralization of IT in ICI

market responsiveness. We, like many other companies, are increasingly concerned about the proportion of our analyst and programming resources which are tied up in the refurbishment and maintenance of 'old' systems.

Our first efforts to design single corporate systems, rather than a multitude of similar divisional systems, were primarily targeted on reducing overall maintenance demand, and saving development effort. This is most easily achieved where the Company demands conformity of practice, in for example such things as common payment structures. The major development in this field is a corporate accounting system, where establishing common data definitions and codes will ensure improved flexibility in data access between the separate parts of the business.

Where no such corporate conformity exists, achieving cooperation proves much more elusive for two reasons. First there is the cost of the 'slum clearance' necessary to accommodate common systems. Second there is the unwillingness on the part of the disparate units to accept 80% solutions, through a conviction that the 20% of difference must overwhelmingly determine the design of each separate Division's systems. Such a view today is no longer tenable because divisional structures are changing, and separate business units from several Divisions are expected to achieve a new international business alignment, irrespective of previous division boundaries.

In this context, it is therefore interesting to reflect on the intense effort expended in the early 1980s on undertaking divisionally-based information systems' surveys, using such techniques as IBM's BSP and James Martin's Information Systems Planning. These techniques, as we used and experienced them, have one major drawback. The answers they provided typically suggested many tens of man-years of effort to bring about something which looked not too dissimilar from the corporate integrated database, longed for in the middle 1970s. The customer, who the systems analyst presumed to be desperately in need of better information, could be promised a substantially more flexible and relevant information source, but only after a lengthy gestation period. This 'jam tommorrow' argument has long damned the MS Function. An Information Engineering approach, by definition, assumes that the current organizational boundaries have a strong business relevance. However in practice and seen over time, the Company organization was, and is, in a continual state of flux.

Strategic IT

The topic of identifying and implementing Competitive Advantage IT opportunities is much more difficult. Within ICI we have tried most of the research and teaching 'recipes' emanating from the business schools

(Earl, 1986; Porter and Millar, 1985; Rockart, 1979; Feeny and Brownlee, 1986; and McFarlan, 1984) together with some variants and experiments of our own. The diverse nature of our many businesses (from commodities to consumer products) and the very wide range of industrial sectors into which we sell, means we have the opportunity to explore every sector of the McFarlan Strategic grid.

Rather than detail the history of our experience and the many blind alleys we have encountered, I have chosen to describe the principle lessons we have learned.

Strategic IT Lessons

The key message from our experience is that 'identifying and exploiting Strategic IT is all about innovation and the management of change. In our work with ICI business teams we have learned at the outset to categorize their motivation for change. The matrix in Fig. 8.3 is based on our experience that management motivation for change and perceived business pain in each business unit influence attitudes to the competitive potential of IT. Unless the business unit management are 'innovative' or 'hungry' you could well be wasting effort.

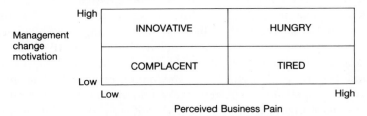

Fig. 8.3.   Management Style

Organization Development experts tell us that change requires pain. They also teach that there are four key stages an individual must go through if change is to occur:

1. I know   communication of ideas
2. I understand   'what I need to do'
3. I can   given necessary skill
4. I will   motivated

Whilst communication is a relatively straightforward process, we have found that any amount of exemplars rarely lead to an 'understanding' of 'what I need to do'. The understanding stage we have found to be by far the most difficult. The problems of understanding are compounded by the 'language' barrier between the Business and MS Function. Success at this stage should spawn some creative IT ideas and the problem then becomes one of managing Innovation.

The research work of Runge at the Oxford Institute of Information Management confirmed for us that the critical success factors for Strategic IT are the same as those previously identified for innovation in science and technology, namely:

1. The need for a *Champion*—provide 'umbrella' and resource
2. the importance of *Feedback*—listen to customer
3. the need for a *New Venture Approach*—'buck' the system
4. extend from the *Familiar*—minimize unnecessary risk.

Having found a Champion it is important that he manages the development of Strategic IT like any New Ventrure, ie. provide resources and be patient. However, here we encounter a problem. If an IT development is to become strategic it must have a discernible effect on the profit of the firm. This implies a sizeable investment before success can be demonstrated, but senior management are reluctant to commit large investments until the New Venture 'proves' its worth. This is connected to the problem of 'Understanding'. If you want sympathetic response talk to a New Venture Manager!

After examining several proprietary methodologies for identifying strategic IT opportunities, we found the Critical Success Factor approach most to our liking and have used it successfully with many business units. Our experience with these businesses has been that such an approach offers considerable advantages over the previous methodologies. In particular, most of the business executives involved have found it an excellent process for identifying those areas where action plans are critically necessary, and in forging business team cohesion in the prioritization of the resource to be applied.

The Management Services function has also benefited from the approach in being able to demonstrate a greater business sensitivity and by being welcomed as an integral part of the business team in devising the short-term action plans. Sadly, however, the IT pull-through has not been as strong as I had hoped for. Some of my colleagues tell me this is because I'm too impatient—there seems to be an unavoidable delay between the seeding and germination of Competitive Advantage IT ideas.

One of ICI's IT applications, 'Wheat Counsellor', has become a well known exemplar of strategic IT. Counsellor is an expert system helping the farmer to optimize his wheat treatment by selecting pesticides and complementary products. This was one of our first attempts at Strategic IT and was a technically led project initiated by 'selling' to a business 'exciting leading edge IT technology'. However we didn't go through the process I've just described. The cost and delays in delivering the technology strained our credibility. We discovered the hard way that Strategic IT needs to be business-led. By being on the 'leading edge' of technology we learned a lot about building expert systems and as a result spun off a joint venture company marketing expert system shells, ISI Ltd.

Epilogue

Returning to the opening theme, 'IT Strategy vs. Strategic IT', I hope I have given a flavour of the distinctive difference between the two. In particular, there is a substantial difference in management styles implied. Tension arises when the 'New Venture' manager of Strategic IT 'bucks the system' and crosses the institutional manager of IT Strategy.

References

Earl, M. J. (1986), 'Formulating Information Technology Strategies', in Piercy, N. (ed.), *Management Information Systems: The Technology Challenge*, Croom Helm.

Feeny, D. F., and Brownlee, C. G. (1986), *Competition in the Era of Interactive Network Services*, Oxford Institute of Information Management research paper **RDP 86/17**, Templeton College, Oxford.

McFarlan, F. W. (1984), 'Information Technology Changes the Way You Compete', *Harvard Business Review*, May–June.

Porter, M. E., and Millar, V. (1985), 'How Information Gives you Competitive Advantage', *Harvard Business Review*, July–August.

Rockart, J. F. (1979), 'Chief Executives Define Their Own Data Needs', *Harvard Business Review*, March–April.

Runge, D. (1985), *Using Telecommunications for Competitive Advantage*, unpublished D. Phil. thesis, Oxford University.

9

Formulation of Information Systems Strategies: Emerging Lessons and Frameworks

MICHAEL J. EARL[1]

Oxford Institute of Information Management, Templeton College, Oxford

Introduction

The formulation of Information Systems (IS) Strategies has become the dominant concern of Information Technology (IT) Managers in large organizations (Earl, 1983; Dickson *et al.*, 1984). This paper is based on both research and advisory work in large European and North American firms who have been attempting to 'put strategy into information systems and IT' over the last three to five years. The reasons they embark upon this exercise seem to be four-fold:

1. Pressures exerted in their sector—often the enabling potential of new technology helping to change the definition, boundaries and activities of the sector, particularly when the sector is undergoing major structural change due to deregulation, global competition, or concentration.
2. The pursuit of competitive advantage—usually the desire to seek the competitive opportunities from IT which management has head about elsewhere.
3. The alignment of IT with business needs—the widespread desire to ensure that investment in IT is consistent with business strategy.
4. A means of revamping the IT function—often the opportunity to change the basis of IT and IS by raising their profile, putting them on a strategic plinth, and reasserting top management direction.

Consequently, as I reported in 1983, the majority of large firms now possess a strategic or long-range plan for IS but, contrary to many prescriptions (Kantrow, 1980; Scott Morton and Rockart, 1984), they are less often formally linked to the business strategy or long range plans. Indeed most firms would admit that they are still experimenting in, and learning about, the formulation of IT strategies. What is clear from my research and experience is that four crucial lessons have to be learnt. These can be stated as follows:

[1] The author is grateful to ICL Limited for funding his research in this area.

1. IT strategy and IS strategy are different.
2. No single strategy formulation methodology will work.
3. IS strategy mode depends on the sector.
4. IS strategy is formulated in stages.

These findings, their implications and the frameworks derived from them are all *interpretative*. They are based on case study investigation and action research.

Levels of Strategy

As executives search for IT strategy formulation methodologies which provide a substantive and ongoing procedure for both directing the application of IT and gaining strategic advantage from it, a common confusion can be found. This exists partly because of the loose terminology of planning and strategy in discourse and the literature, partly because organizations are still learning how to plan IT and partly because senior management tends to be concerned about both technology policy issues and business needs and about both planning information resources and controlling them. The delineation in Fig. 9.1 between ends and means or between applications and delivery is

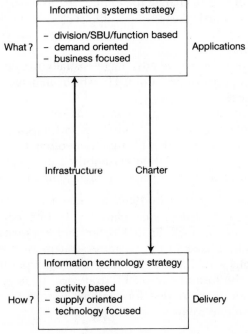

Fig. 9.1. Information Systems and Information Technology Strategies Delineated

intended to clarify concepts and practice in strategy formulation. The issue of what should we do with the technology, I term the Information Systems Strategy, whilst questions of how do we do it, I term the Information Technology Strategy.

In business it is not unusual to find general managers with inadequate experience and qualifications addressing the delivery strategy and IS executives, who cannot know all about business needs trying to drive the applications strategy. It is common to find steering committees quite confused about which of these levels of strategy is their concern. Of course the two levels are not entirely separable—application needs suggest the charter for the IS function and the technology posture provides the infrastructure which underpins applications. Indeed, Lucas and Turner (1982) contend that 'effective control of information processing' (much of which can be achieved through the delivery strategy) 'is a necessary prerequisite to the integration of technology with strategy' (applications strategy). Nevertheless, the two levels of strategy are distinct in terms of focus, organizational responsibility, methodology, and timescale.

The IS strategy is concerned primarily with aligning IS development with business need and with seeking competitive advantage from IT. Thus, in principle, it is formulated wherever business—especially product–market—strategy is formulated, typically at the level of the strategic business unit. In large and complex organizations, therefore, there may be several IS strategies and they will be the ultimate responsibility of each business unit's executive management. These strategies may be formulated through a planning methodology and should relate in some way to the business strategy. They will comprise a mix of short-term essential and tactical applications, medium-term business driven needs and longer-term visionary investments.

The IT strategy is concerned primarily with technology policies and with procedures for 'putting the management into IT'. This strategy becomes the charter, guidelines and modus operandi for the IT function. It is heavily influenced by the IT professionals, but with top management involvement in order to ensure the function is directed and managed in line with the organization's needs, style and structure. There are likely to be fewer IT strategies than IS strategies in large and complex organizations, perhaps only one in a centralized business. The IT strategy evolves continuously and comprises a mix of objectives, policies, and procedures adapting to meet business needs, technological change, and organizational learning.

This delineation of strategies is consistent with strategic management theory in general. Table 9.1 suggests the correspondence. The IS and IT strategies together become the activity strategy for the IT function, just as finance, personnel, etc. will have their activity strategies.

Table 9.1.　*Strategy levels*

Level	Focus	Responsibility	IS/IT Linkage
Corporate	Global Business Portfolio	Board	IS Mission and Charter
Business	Product–Market	SBU Management	IS Needs and Priorities
Activity (The IT Function)	*a.* Applications	SBU Management and IT Management	Applications Development Portfolio
	b. Delivery	IT Management and Top Management	IT Policies and Procedures

The remainder of this paper is concerned with formulation of the IS strategy, assuming it has been uncoupled from the delivery or IT strategy. The result we seek is the contents list depicted in Fig. 9.2. In many ways this is closer to the 'shopping list' pilloried by consultants than to the 'intergalactic systems charts' they often favour. However, to qualify as a strategy, the contents list must satisfy three criteria:

1. the relative spending on each area needs to be agreed,
2. the relative priorities of each area and application need to be agreed,
3. each application, except mandatory ones, should be strategically justified.

In the next section, the more difficult question of how to derive this applications development portfolio—a term coined by McFarlan (1984)— is addressed.

Mandatory applications	Stategic applications	Infrastructure developments	System renewals	R&D/ experiments	Maintainance and enhancement	Niche developments

Fig. 9.2.　Applications Development Portfolio

A Three-Pronged Attack

Organizations' perceived need to plan IS, together with the more recent desires to align IS development with business plans and exploit IT strategically, have spawned several methodologies for strategy formulation and prompted some evaluative research. Early work borrowed from long range planning, proposing approaches such as PPBS and arguing the benefits of top-down versus bottom-up philosophies (McFarlan, Nolan and Norton, 1973). Later work proposed general frameworks to discover business strategy and interpret it into IS needs (King, 1978) or to analyse internal and external environments, strengths and weaknesses, and business objectives to formulate IS goals (McLean and Soden, 1977). More recently, more structured techniques have been developed both by academics and consultants, one example being the 'critical success factors' approach (Bullen and Rockart, 1984) which seeks to logically derive business goals, critical success factors needed to achieve the goals, and IS requirements needed to support or deliver the critical success factors. At the same time computer manufacturers have continued to develop or enhance their planning tools, an example being IBM's 'Business Systems Planning'.

Evaluative work has sought to discover when, how, and whether these methods work, for example Shank *et al*.'s (1985) appraisal of 'critical success factors' and McLean's (1983) comparison of this method with Business Systems Planning. Useful guidelines are beginning to emerge, but in general the conclusions seem to be that most techniques work in the appropriate context, with skilled analysts and in a supportive environment. Sullivan (1985), however, recently has argued for a contingency approach where he proposes that different methods suit different contexts, the key determinants being how diffused are the organization and its technology and how infused (how well developed and important) are the applications. Pyburn (1983) also derived a situational approach when he suggested three different approaches to IS strategic planning dependent on factors such as business environment, technological context, management style, and organizational structure.

My own work suggests a more complex approach is needed. The resultant framework however does have a contingent implication. A *multiple methodology* is proposed because in practice a firm's management is seeking a way forward bearing three questions in mind: (a) what are our business needs, (b) what are the technology opportunities, (c) what is our capability and current position? Fig. 9.3 depicts this multiple approach, suggesting that a three-pronged attack is required to derive the applications development portfolio proposed in Fig. 9.2. My model here, therefore, implies that no single methodology is likely to satisfy these three concerns or always to be the preferred approach.

The desire and need for a formal attempt to match IS investment with business needs is met by leg one of the model. It proposes the identification of business plans and goals, followed by deduction of IS/IT needs using an analytical approach with a formal methodology and requiring inputs from a coalition of line, general, and IS managers. Essentially 'top-down' it 'puts the business into IS'. Commonly, business plans and goals are not formally available or are ill-defined and rarely will be expressed in terms easily translated into IS/IT needs. Thus a formal methodology is required to both elicit business strategy and derive IS needs. The properties required are that it is easily understood and used

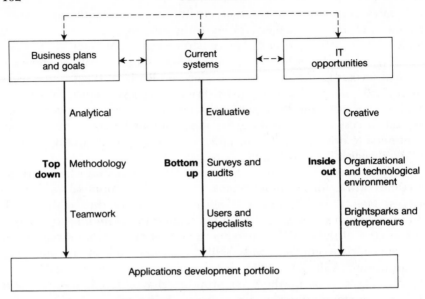

Fig. 9.3. IS Strategy Formulation; A Multiple Methodology

by line and general managers, it can cope with varying robustness of business strategy, it does not look as if the exercise is defining or redefining business strategy, it does not consume too much time or resource, it can be repeated as circumstances inevitably change and, as a result of these needs and because it could not achieve anything else, it points to directional IS needs and not detailed specifications. The 'critical success factors' approach seems to possess some of these qualities (Bullen and Rockart, 1984) and from my own experience is particularly valuable when prior strategy analyses have been done, but also provides a workmanlike solution where strategic understanding is low. Fig. 9.4 displays a slightly generalized example of the critical success factors approach by conflating two actual cases of the method.

The first step involves identification and agreement of business objectives for the SBU. Working from interviews and documents, clear and firm objectives (perhaps goals in planning parlance) are stated. Next the factors critical to success in achieving these goals are explicated. This involves interviews with the executive management and crucial alignment phase to ensure the critical success factor set is agreed by the whole management team. These can be further factored into critical processes or activities. Next the information system supports which these critical success factors require are determined, whether through the application of technology in products and processes or the development of information systems for co-ordination and control of activities and for management decision-making.

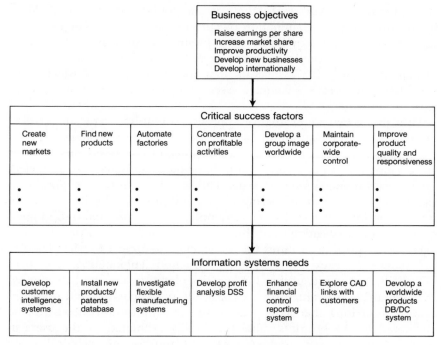

Business objectives
Raise earnings per share Increase market share Improve productivity Develop new businesses Develop internationally

Critical success factors						
Create new markets	Find new products	Automate factories	Concentrate on profitable activities	Develop a group image worldwide	Maintain corporate-wide control	Improve product quality and responsiveness
• • •	• • •	• • •	• • •	• • •	• • •	• • •

Information systems needs						
Develop customer intelligence systems	Install new products/ patents database	Investigate flexible manufacturing systems	Develop profit analysis DSS	Enhance financial control reporting system	Explore CAD links with customers	Devolop a worldwide products DB/DC system

Fig. 9.4.   A Critical Success Factors Approach

My research indicates that, in the UK, managers have found this approach especially valuable in setting and agreeing objectives and in deriving critical success factors across the business. The jump to determining information systems needs seems to be more difficult. However, the direction and priorities for IS development do become apparent. Furthermore, if preceded by management education on IS and strategic advantage and followed-up by systems analysis or feasibility studies, often aided by prototyping to test out ideas, more focused identification of IS needs can result. These findings largely coincide with those of Boynton and Zmud (1984) and Shank *et al.* (1985) in the USA.

Leg two of the model in Fig. 9.3 is more bottom-up. Whilst this may not seem strategic, most organizations when they begin or renew their attempts to plan IS strategically need to understand and evaluate their *current* IS investment. This is for several reasons. It may be important to demonstrate the quality and coverage of IS hitherto in order to gain, retain or work for credibility. Further, top managment often is not informed about the current IS position of the business and requires confidence both of understanding IS and of the firm's IT capability before it will approve any major IS investment. Then IS strategies are rarely developed from a greenfield site but have to recognize the strengths and weaknesses of the current applications portfolio. More important perhaps, examination of current systems may suggest either that some could already be better exploited for strategic advantage or be built upon to yield significant added value. Indeed, our research (Runge and Earl, 1987) suggests that many applications which have provided competitive advantage were in fact evolutionary add-ons to existing systems.

Thus in leg two, an evaluative approach is required, typically satisfied by commissioning an audit or survey of current systems. Several techniques exist but two sets of questions need to be asked. First, what is the existing *coverage* of systems—both basic business systems and management decision and support systems. This seemingly mundane question is significant because in answering it, gaps by function, by IS type, or of integration may be revealed. For example, it is not unusual to find good coverage in accounting and huge gaps in marketing, or extensive exception reporting facilities for management support but few enquiry or analysis features, or adequate production, engineering, and sales systems but poor integration for logistics planning and market-oriented manufacturing. Coverage surveys basically map activities and decisions against functions. Secondly, each current application needs to be examined for its business value (preferably evaluated by the users in terms of impact, use, and ease of use) and for its technical value (preferably by the IT specialists in terms of reliability, maintainability, and cost). Evaluation can be both current and potential. It also may be useful to appraise the capability of the organization to develop further, considering such factors as user awareness, much as implied by Gibson and Nolan's (1974) model of the stages of EDP growth. Leg two analysis clearly may not only identify strategic developments but also help determine what developments are mandatory, which systems need renewing, where basic business systems gaps need to be filled to complete infrastructure, and which applications should command most maintenance and enhancement effort.

Leg three of the model is of quite different character. In our research at the Oxford Institute of Information Management, we have been investigating what enables firms to spot and develop opportunities from IT which give them competitive advantage that can be sustained. Building on these studies particularly those of my colleagues Runge, Feeny and Lockett, respectively, it seems clear that we can learn more from the lesson of successful industrial innovation than from the nostrums of IS administration. Seven patterns emerge from these studies:

1. Competitive ideas often arise by chance: a commercial manager perhaps recognizes that a customer's or a supplier's information or

service problem can be solved by IT; or maybe an indea has existed for some time, perhaps as a partial technological solution, for which a problem of opportunity suddenly appears.

2. Many competitive advantage IT applications develop incrementaly: perhaps a system which addresses an internal need is seen to have potential value for customers, suppliers, or allies; perhaps the strategic context changes so that a once 'ordinary' application becomes crucial.

3. Many competitive advantage systems are developed outside the formal IS management process: local, departmental, 'do it yourself', or unapproved applications are developed quickly to meet a pressing need or timely opportunity.

4. IT innovations often require both a product champion and sponsor: the originator of the competitive advantage idea has to find a superior to back or champion the application (frequently against the official IS department); they then have to find a sponsor, that is someone who commits, provides, or diverts resources for the project.

5. Hybrids are potential innovators: the originator and prosecutor of an idea quite frequently is a former IS professional now working in a line or staff/function, who sees that an opportunity or problem can be addressed through IT, knows roughly what is involved and is able to locate specialist expertise to help him.

6. User involvement is often high in competitive advantage systems; this includes soliciting of ideas, testing out prototypes, good practical training, and encouragement of user-led projects,

7. The business consequences of IT application, if successful, must be analysed; whether at origination or subsequent implementation the implications for competitive strategy and the management responsibilities must be fully considered.

In short, the third leg of the model is concerned with innovation through IT, a creative process whereby hybrids or brightsparks, backed by product champions and system sponsors, exploit often existing systems with informal or no support from the IT function but with high user involvement for hitherto unforeseen competitive advantage. Appropriate organizational environments have to be designed therefore to make sure new ideas flourish, are supported and are understood.

However it is also apparent that opportunities can be fostered and facilitated by an appropriate technological environment. We have case evidence that by 'taking IT to the people', users may develop strategic or innovative applications themselves. Examples include providing user-friendly, firm-specific personal computing menus, aids and application generators, investing in professional-specific or industry-specific expert system shells or developing viewdata utilities for executives to customize. It is interesting to note that creating an organizational and technological environment to promote opportunities suggests giving away degrees of IT resource and IS responsibility, informally or formally, to the users. Much of the logic behind the niche segment of the applications development portfolio rests on these findings. That is to say that a proportion of the IS budget may be allocated to exploitation of particular technologies by particular user groups.

The more general implications of leg three are that 'brightsparks' need to be recruited, retained, and encouraged in key commercial and operating posts. Product champions who will become IS entrepreneurs need to be placed in potentially strategic areas of the business or in positions suggested by critical success factor analyses and systems coverage audits. IS management practices and IS managers need to recognize that 100% formalization of IS planning and control can be dysfunctional and that user involvement in the earliest stages of systems work may yield unexpected business benefits. In other words, we look for impetus from inside the organization, ie. 'inside out'. The general principle therefore is to design an organizational and technological environment which enables innovations to happen.

Each of the three legs of the model in Fig. 9.3 has been described so far from a largely internal perspective. By definition, a strategic approach to planning IS, and in particular the search for competitive advantage from IT, also require an external perspective. Especially in sectors undergoing great change, leg one must address the competitive environment. Inclusion here therefore of a threats and opportunities analysis of the firm's competitive forces may suggest other critical IS needs and/or exposures. Porter's (1980) five factor framework of new entrants, suppliers, customers, rivals and new products provides a useful structure. Likewise in leg two, it may be important to assess competitors' and potential competitors' IS, using a strengths and weaknesses approach. This may take two or three years before a reliable picture is built and practicable intelligence mechanisms installed. Finally, in leg three, opportunity suggestion may be prompted by collecting and analysing exemplars from other industries and writing scenarios of the future of the firm's particular sector. Thus the external perspective can be superimposed on the three-legged model of IS strategy formulation as in Table 9.2.

This three-legged multiple methodology recognizes that alignment of IS strategy with business needs is essential, that innovation and ideation are more a process of fermentation and opportunism than of structured analysis and that many vital IS developments and much of what is feasible are identified by examining today's inherited position. For these reasons, I have concluded that no one methodology works; that is to say no single method alone. Each leg is necessary but not sufficient. A

Table 9.2. *External Perspective and IS Strategy Formulation*

	Leg		
	Top-down	Bottom-up	Inside-out
Technique	Opportunities and Threats Analysis	Strengths and Weaknesses Appraisal	Exemplars and Scenarios

three-pronged attack is required; indeed the top-down key may provide contextual understanding and prioritizing so that the inside-out leg is more effective and focused. The bottom-up leg is required as a foundation for top-down and inside-out approaches. Furthermore the three-pronged attack is required to cope with ever changing external demands, variability of internal capability, the stage of an organization's IT historiography and the pace and breadth of technological change. In particular the emphasis may differ over both space and time; these complications are addressed in the next two sections.

A Sectoral View

In researching large companies' approaches to IS and IT strategy formulation, I discovered early on that (a) significant differences existed in different firms, (b) IS strategy formulation inherently seemed a more complex matter in some firms than others, (c) approaches adopted in practice did not always match either popular prescriptions or the accounts in cases documented in articles. The first explanation of this appears to be sectoral. It became clear that in organizations where IT was perceived to be a strategic resource, three different expressions of this exist. For some, they see that in their sector IT has become the means of delivering goods and services; examples include banking and, increasingly, retailing. For others, they appreciate that their business strategies increasingly depend on IT for their implementation; examples being manufacturing sectors fighting global competition for survival, especially automobile manufacturers. For a third group, management believes that IT potentially provides new strategic opportunities in certain areas of the business and is driving for them; many chemical and consumer product companies seem to belong to this category. I label these sectors the delivery, dependent, and drive sectors as in Table 9.3. (Firms where IT has no strategic significance, or where this is the perceived condition, I collate under the 'delayed' label.)

In Delivery firms, it seems rather than work out business needs, strive for strategic clarity or adopt a top-down approach, much of the thinking behind IS strategy formulation is technological. It is concerned with laying down telecommunications networks, rationalizing data standards,

Table 9.3. *Sectoral Classification*

Strategic Condition	Characteristic	Metaphor
IT is the means of delivering goods and services in the sector	Computer-based transaction systems underpin business operations	Delivery
Business strategies increasingly depend on IT for their implementation	Business and functional strategies require a major automation, information, communications capability and are made possible by these technologies	Dependent
IT potentially provides new strategic opportunities	Specific applications or technologies are exploited for developing the business and changing ways of managing	Drive

investing in hardware architectures and developing a sound basic business systems foundation. In other words the IS strategy mode is *infrastructure-led*. Sometimes criticized as being non-strategic, uncoupled from business, back-office-oriented and technologists-controlled, this mode does appear more rational on closer analysis.

Often top management in these firms recognized that IT was becoming crucial both to the capability of the firm and the operations of the sector but had less clear views on what was required. The IT function had to second guess where to invest and was safe in ensuring the firm could connect to the emerging sector IT infrastructure, in building transaction databases to support business systems and MIS and in developing efficient and updatable basic systems upon which new services and products could be quickly built as needs become apparent. Such has been the typical posture of many UK banks' IT functions. An infrastructure-led approach worked because the sector's infrastructure was becoming IT-based. A firm in a delivery sector became exposed if its computer network failed, was inefficient if it did not automate its internal operations, and inflexible in its product development and customer service if it had poor infrastructure. Only later then do more business-driven approaches to IS strategy formulation become both more necessary and feasible.

In firms in the dependent sector, it is generally discovered that business and functional strategies require major support from IS and/or depend on IT. Once business imperatives are worked out, IT and IS are seen to be obvious enablers for growth or survival. Indeed, in one automobile firm, it was the explication of critical *survival* factors that pinpointed the area for IT investment; robotics and CIM to improve productivity and quality in manufacturing, CAD/CAM to improve design and market-oriented flexibility, and data communications to improve the effectiveness and efficiency of distribution. In other words, as shown in Table 9.4, in contrast to the infrastructure approach of the delivery sector, firms in the dependent sector can easily adopt a *business-led* IS strategy mode. Here IS strategy can be a derivative of business strategy, whereas for delivery firms IS strategy requires more vision, carries more risk and in some senses due to its infrastructure qualities, is intertwined with, and an inherent part of, business strategy.

Table 9.4. *IS Strategy Modes*

Strategic condition	Sector metaphor	Strategy mode
IT is the means of delivering goods and services in the sector	Delivery	Infrastructure-led
Business strategies increasingly depend on IT for their implementation	Dependent	Business-led
IT potentially provides new strategic opportunities	Drive	Mixed

In short, in dependent firms I found that the normative prescription of deduce or derive the IS strategy from the business strategy was being applied and could be made to work. Furthermore general management finds IS strategy formulation not so complex or threatening as in the other two sectors. It should be pointed out, however, that the business-led mode does not imply that infrastructure is unimportant. Indeed, it may turn out to be a major element of the firm's capital investment—but the nature of the infrastructure is more obvious and the financial implications more quantifiable because there is a clearer business case.

In the drive sector, firms are searching for less obvious strategic gains, although the rewards for success can be high if they outwit the competition. Because there is no sector infrastructure push and fewer business dependencies, IS strategy formulation in drive firms is the most difficult. The most likely mode here seems to be *mixed*—a combination of infrastructure investment and business direction, or put another way, a mix of technological push and demand pull.

In these firms, the drive for opportunities is seen to require both awareness of IT possibilities and ability to implement them by taking infrastructure to the user community. Such infrastructure includes end-user computing, communications networks database environment, software tools, and IT training. At the same time, so that good opportunities are not thrown away or under-exploited, and also to ensure that IT developments which are inconsistent with the firm's strategy do not gain momentum, a framework of business direction is often provided. Such frameworks are built by encouraging IS plans to be linked with long range plans, experimenting with critical success factor exercises or similar and investing in management education on IT and strategic advantage.

In drive firms, whilst the chief executive may be pushing the IT initiative, it is the IT Director or equivalent who has to work out most of the 'how' and lead from behind on much of the 'what'. This is because the IT needs and opportunities are not so obvious and the organization therefore requires much more leadership and help. The case for IT investment is more difficult and the benefits more dispersed and perhaps slower to accrue. Because the IS strategy mode is mixed, several methodologies may be attempted over time. Inevitably, however, there has to be some 'up-front' investment in both hard and soft infra-structure.

Whilst many practitioners tend to recognize this three-way strategy modes classification, the puzzle which falls out is how does my three-legged methodology fit? The reconciliation is summarized in Table 9.5.

Table 9.5.   *Strategy Modes and Methods*

IT strategy mode	Emphasis in strategy formulation
Infrastructure-led	Bottom-up/Leg 2
Business-led	Top-down/Leg 1
Mixed	Inside-out/Leg 3

For infrastructure-led firms, the obvious clues on what to do are to be found in the current systems of the business and its sector. Thus, a bottom-up emphasis tends to hold sway over time. However, this will be limited unless connected to some vision of the future and so from time to time a top-down attack may pay off and inside-out initiatives may extract unforeseen advantage from the infrastructure investment.

In business-led firms, most of the direction and much of the application development portfolio can be derived by top-down means. Here the alignment of IS with business needs is the main concern. However, over time, the cumulative investment in IS will require a thorough survey of a bottom-up nature and there may be areas of the business where inside-out approaches may be worthwhile in the hope of finding unique competitive advantage from IT.

In mixed firms, it is clear that the multiple methodology of all three legs will be required over time. It is likely, however, that the propositions of the inside-out leg will have to be adopted continuously, for the mixed approach is concerned with creating an environment for IT opportunities.

The Time-Dimension

Most large UK firms have been experimenting with IS/IT strategy formulation for two to five years. They have often adopted different approaches over this period and find that the benefits they orginally anticipated take four to five years to materialize. Indeed, the early benefits of IS strategy formulation seem to be 'soft'—that is improvement in top management support, user communication, IT functions understanding of the business, and business planning in general, rather than cultivation of IS strategic plans tightly linked to business strategy or gaining of major competitive advantage (Earl, 1983).

Moreover, one reason why I conclude that multiple methodologies are required for IS strategy formulation is that firms seem to learn how to plan IS strategically in an evolutionary fashion. This involves extracting the relevant and appropriate features of different approaches in stages. Eventually it seems that the firm recognizes that multiple methods are required and that IS strategy formulation is a complex matter where the hard product of robust strategic IS plans will result some time after the early process benefits. It may therefore be sensible to plan how to plan in the spirit of the stage model idealized in Table 9.6.

Typically, for reasons outlined earlier, most organizations need to understand their current position before they can advance or have the confidence to do so. The first round of strategy formulation thus tends to be a bottom-up mapping exercise. Top management then is anxious to ensure IS development is aligned with business needs and that priorities are clear in allocating scarce IT resources. Here in stage two top-down methods become essential but have to wrestle often with poorly defined business plans and needs. After some groping for top-down direction, a structured methodology—such as critical factors—is often adopted. Subsequently the enormity of the problem is apparent and the applications development portfolio becomes a set of management compromises between development and maintenance, risks and rewards, infrastructure and applications and long-term and short-term, with the recognition often that the business has been changing so that reassessment of fundamentals may be required. At the same time the pointers which have emerged from the top-down analysis normally need detailed investigation. Either feasibility studies or systems analysis are required or perhaps prototyping experiments are commissioned.

Eventually top management and/or IS Management become concerned that not enough competitive advantage have been discovered and realized from IT. Few opportunities may have been highlighted by earlier approaches and some potential strategic systems may be seen to have been under-exploited. The emphasis now is on complementing the analytical and evaluative thrusts of earlier phases

Table 9.6.　*Planning in Stages*

Factor	Stage				
	One	Two	Three	Four	Five
Task	IS/IT mapping	Business direction	Detailed planning	Competitive advantage	IT-Strategy connection
Objective	Management understanding	Agreeing priorities	Shaping the portfolio	Finding opportunities	Integrating IS and business strategies
Direction/ involvement	DP/IT lead	Senior management drive	Mainly users and IS involved	Executive management and users	Coalition of users, general management and IS
Methodological emphasis	Bottom-up survey	Top-down analysis	Matching top-down and bottom-up plus investigations and prototypes	Inside-out processes	Multiple methods accepted
Administrative context	Inexperience/ unawareness	Inadequate business plans	Complexity apparent	Impatience	Maturity

with the processes required of the inside-out approach. A few UK firms have entered this fourth-stage and have talked to the Oxford Institute of Information Management about their disappointments so far and what new technologies can be applied. Our response has been to discuss organizational processes as well as management technologies. In the fifth and hopefully final stage, not only may the connection between IS and business strategies be widely understood but business strategy formulation may now include IS strategic planning and regard IS development as naturally part of strategy implementation. Here the complexity of IS strategic planning is recognized in the adoption of multiple methods. The organization could be impatient by now; fortunately if it is still committed to IS strategy formulation, the key actors will have learnt what can be realistically expected and how to manage both expectations and the methods.

For some organizations embarking on IS strategy formulation, this scenario may seem dispiriting. However, there are some comforts available! Typically different businesses or SBU's in the organization have different historiographies. Thus one business or division may already through earlier attempts be at the equivalent of stage three or four. Others may be ready to embark on the top-down attack of stage two and immature or newly-acquired businesses may need the IS mapping characteristic of stage one. This is another reason why IS strategy should be formulated at business unit level—experience varies within organization.

Conclusion

My research and experience suggest that IS strategy formulation is a complex process. In seeking to align IS with business needs, exploit IT for competitive advantage or revamp the IT function, the exercise seems to produce early benefits of understanding and commitment and later benefits of strategic capability. However, strategy formulation in general and IS on the whole have one important common attribute: simplistic and universal techniques rarely work. The lessions that can be drawn to date can now be repeated in straightforward terms;

1. Separate IS strategy from IT strategy formulation—to start with.
2. Position yourself—sectors and experience differ.
3. Adopt multiple methods—a three-pronged attack is required.
4. It takes time—but there are early management benefits.

These are four practical lessons for those embarking upon or engaged in IS strategy formulation. Frameworks built upon these lessons have been suggested and should provide ways forward for practitioners and consultants and directions for further research.

References

Bullen, C. V., and Rockart, J. F. (1984), *A Primer on Critical Success Factors*, CISR working paper No. 69, Sloan School of Management, MIT.

Boynton, A. C., and Zmud, R. W. (1984), 'An assessment of Critical Success Factors', *Sloan Management Review*, **25, 4**.

Dickson, G. W., Leitheiser, R. L., and Wetherbe, J. C. (1984), 'Key Information Systems Issues for the 1980s', *MIS Quaterly* **8, 3**.

Earl, M. J. (1983), 'Emerging Trends in the Management of New Information Technologies', In Piercy, N. (ed), *The Management Implications of New Information Technologies*, Croom Helm.

Feeny, D. F., and Brownlee, C. G. (1986), *Competition in the Era of Interactive Network Services*, Oxford Institute of Information Management research paper RDP 86/17, Templeton College, Oxford.

Gibson, C. F., and Nolan, R. L. (1974), 'Managing the Four Stages of EDP Growth', *Harvard Business Review*, January–February.

Ives, B., and Learmouth, G. P. (1984), 'The Information System As A Competitive Weapon', *Communications of the ACM* **27, 12**.

Kantrow, A. M. (1980), 'The Strategy–Technology Connection', *Harvard Business Review*, July–August.

King, W. R. (1978), 'Strategic Planning for MIS', *MIS Quarterly* **2, 1**.

Lockett, M. (1978), *The Factors Behind Successful IT Innovation*, Oxford Institute of Information Management, research and discussion paper RDP 87/9, Templeton College, Oxford.

Lucas, H. C., and Turner, J. A. (1982), 'A Corporate Strategy for the Control of Information Processing, *Sloan Management Review*, Spring.

McFarlan, F. W. (1984), 'Information Technology Changes the Way You Compete', *Harvard Business Review*, May–June.

——, Nolan, R. L., and Norton, D. P. (1973), *Information Systems Administration*, Holt, Rinehart, and Winston Inc.

McLean, E. R. (1983), *Strategic Planning for MIS: An Update*, Information System Working Paper 4–83, Graduate School of Management, UCLA.

——, and Soden, J. V. (1977), *Strategic Planning for MIS*, J. Wiley.

Porter, M. E. (1980), *Competitive Strategy*, The Free Press, New York.

——, and Millar, V. (1985), 'How Information Gives you Competitive Advantage', *Harvard Business Review*, July–August.

Pyburn, P. J. (1983), 'Linking the MIS Plan with Corporate Strategy: An Exploratory Study', *MIS Quarterly* **7, 2**.

Runge, D. (1985), 'Using Telecommunications for Competitive Advantage', unpublished D. Phil. thesis, Oxford University.

——, and Earl, M. J. (1987), *Using Telecommunications-Based Information Systems for Competitive Advantage*, Oxford Institute of Information Management research paper, RDP 87/1, Templeton College, Oxford.

Scott Morton, M. S., and Rockart, J. F. (1984), 'Implications of Changes in Information Technology for Corporate Strategy', *Interfaces* **14, i**.

Shank, M. E., Boynton, A. C., and Zmud, R. W. (1985), 'Critical Success Factor Analysis as a Methodology for MIS Planning', *MIS Quarterly*, **9, 2**.

Sullivan, C. H. Jun. (1985), 'Systems Planning in the Information Age', *Sloan Management Review* **26, 2**.

Managing IT Strategy

FOREWORD

The previous section focused on formulation of IT strategy. In section four, the issue is how to manage and implement IT strategies. For it would seem that for IT strategies to be credible in formulation and successful in implementation, they must be managed. As one corporate planner put it to me during a research project some years ago 'Our [business] strategy in 1970 was brilliant—it could not be faulted. The only trouble was we never implemented it'. What needs to be avoided in IT strategic planning is that 1970s syndrome of business strategic planning—elegant plans produced by the planners for the planners, but which have little or no impact on the business.

Putting the management into IT strategy therefore is addressed in this section at three levels. For in reality one suspects that like most planning, IT strategy formulation has to go on all the time, focusing on diverse issues, differing at various levels of the organization, blending short-term and long-term horizons and adopting and adapting several methods. It is neither neat and tidy nor comprehensive and integrated. As Scott Morton suggests earlier, it is 'messy'. So recognizing that we are dealing with messes is important, but messes have to be managed if they are to serve some overall purpose.

In Chapter 10, Galliers reports on an empirical survey of information systems planning practice and experience in the UK. There has been a dearth of empirical work, perhaps only Martino (1983), Doll and Ahmed (1984), and Grindley (1985) having executed investigations—albeit sometimes rather simple—across large samples. Most work has been prescriptive either presenting particular methods or approaches, for example Shank *et al.* (1985) and King (1975), respectively, or interpreting and judging various researchers or cases for example Earl (1987) or Pyburn respectively. Yet if IT strategy formulation is to be connected into the organization, the managers leading the exercise need not only to be informed on general practice and experience but be equipped to answer questions like what are our objectives in IT strategy formulation, which methods fit these projectives, who should be involved and what factors are likely to be critical to success? Thus surveys, like that of Galliers, if they represent the population at large—or a relevant segment of it—can help us manage the IT strategy formulation process by pinpointing likely errors and guiding us on what might work in our particular situation.

Matheson next addresses the issue of implementation. His account is in some ways a special case. The strategy for computerizing personal income tax became a *major* project, in the terminology of project management, and it was subject to all the political uncertainties encountered in the public sector. Out of this extremity, however, emerged some ways of managing strategic IT projects. These included use of outside bodies, creation of a high-level steering committee, combining responsibility for advice and direction with responsibility for action and implementation, and use of more operational planning and control tools. The Inland Revenue's IT strategy does not sound like one that is long on recommendations and short on implementation.

Finally Lockett tackles a contemporary technology issue. In the sense earlier hinted at by Seddon and delineated by Earl, Lockett is concerned with IT strategy in its 'how' and 'functional' sense rather than its 'what' and 'business' sense. In 1987, many organizations are discovering that they need a strategy—that is policies, procedures, standards, guidelines, architectures, responsibility agreements, longer-term frameworks—for end-user computing. Lockett's research suggests what is and is not necessary and feasible as personal computing, information centres, and some aspects of office automation converge. Thus a strategy for end-user computing can be seen as a microscom of the large issue of formulating an IT strategy, in its delivery of 'how' or functional sense. As a lead into the next section, Lockett also observes that end-user computing eventually becomes not so much a technological matter as an organizational issue.

References

Doll, W. J., and Ahmed, M. V. (1984), 'Objectives for Systems Planning', *Journal of Systems Management* **35, 12**.

Earl, M. J. (1987), 'Information Systems Strategy Formulation', in Boland, R. J., and Hirschheim, R. A. (eds), *Critical Issues in Information Systems Research*, J. Wiley.

Grindley, C. B. (1985), *Information Technology Strategy Studies*, Price Waterhouse, London.

King, W. R. (1975), 'Strategic Planning for Management Information Systems', *MIS Quarterly* **2, 1**.

Martino, C. A. (1983), *Information Systems Planning to Meet Objectives: A Survey of Practices, 1983*, Cresap, McCormick, and Paget, New York.

Pyburn, P. J. (1983), 'Linking the MIS Plan with Corporate Strategy: An Exploratory Study', *MIS Quarterly*, June.

Shank, M. E., Boynton, A. C., and Zmud, R. W. (1985), 'Critical Success Factors as a Methodology for MIS Planning', *MIS Quarterly* **9, 2**.

10

Information Technology Strategies Today: The UK Experience

School of Computing and Quantitative Studies, Western Australian Institute of Technology

Introduction

Despite the growing interest in and perceived importance of information technology strategy (ITS) formulation, little empirical evidence exists on the approaches actually adopted. Nor is there evidence about either those factors which appear to lead to successful IT strategies, or the efficacy of different approaches in different circumstances. Prior to the commencement of the research described here, only seven instances of empirical research designed to provide some insight as to how ITS strategies are formulated had been carried out.

Of the seven studies identified, five were based in the United States of America and two in the United Kingdom. With just one exception, the three studies based on reasonably large sample sizes lack comprehensiveness in their treatment of the subject matter, covering aspects only of the topic. The remaining four base their conclusions on small samples and in two of these cases—by the admission of the researchers concerned—the sample populations studied are unlikely to be representative of the general situation.

A summary of the published empirical research on the subject carried out prior to 1986 is provided as Table 10.1. As can be seen, the focus has been primarily on the viewpoints of information systems managers and, to a lesser extent, senior management. Having said this, however, none of the surveys has apparently contrasted the views of the two groups. In addition, there is no evidence to suggest that the views of consultants and academics with expertise in this topic area have been sought and there is a total lack of evidence as regards the impact of IT strategies on organizational performance.

While there has been a considerable amount of attention paid in both the academic and professional information systems literature to the topic of ITS formulation, and given that little investigative research of

Table 10.1.   *Summary Details of Empirical Research in Information Technology Strategy Formulation prior to 1986*

Year (Country)	Researchers	Research Method(s)	Sample						Role			Focus
			Size	Organizations								
				Public	Private	Large	Medium	Small	Senior Management	IS Management	Consultants/ Academics	
1977 (US)	McLean & Soden	Conference Survey & Discussion	20	✓	✓	✓	✓	✓		✓		Objectives, end-products, attributes of approaches used, pitfalls.
1981 (US)	Pyburn (see also Pyburn, 1983)	Case Study; inc. questionnaire & structured interviews	8		✓	✓	✓		✓	✓		Whether reviews take place, relationship with corporate planning, need, performance measures of IS department, style of management decision making, volatility of environment, complexity of IS organization.
1982/3 (UK)	Earl	Questionnaire survey (attendees on IT management courses)	42		✓	✓			✓	✓		Trends in IT planning, benefits, problems.

Year	Author	Method	No.						Main areas of study
1983	Martino (Cresap, McCormick, & Paget)	Postal survey	334	*	√		√	√	Content, problems, benefits, success factors, time horizon, responsibility, characteristics of process, frequency.
1984 (US)	Doll & Ahmed	Postal survey	445	√	√	√	√	√	Objectives for ITS studies.
1985 (US)	Sullivan	Interviews	37	√	√		√	√	Correlation between organizational features and their impact on the successful application of particular ITS approaches (deployment and strategic impact of IS).
1985 (US)	Grindley (Price Waterhouse) (see also Cane 1985)	Postal survey	340	√	√	√	√	√	Whether an IT strategy study has been or is undertaken or whether one is planned. Reasons for and problems in IT strategy studies.

* While the report of the survey indicates that 9% of the respondents were 'service, government and other' organizations, no public authority appears in the list of respondents cited in the report.

Source: Galliers 1986a,c.

the kind described above has been undertaken, the great proportion of published material on the subject falls into the following sets:

1. An explanation of a particular approach based on personal experience and case study evidence (e.g. Rockart, 1979; Saaksjarvi, 1980; Henderson *et al.*, 1984; Johnson, 1984; Galliers, 1985*a*; Shank *et al.*, 1985).
2. Intuitive argument leading to conceptual frameworks or proposed approaches (e.g. Lincoln, 1975; King, 1978; Davis, 1982; James, 1984; Ward, 1986).
3. A comparison of approaches (e.g. McNurlin, 1979; Zachman, 1982; Orden, 1985).

In addition, some empirical testing of models and theories has been attempted, for example of Gibson and Nolan's (1974) Stages of Growth model (Benbasat *et al.*, 1984; King and Kraemer, 1984), but the great majority of the evidence, while for the most part providing useful insights into aspects of the subject, is patchy, far from comprehensive and at times speculative (Galliers, 1986*a,c*). Given this background it was decided to embark on a major piece of investigative research[1] as to the current state-of-the-art of ITS formulation in the UK. Two important factors impacted on the research design: one related to the need to obtain information from as wide a constituency as possible; the other arose from the recently completed UK-based survey by Grindley (1985) which had focused on only a few aspects of the topic area, namely:

1. whether or not an ITS study has been undertaken in the last five years or was being contemplated;
2. whether an IT plan was actually in existence at the time;
3. the reasons for such a study taking place or not having been attempted, and
4. the major problems encountered.

As Grindley had been able to obtain evidence from 340 organizations, it was decided that despite the likelihood of significantly reducing the sample size, the research would aim to be far more comprehensive in its coverage than he had attempted. It would aim to test the major conclusions drawn from both the empirical studies previously reported and from the 'conventional wisdom' contained in the literature and of ITS practitioners.

---

[1] A call for increased research efforts in the field of ITS formulation was made at a research colloquium hosted by the Harvard Business School in 1984 (McFarlan, 1984*a*). The point was repeatedly made that research in this topic area should initially be investigative since so little empirical evidence exists (Nolan, 1984; Davis, 1984) but that later longitudinal field research would be required with a view to testing the tentative conclusions drawn from the earlier studies (Ashenhurst, 1984). This is a point taken up later in this paper.

The Research Methodology

Given the arguments regarding the relative strengths and weaknesses of various information systems research methodologies (see, for example, Galliers, 1985*b*), it was decided to devise a research programme which would incorporate a number of approaches most suited to the study of ITS formulation. Given the lack of empirical evidence, an initial aim would be to identify the approaches to ITS formulation which are being attempted, the characteristics of organizations using these approaches and views of practitioners, consultants, and management as to the effectiveness of the planning effort. Given the investigative nature of this phase of the research, it was decided that a survey approach would be adopted with a view to identifying the current, past, and intended approaches to ITS formulation within as wide a range of organizations as could be persuaded to complete a fairly lengthy questionnaire. The choice had to be made between a short and relatively superficial questionnaire which would doubtless attract a reasonably high rate of response, but which would leave many questions unanswered, and a more lengthy and comprehensive questionnaire which could doubtless deter a substantial number of organizations from responding.

However, given the limitations of the survey method, the depth of analysis needed to be added to the breadth which would hopefully be forthcoming from an analysis of returned questionnaires. A series of structured interviews with consultants undertaking ITS assignments on behalf of client organizations and with people responsible for ITS within their own organizations was therefore planned as a precursor to the design of the questionnaire and following the analysis of returned questionnaires. This was in order to:

1. aid questionnaire design;
2. follow up tentative conclusions which would be drawn from an analysis of the returned questionnaires.

The design of the questionnaire was also made possible by a thorough review of the literature both in terms of the existing empirical evidence and in terms of the 'conventional wisdom'. In addition, a thorough review of the Management literature on the broader topic of strategy formulation was also undertaken with a view to incorporating lessons learnt from this experience into the treatment of ITS formulation. A draft questionnaire was produced and sent to a number of practitioners for comment. Revisions were made in the light of these comments and a final format produced. The final questionnaire was divided into three sections:

Part A: Asking questions of a background nature concerning the organization itself (size, industry, environment, corporate planning and management practices, information systems, and technology utilization) and the respondent (job title, involvement in ITS formulation).

Part B: Relating to the ITS effort (aspects of the approach used, objectives linkage with corporate planning, reasons for undertaking such studies and for the choice of approach, outcomes, the extent to which formal reviews have been undertaken).

Part C: Seeking opinions as to the efficiency of the ITS approach used (the extent of success or failure, success measures, factors contributing to successful/unsuccessful ITS).

A second form of questionnaire was also devised for distribution to consultants covering much of the above material but with fewer questions relating to the organization itself and more relating to the number and growth of ITS assignments with which they had been involved. This enabled a comparison of attitudes/perceptions to be made between those concerned with ITS within their organization and those who had undertaken ITS studies on behalf of client organizations: a comparison which had apparently not previously been attempted. Analysis of the data was undertaken using the SCSS (Conversational Statistical System) package which is the interactive complement to SPSS (Statistical Package for Social Sciences) utilizing some of the more commonly used statistical techniques such as univariate statistics (descriptive statistics and frequency counts), correlation, and cross tabulation.

Summary results from the analysis of returned questionnaires were then sent to all respondents with a view to:

1. providing them with information which may be of use in future ITS studies:
2. enabling a revision of views in the light of the response of others (i.e. a kind of postal Delphi study).

These results were also sent to Chief Executive Officers of the respondent organizations with an invitation for them to provide their viewpoints by completing a brief questionnaire which highlighted the major results from the first phase. In this way, a comparison was made possible between the viewpoints of those responsible for the process of ITS formulation within or on behalf of organizations and senior management. Again, this is a comparison of views not previously researched.

Outcomes from the survey phase of the overall research programme include an identification of the range of objectives for ITS studies associated with different viewpoints (senior management, information systems management) and associated performance measures. In addition, candidate key factors which contribute to ITS success (or failure) given certain organizational and environmental conditions, are being identified as are opinions as to the efficacy of various approaches and trends as regards the level of satisfaction with IT strategies.

The survey reported here is being followed up by a similar exercise in Australia to seek transitional comparisons and then by action research studies to test out ideas for success in IT strategy formulation suggested by they surveys.

Research Data

While collection of the data arising from the follow-up survey of senior management is still proceeding and detailed analysis of all the data obtained has yet to be completed, a number of significant conclusions can already be drawn. These relate to the following aspects of ITS formulation as currently practised in the UK:

1. occurrence of ITS formulation studies,
2. reasons for undertaking ITS studies,
3. aspects (including outcomes) of the ITS formulation process,
4. factors perceived to be most important in formulating an ITS,
5. factors perceived to present problems in formulating an ITS,
6. proposed measures of performance for ITS and the perceived impact of ITS,
7. ITS formulation within a competitive strategy framework.

Before reporting on these findings, however, some background as to the participating organizations should first be provided. A total of 131 completed questionnaires were received which represented a response rate of approximately 15%. Given the length and complexity of the questionnaire and the fact that no advanced notice was given, nor any follow-up attempted, this was considered to be more than reasonable, and perhaps could be taken to indicate the high level of interest in the subject.

No restriction was made regarding the size of organization partici-pating in the survey, nor the industrial sector to which it belonged. As can be seen from Fig. 10.1, however, manufacturing and financial/ professional service organizations predominated, and the great majority of organizations had a turnover (or budget in the case of the public sector) in excess of £50m (79%) and employed in excess of 1,000 staff (78%) in 1985.

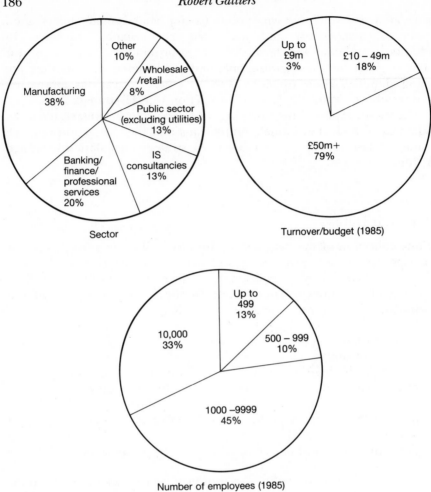

Fig. 10.1. Aspects of the Organizations Participating in the Survey

Occurrence of ITS Formulation Studies

Given the length and complexity of the questionnaire, it is most likely that there was a marked bias in favour of those organizations with an ITS or considering undertaking a study. This is true even though all organizations were asked to complete the questionnaire despite the fact that they might not in fact undertake ITS studies. It would be unwise, therefore to read too much into the fact that 84% of those surveyed attempt IT planning, with only 4% having never undertaken IT planning nor intending doing so. A more accurate picture of the extent of ITS formulation in UK organizations is likely to be provided by the study undertaken by Grindley (1985) since the survey instrument used was far less comprehensive than the author's and therefore likely to deter fewer 'non-ITS' organizations. Grindley found that in only 55% of instances was there an ITS in existence at the time of his study, while in 64% of cases an ITS study had been attempted in the previous five years. 26% of organizations surveyed were considering undertaking an ITS study (Cane, 1985).

The figures as regards the regularity, or otherwise, of such exercises in organizations actually undertaking ITS studies are more likely to be accurately portrayed by the findings from the author's survey, however. These are compared with the incidence of corporate planning studies in Table 10.2. As can be seen, ITS studies tend to be more likely to be undertaken on an occasional or irregular basis than is the case of corporate planning, but in both cases, annual or continual planning is most likely to take place.

Table 10.2.   *A Comparison of the basis on which ITS and Corporate Planning Studies are undertaken*

Basis	ITS %*	Corporate Planning %
Occasionally/Irregularly	24	14
Annually/Continually	60	79
Every 2 years or more	4	5
(Re) considering	13	2

* Excluding organizations not undertaking ITS studies.

It would also appear likely that in most instances involvement in ITS studies in UK organizations is only a relatively recent phenomenon. This is indicated not only by the reported length of organization experience in ITS formulation (see Fig. 10.2) but also the reported growth in ITS studies on the part of IS consultancies (see Table 10.3).

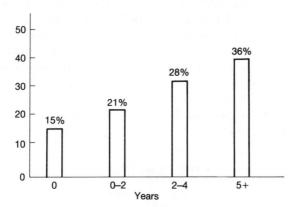

Fig. 10.2. Length of Organizational ITS Formulation Experience (Source: Galliers 1986*b*)

Table 10.3.   *Reported growth in ITS studies by
UK consultancies*

Growth %	1983–5	1985
0–9	0%	25%
10–29	42%	17%
30–49	17%	50%
50–99	33%	0%
100+	8%	8%

As can be seen, only a third or so of the organizations studied have
experience of ITS formulation stretching over five years or more. In
addition, practically 60% of consultancies report a growth in ITS assignments of up to 50% over the past three years, with over 40% reporting
even higher growth rates. In 1985 alone, growth rates of up to 50% were
reported by over 90% of the consultancies.

Reasons for Undertaking ITS Studies

The motivating factors contributing to the increased interest in and
incidence of ITS studies has been the subject of research in both the US
and the UK (notably, McLean and Soden, 1977; Doll and Ahmed, 1984;
Grindley, 1985). A summary of the findings from these three studies,
compared with those of the author is provided as Table 10.4.

While there is clearly some measure of consistency between the results
of the four studies (most notably between the two US studies), it has to
be said that there is a range of opinion as regards why ITS studies
should be undertaken. Given that this range of opinion could potentially
lead to the need for different approaches to ITS formulation, the author
decided to attempt to obtain the views of senior management as regards
their reasons for undertaking ITS studies. While only a proportion of
the questionnaires sent to senior managers has as yet been returned, it is
interesting to note that the single most important reason given thus far
for having an ITS is matching information systems with business needs
and therefore confirms the views given by ITS practitioners. Resource
considerations, such as co-ordinating and prioritizing developments,
while important, are seen as being of secondary importance in comparison (see Table 10.5).

Aspects of the ITS Formulation Process

There would appear to be quite a diversity in approach to the ITS
formulation process as undertaken in UK organizations. This is
illustrated, in part, by the differences in the composition of project
teams (see Fig. 10.3). The number of personnel involved varies from just

Table 10.4. *A Comparison of the Major Reasons Behind Information Systems Planning in the US and UK. (Source: Galliers 1986c)*

Objective/Reason*	Ranking			
	US		UK	
	McLean/Soden (1977)	Doll/Ahmed (1984)	Grindley (1985)	Galliers (1986)
Improved user involve- ment/understanding	1	1	2	—
Improved IS	3	3	—	4=
Creation of applications portfolio (prioritized)	4	2	—	6
Improved adaptability of IS	—	4	—	—
Creation of corporate database(s)	—	5	—	—
Improved software management/resource allocation	2	6	—	2
Reduced maintenance costs	6	7	—	—
Improved decision making	5	—	—	—
Matching IS to business needs/clear accept- able IS plan	—	—	1	1
Improved co-ordination of IS developments	—	—	—	3
'Sound management practice'	—	—	—	4=
Concern *re* mainframe strategy	—	—	3	10
Implications of telecom- munication growth	—	—	4	—
Reduced backlog	—	—	5	—

* Some of the objectives/reasons have been combined to enable closer comparisons to be made.

Table 10.5. *Importance of Reasons for Undertaking ITS Studies*

Reason	Senior Management		IT Planners
	Rank	Mean (max: 4)	Rank
Matching IS to business needs	1	3.37	1
Coordinating IS developments	2	3.05	3
Resource considerations (accountability, justification, ROI)	3	3.00	2
Need to prioritize IS development (increased demand, limited resources)	4	2.82	6
Need for effective IS/Past IS failures	5	2.50	4=

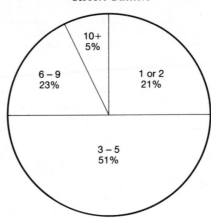

Fig. 10.3. The Size of UK ITS Teams (Source: Galliers 1986*b*)

one or two to over ten, although three to five team members appears to be the norm.

The leadership of UK ITS teams also varies to some extent. While in practically two-thirds of the situations studied, leadership was the province of an information systems professional, management took the helm in a third of the cases. This is in contrast to the opinion expressed by IT planners, consultants, and senior managers, all of whom believe that, for the most part, a senior executive rather than an IS representative should head up the ITS team. On a scale of 1 to 4, IS respondents scored management 2.976 as opposed to 2.723 for themselves; while the emphasis was even more pronounced on the part of consultants: 3.000 to 1.353 (Galliers, 1986*b*, p. 37). Senior managers voted 54% to 23% that leadership should be taken by management as opposed to an IS professional.

Further variations in approach are illustrated by the time horizon (cf. Land, 1982) for the ITS and the time taken to complete a study. Table 10.6 provides a summary of the reported time horizon for an ITS as compared to a corporate plan. Note that this is generally less for the former as compared to the latter, quite probably due in no small part to the constant changes taking place with respect to the technology.

Table 10.7 compares the amount of time now taken to complete ITS studies with the organizations' initial experience. While there are still

Table 10.6.   *The Time Horizon of ITS Strategies and Corporate Plans*

Time horizon (years)	ITS %	Corporate Planning %
Up to 2	31	12
3–5	64	80
6+	4	9

Table 10.7. *The length of ITS studies: Current vs. Initial Practice*

Length of Study	Currently %	Initially %
Continuous process	5	5
Up to 1 month	8	7
1–2 months	33	16
3–5 months	41	40
6 months–1 year	9	23
1+ years	4	9

significant differences in practice, the great majority of studies now take less than six months to complete, or are a continuous process (87%).

The variety in approach adopted to ITS formulation by UK organizations is not limited to questions of team format and timing alone, however. Even more significant are the variations in the manner in which studies are conducted and the actual outcomes from the process. As can be seen from Fig. 10.4, in-house approaches tend to out-number the well-known or proprietary methodologies by over 3:1—a remarkably similar statistic to that reported in the US by Martino (1983). A significant proportion of the approaches adopted (27% and 20% respectively) might be described as either reactive (i.e. they are little more than an attempt to match the supply of information systems and technology with demand) or informal (i.e. they are *ad hoc* in nature with little real pattern and unclear objectives).

As regards reported outcomes from the ITS formulation process, there is clearly a heavy emphasis on such aspects as identifying the information needs of the organization and an associated, prioritized, applications portfolio. Similarly, identification of the required resources associated with the ITS (finance, staff, equipment) feature prominently.

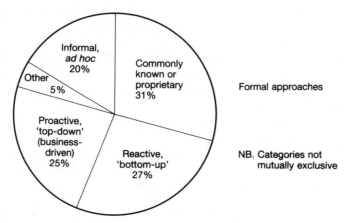

Fig. 10.4. Approaches to ITS Formulation Adopted by UK Organizations

Having said this, one is also struck by the fact that, for example, organizational issues associated with the ITS feature in only 60% or so of instances and reduced costs and/or backlogs arising from the ITS process occur infrequently (in 36% and 23% of cases respectively).

The latter provide a further illustration of the different motivational factors that exist on the part of IT planners and consultants as compared to senior management. While a reduction in costs is ranked as being relatively unimportant by consultants (1.765 on a scale of 1 to 4), senior management perceive this to be a more significant issue (2.556). Similarly, a reduction in the IS development/maintenance backlog is given a rating of 2.118 by the consultants, 2.519 by IT planners, and 2.737 by senior management.

One final comment regarding outcomes from the ITS formulation process might usefully be made. While 85% of ITS practitioners reported information systems closely aligned to corporate objectives as an important outcome, a mere 20% claimed that realignment of IT was a reason for undertaking an ITS study in the first place and only 10% claimed that their ITS planning was fully integrated with the business plan.

Factors Perceived to be Most Important in Formulating an ITS

In line with the above discussion regarding the perceived importance of certain outcomes of the ITS formulation process, it would appear that IT planners believe the process of planning itself, provided there is sufficient management involvement, is of prime importance, since improved relationships and communication between management and the IS function are likely to result (Galliers, 1986*b*, p. 37). Table 10.8 provides a summary of the factors deemed important by IT planners and consultants. Note that over half the factors listed relate to the importance of management participation in the process. The significance of this has apparently not been lost on senior management. They rank their involvement in the process as the single most important factor in contributing to successful ITS studies, giving it a score of 3.895 on a scale of 1 to 4.

In addition to their involvement in the process, senior management also view the need for a very close link between ITS formulation and corporate planning/business objectives as the second most crucial success factor, rating this at 3.632 on a scale of 1 to 4. In practice, however, they reported the two processes as being inextricably tied in only 22% of cases (as compared to the 10% of cases reported by IT planners), a problem that is perhaps exacerbated by the fact that business/corporate planners tend not to play an active part in the ITS

Table 10.8.　*Views on Factors Critical to Successful ITS Planning*

IT Planners			Consultants		
Rank	Mean (max: 4)	Success factor	Rank	Mean (max: 4)	Success factor
1	3.756	Commitment of senior management	1	3.882	Involvement of senior management
2	3.663	Involvement of senior management	2—	3.765	Commitment of senior management
3	3.537	Involvement of senior & user management	2—	3.765	ITS planning based on corporate objectives
4	3.482	Improved under-standing between management & IS function	4	3.750	Involvement of senior & user management
5	3.465	Review of IT strategies	5	3.706	ITS planning approach based on future scenarios
6	3.419	ITS planning approach includes opportunity to debate alternatives	6	3.687	Process/outcomes well supported by IS management function
7	3.412	CIO part of senior management team	7	3.647	Review of IT strategies

formulation process. In over half the instances reported, business/corporate planners are never involved, while senior management believe that they should either be full-time members of the team (37%) or part-time members (32%) or at least act in an advisory capacity (32%).

Third in senior management's list of critical success factors for ITS (scoring 3.474) was the need for formal reviews of the ITS formulation process and the outcomes of the process. Alarmingly, such reviews were reported in only 11% of cases—just 6% if the responses from the consultancies are excluded.

Factors Perceived to Present Problems in Formulating an ITS

Major pitfalls to successful ITS planning which require to be avoided are summarized as Table 10.9 and are compared with the findings of other researchers in the US as well as the UK. For the most part, the pitfalls are the converse of the critical success factors given in Table 10.8. Other factors contributing to failure include the lack of planning experience and credibility of IT planning personnel; the lack of a clear business plan/direction for the company; reliance on reactive ITS formulation

Table 10.9. *Problems/Pitfalls in Undertaking ITS Studies*

Problems/Pitfalls in ITS Formulation	Ranking				
	US		UK		
	McLean/Soden (1977)	Martino (1983)	Earl (1983)	Grindley (1985)	Galliers (1986)
Lack of business plan/direction	3	1	1	1	3
Lack of time	7	2	—	—	—
Insufficient staff	3	—	—	5	—
Lack of planning experience/credibility	6	4	3	6	2
Technical/environmental change	—	5	4	4	6
Poor commitment to planning/change	1	6	—	—	1
Lack of top management involvement/support	9	—	—	3	4
Planner over-optimism	2	—	—	—	7—
Bottom-up/IT-led planning	4	—	—	7	5
Inadequate formal planning procedures	5	—	—	—	—
Policies ignored	8	—	2	—	—
Agreeing priorities	—	—	2	—	—
Inflexibility/rigidity of ITS	—	—	—	—	7—
Organizational structure	—	—	5	—	—
Measuring benefits	—	—	—	2	—

(used in over one quarter of the organizations surveyed); planner over-optimism; difficulties in measuring the benefits of IT and the impact of the ITS, and the inflexibility of the ITS itself.

One additional problem, cited in the four most recent studies conducted on either side of the Atlantic, not thus far mentioned, is the rate of technological and environmental change. Whilst this is clearly a problem which will not go away, it is exacerbated by planning procedures which do not include environmental scanning techniques and the results of futures research in the area of technological change.

Proposed Measures of Performance for ITS and the Perceived Impact of ITS

The IT planners and consultants were asked to propose means by which the success and/or impact of the ITS formulation process might usefully be measured from the point of view of senior management, user management and IS management. They were also asked to assess the extent of success or failure of ITS formulation in their own organization. The opinions given were then reported to senior management who were asked to indicate the extent of their agreement or disagreement. The proposed measures of performance are summarized as Table 10.10 and an assessment as to the relative success of ITS formulation is presented as Table 10.11.

While it is reassuring to note the level of agreement on the part of IT planners/consultants and senior management with respect to appropriate measures of success for ITS from the viewpoint of the latter group, there is clearly much less agreement between the two groups when it comes to the user/middle management viewpoint. While IT planners/consultants believe that the principal measure of success in this case should be a clearer view of overall information systems requirements leading to agreed priorities, senior management have a more pragmatic outlook. They believe that user/middle management would be more interested in improvements in the information systems themselves and in their involvement/satisfaction with the systems development process. It may be the case that the IT planners/consultants' viewpoint, in part at least, reflects a degree of 'wishful thinking'.

No senior management viewpoint on what should be success measures for ITS from the Information Systems Management viewpoint was obtained. However as a group, the IT planners/consultants appeared to be most interested in arriving at clear, achievable plans and improved understanding between themselves and management as a result of the ITS formulation process.

Table 10.11 presents a summary of the views of IT planners,

Table 10.10.　*Proposed Measures for Assessing the Impact of the ITS*

Measure of success	Ranking	
	Planners/Consultants'	Senior managers'
(User/middle management viewpoint)		
Clearer view of overall corporate IS requirements/objectives leading to agreed priorities	1	3
Improved, more effective IS	2	1=
Improved user involvement/satisfaction with IS development process	3	1=
Improved support from senior management and the IS function for required IS developments	4	5
Greater influence in setting IS priorities	5	4
(Senior Management Viewpoint)		
Improved awareness of IS/IT issues and of justification for IS developments/acquisitions	1	1
Improved control/review of IS development/investment decisions	2	2
Agreed IS priorities between departments	3	4
Improved service from IS department (easier access, more effective IS)	4	3
Standard approach to IS developments throughout organization	5	5
(IS Management Viewpoint)		
Clear, achievable plans/objectives	1	—
Improved understanding/communication between management and the IS function	2	—
Improved IS resource allocation	3	—
Focused IS developments (agreed priorities)	4	—
Improved support for IS developments (IS projects more easily justified/approved)	5	—

Table 10.11. *Views of IT Planners, Consultants and Senior Managers on the Relative Success of ITS Planning and its Impact on Senior and User Management and on the IS Function*

	Senior management viewpoint			User/middle management viewpoint			IS management viewpoint			Overall		
	Successful	Unsuccessful	Mean Max: 4	Successful	Unsuccessful	Mean Max: 4	Successful	Unsuccessful	Mean Max: 4	Successful	Unsuccessful	Mean Max: 4
IT Planners	59%	42%	2.59	55%	46%	2.58	66%	35%	2.74	—	—	—
Consultants	93%	7%	3.57	86%	14%	3.21	100%	0%	3.21	—	—	—
Senior management	65%	35%	2.71	69%	31%	2.69	—	—	—	64%	36%	2.64

consultants and senior management on the relative success of ITS formulation efforts from the viewpoint of senior management, user/ middle management and information systems management. Senior managers were also asked to provide an indication of the overall impact of ITS on their organization as they saw it.

It is reasonable to conclude that ITS meets with a degree of success in a majority of organizations, yet these efforts are not particularly well received in far too many instances. Bearing in mind the likely bias in favour of ITS on the part of the respondents to the survey, this conclusion may well turn out to be an over-statement of the success of ITS as currently undertaken in the UK. It is also reasonable to conclude that ITS Consultants have, on the whole, an inflated opinion of the impact of ITS on organizational performance, whereas IT Planners possibly slightly underestimate the positive outcomes from their efforts.

ITS Within a Competitive Strategy Framework

An alarming conclusion to be drawn from the author's research is that, despite the many examples of IT being used for competitive advantage (Harvey, 1986; Marchand and Horton, 1986; McFarlan, 1984b; Porter, 1985; Strassman, 1985), there is little, if any, evidence to suggest that this occurs as an outcome of the ITS formulation process as currently practised in the UK.

It has been argued (Ward, 1986; Sinclair, 1986) that there are three major domains of ITS formulation, concerned with matters of efficiency, effectiveness, and competitiveness: the first having its prime focus in the information systems function, the second across the organization as a whole, and the third focused on the organization's environment.

The author reviewed the descriptions of the ITS approaches adopted by UK organizations in terms of efficiency, effectiveness, and competitiveness and the results of this review are summarized as Table 10.12. While 73 organizations of the 114 surveyed (64%) listed a range of information systems which they claimed provided their organizations with a competitive edge, in only 5 instances (6%) could it be construed that the ITS formulation process included considerations of competitiveness.

The evidence presented above would tend to confirm that the focus of the ITS planning effort in UK organizations is concerned with internal issues of efficiency (such as reducing head count, down time, or production costs) or of effectiveness (such as aligning the ITS with current business practices or corporate plans). It may be that improved competitiveness is a by-product of the ITS formulation process but it would appear that if this does occur, it is likely that competitive advantage is gained as much by chance as good planning (Galliers, 1987).

Table 10.12. *The Focus of ITS Planning Efforts in UK Organizations in terms of Efficiency, Effectiveness, and Competitiveness*

Focus of ITS Planning	Organizations excluding consultancies[1]	Total Sample[2]
Competitiveness (market place)	5 (6%)* 0 (0%)**	6 (6%)* 0 (0%)**
Effectiveness (company)	64 (76%)* 29 (35%)**	78 (78%)* 38 (38%)**
Efficiency (IS function)	51 (61%)* 20 (24%)**	59 (59%)* 23 (23%)**

* Not mutually exclusive.
** Instances where this is the focus of the approach.
[1] Sample size: 114 less 30 instances where no ITS formulation approach is cited or it was impossible to judge the focus in terms of efficiency, effectiveness or competitiveness (i.e. 84 organizations).
[2] Sample size: 101 organizations (84+17 consultancies).

Summary

This paper has attempted to show that despite the heightened interest in ITS, there is still limited empirical evidence available on which to base current and future practice. Because of this lack, research has been described which aims to improve our understanding of what makes for sound ITS practice.

Tentative conclusions from this partially completed UK-based survey and case study research have been presented. In the main, these relate to the variety of approaches adopted in, and motivation for, undertaking ITS studies in the UK. In addition, the importance given to management involvement in the process and the strong link necessary between ITS formulation and corporate planning have been stressed. Major problems which are likely to reduce the chances of successful ITS planning have also been identified and in addition to the converse of the success factors cited, these include the lack of pro-active ITS planning and the lack of planning experience and credibility amongst those information systems personnel involved in the process. The lack of competitive considerations in current ITS practice in the UK has also been noted, as has the almost total lack of a review of either or both the ITS formulation process and outcomes from that process in UK organizations.

Overall it may reasonably be concluded that ITS formulation in the UK has met with a degree of success but that there would appear to be ample opportunity for improving the practice. An on-going research programme has been proposed which is designed to provide ITS practitioners with firmer evidence on which to base their decisions with a view to improving the efficacy of the approaches adopted.

References

Ashenhurst, R. L. (1984), Conclusion to Part IV (Information Systems Technology and Corporate Strategy)', in McFarlan (1984*b*).

Benbasat, D. A. S., Drury, D. H., and Goldstein, R. C. (1984), 'A Critique of the Stage Hypothesis: Theory and Empirical Evidence', *Communications of the ACM* **27, 5**.

Cane, A. (1985), 'Credibility Gap "Deters Corporate Strategy on IT"', *Financial Times*, 27 November, p. 19.

Davis, G. B. (1982), 'Strategies for Information Requirements Determination', *IBM Systems Journal* **21, 1**.

—— (1984), 'Conclusion to Part III (Management of the Information Systems Resource)', in McFarlan (1984*b*).

Doll, W. J., and Ahmed, M. V. (1984), 'Objectives for Systems Planning', *Journal of Systems Management* **35, 12**.

Earl, M. J. (1983), 'Emerging Trends in Managing New Information Technologies', Oxford Centre for Management Studies, research paper 83/4; reproduced in N. Piercy (ed.), *The Management Implications of New Information Technology*, Croom Helm, London, 1986.

Galliers, R. D. (1985*a*), 'Providing a Coherent Information Planning Environment to Meet Changing Organisational and Individual Information Needs: A "Soft Systems" Approach', WAIT working paper, January.

—— (1985*b*), 'In Search of a Paradigm for Information Systems Research', in Mumford, *et al.* (eds.).

—— (1986*a*), 'Research in Information Systems Planning', WAIT working paper. April.

—— (1986*b*), 'A Failure of Direction', *Business Computing and Communications*, July–August.

—— (1986*c*), 'Towards an Understanding of Factors Critical to Successful Information Systems Planning: A Manifesto for Australian-Based Research', *Australlian Computer Journal* **18, 4**.

—— (1987), 'Information Systems and Technology Planning within a Competitive Strategy Framework', in P. Griffiths (ed.), *The Role of Information Management in Competitive Success*, Pergamon Infotech State of the Art Report, Maidenhead, Berkshire, (forthcoming).

Gibson, C., and Nolan, R. L. (1974), 'Managing the Four Stages of EDP Growth', *Harvard Business Review* **52, 2**.

Grindley, C. B. B. (1985), *Information Technology Strategy Studies*, Price Waterhouse, London.

Harvey, D. (1986), 'Travelling to the TOP', *Business Computing and Communications*, December–January.

Henderson, J. C., Rockart, J. F., and Sifonis, J. G. (1984), *A Planning Methodology for Integrating Management Support Systems*, MIT CISR working paper No. 116, September.

James, P. M. (1984), 'Strategic and Long-Range Information Resource Planning', *Auerbach Data Processing Management* **1–03–17**.

Johnson, R. J. (1984), 'Enterprise Analysis', *Datamation*, 15 December.

King, W. R. (1978), 'Strategic Planning for Management Information Systems, *MIS Quarterly* **2, 1**.

—— and Kraemer, K. L. (1984), 'Evolution and Organizational Information

Systems: An Assessment of Nolan's Stage Model', *Communications of the ACM* **27, 5**.

Land, F. (1982), 'Adapting to Changing User Requirements', *Information and Management* **5**.

Lincoln, T. J. (1975), 'A Strategy for Information Systems Development', *Management Datamatics* **4, 4**.

Martino, C. A. (1983), *Information Systems Planning to Meet Objectives: A Survey of Practices, 1983*, Cresap, McCormick, and Paget, New York.

Marchand, D., and Horton, F., Jun. (1986), 'Existing Information Resources Can Give You Competitive Edge', *Computerworld*, 26 May.

McFarlan, F. W. (ed.) (1984*a*), *The Information Systems Research Challenge*, Harvard Business School Press, Boston, Mass.

—— (1984*b*), 'Information Technology Changes the Way You Compete', *Harvard Business Review* **62, 3**.

McLean, E. R., and Soden, J. V. (1977), *Strategic Planning for MIS*, Wiley, New York.

McNurlin, B. C. (1979), 'What Information do Managers Need?', *EDP Analyzer* **17, 6**.

Mumford, E. *et al.* (eds.) (1985), *Research Methods in Information Systems*, North-Holland, Amsterdam.

Nolan, R. L. (1979), 'Managing the Crises in Data Processing', *Harvard Business Review* **57, 2**.

—— (1984), 'Managing the Advanced Stages of Computer Technology: Key Research Issues', in McFarlan (1984*b*).

Orden, A. (1985), 'Evaluation of Methodologies for Information Services Strategic Planning', (in manuscript).

Porter, M. E. (1985), *Competitive Advantage*, Free Press, New York.

Pyburn, P. J. (1981), 'Linking the MIS Plan with Corporate Strategy: An Exploratory Study', *MIS Quarterly* **7, 2**.

Rockart, J. F. (1979), 'Chief Executives Define their Own Data Needs', *Harvard Business Review* **57, 2**.

Saaksjarvi, M. (1980), 'Framework for Participative Systems Long Range Planning', in H. C. Lucas, Jun., *et al.* (eds.), *The Information Systems Environment*, North Holland, Amsterdam.

Shank, M. E., Boynton, A. C., and Zmud, R. W. (1985), 'Critical Success Factor Analysis as a Methodology for MIS Planning', *MIS Quarterly* **9, 2**.

Sinclair, S. W. (1986), 'The Three Domains of Information Systems Planning', *Journal of Information Systems Management*, Spring.

Strassman, P. (1985), *Information Pay-Off: The Transformation of Work in the Electronics Age*, Free Press, New York.

Sullivan, C. H. Jun. (1985), 'Systems Planning in the Information Age', *Sloan Management Review* **35, 12**.

Ward, J. M. (1986), 'Integrating Information Systems and Business Strategies', *Long Range Planning* (forthcoming).

Zachman, J. A. (1982), 'Business Systems Planning and Business Information Control Study: A Comparison', *IBM Systems Journal* **21, 1**.

11

Implementing an IT Strategy: The UK Inland Revenue

STEVE MATHESON

Inland Revenue

Introduction

This case study describes a large project—the computerization of Pay as You Earn—in order to illustrate the way in which the Inland Revenue is utilizing the converging technologies (computers, telecommunications, and office systems) for the benefit of the Department's work in administration, policy, tax assessment, and collection. Today the main operations of the Department's Taxes and Collection offices are in the course of computerization; pay, personnel records, statistics gathering, and other functions in this field are computerized and the Inland Revenue has a computer-based financial information system. There is growing use of micro- and mini-computers and word processors and the Department has a comprehensive IT Strategy.

The Information Technology Division (M3) of the Inland Revenue has the main responsibility for the Department's IT work with a Head Office in London and two major development centres, at Worthing and Telford. Table 11.1 summarizes the work of these locations. The Worthing Centre is IBM based whilst the Telford Centre is ICL-based.

Table 11.1. *IT Development*

London Head Office	Secretarial/Strategy
	Administration
	Personnel
	Office Systems
Worthing Development Centre	Personnel
	Pay
	Statistics
	Enforcement
	Financial Management System
	Management Information Centre
Telford Development Centre	Assessment and Collection Systems

Computerization of PAYE (COP)

This project is still the largest administrative computing system currently underway within Government. It received Ministerial and financial approval late in 1980 and it remains today on schedule in terms of time and cost. It illustrates well the need in a major project to identify the traditional weak areas in the management of information technology and to determine how they might be overcome in order to provide both effective control and the flexibility essential to cater for policy initiatives.

Throughout this project it has been necessary to recognize and reconcile the drive towards operational efficiency, the flexibility throughout design, development, and implementation to accommodate Ministerial and Departmental changes to the system requirement and the ability within the project to manage and control change of all kinds.

Change has been a major factor in the Department's plans to computerize the PAYE system. In the early 1960s it was evident that this manually intensive process was a prime candidate for computerization of the kind that was available at that time—the big batch process—and the decision was taken in computerize PAYE by establishing nine large computer centres around the country. One centre was built and became operational. Centre 1, at East Kilbride in Scotland, has been handling the tax affairs of employees in Scotland in a batch processing system since 1969. After Centre 1 became operational the whole programme was suspended on the change of Government in 1970 and abandoned the following year. The incoming administration decided that is wanted to look at alternative systems for handling personal taxation. In particular it wanted to consider the possibility of integrating the tax and benefit systems through a scheme known as tax credits. Thus plans to automate PAYE were stopped and work began on the new system. Government changed once more in the election of 1974 and the tax credit scheme was, in turn, abandoned. By that time the combination of very tight public expenditure constraints and the rapid advance of technology made it inappropriate to try to re-establish the old nine-centre programme previously terminated in 1971.

In 1977 the Department investigated computerization once more through the Government cycle of preliminary study, feasibility study and then approval and implementation. A decision was not made until late in 1980 partly because the change of Government in 1979 led to yet another review of the proposals developed in the period 1977 and 1979. It may be a feature of large administrative systems generally that the decision point always takes longer than expected. Decisions are not taken quickly. They are certainly not taken easily.

Approval was given in November 1980 and since then the project has remained on schedule coping along the way with substantial change to the original specification. Its objectives listed in Table 11.2 are being met.

Table 11.2. *Objectives*

Save staff costs
Improve service to public
Improve facilities and job satisfaction
Provide flexibility for change

The Outlook in 1980

Those boldly stated objectives looked more difficult to achieve in 1980, when approval was given, than they do now. It may be worth recalling that the prognosis in 1980 for large Government administrative computer systems was not good. There had been some spectacular time and cost overruns and there was a general expectation of delay for Government computer projects. COP was thought to incorporate considerably higher risk than most. Within Government generally and within the Inland Revenue there was a lack of in-house technical resources experienced in the design and development of network systems, and the ICL mainframe to be used as the basic engine in the processing centres (the 2966) was still at the development stage. There was concern that the design, development, and implementation of the project would take too long (thus inhibiting change) but also that it needed to be extended and cut down in scope in order to minimize risk. In the event the project was approved late in 1980 on the basis that the work would be phased with 44 stand-alone 2966 operational configurations, without machine-to-machine communication, in 12 computer centres across the country by the end of 1987 or early 1988: an extended programme, say to 1990 would provide the national communications and tracing facilities and on-line transmission between processing centres. So the initial project in effect covered a 10-year period as detailed in Table 11.3.

During the feasibility study stage and prior to formal approval, the Department recognized that several factors would be critical for the successful implementation of this programme. The first was that it would be necessary to bring in substantial resources from the private sector, both in the areas of technical support and project control. Two contracts were, therefore, to be let with private firms and the private sector staff engaged were to be incorporated in the line-management structure of the project. In other words, those responsible for giving advice were also to be responsible for implementing it. Secondly, a steering group was established at the highest level of management

Table 11.3.   *Original Timetable for COP*

Preliminary study	1977
Feasibility study	1978–9
Initial ministerial approval	1980
Phase 1	
Procurement and initial design	1980–November 1981
Detailed design and development	December 1981–December 1983
Implementation in pilot offices and review of performance	October 1983–December 1984
Ministerial approval for extension nationwide	July 1984
Delivery and acceptance of balance of first region's equipment	January 1985–March 1985
Implementation of remaining regions	April 1985–Early 1988
Phase 2	
National communications/tracing and on-line machine-to-machine communication	1988–1990

within the Department, chaired by the Permanent Secretary and with representatives from the external agencies involved—the government's Central Computing and Telecommunications Agencies, the Property Services Agency, British Telecom, ICL, and the two consultancy firms. Representation was at Managing Director level. Third, the project was to be run under a single manager and the team re-located to a new town—Telford.

This was the top-down approach through the very high level steering group, acting through a single project manager and with substantial external support. But there was also a bottom-up approach which involved extensive consultation with the Trade Union Sides, pilot schemes, and ergonomic studies. Also a multi-disciplinary team was created incorporating the user from the outset. As a result of this consultation and experiment, the decision was made to minimize the effect of change on staff in local offices, in particular moving from a manual to a computer-based system by mirroring the manual system in the full knowledge that it would be subject to substantial change later on.

The Outturn

In the event, the risks have been contained, the original project has gone well and is more than halfway through implementation and the original two phases have been run into one. Indeed the COP project has been extended very substantially to include the self-employed, through the computerization of Schedule D assessments, known as CODA. The system now being implemented is large, as indicated by Table 11.4.

Table 11.4. *System Outline*

Telford Development Centre
11 processing centres (ICL mainframes)
National Tracing Centre
600 Local Tax Districts all over UK (VDUs, printers)
900 British Telecom circuits
25,000 ICL visual display terminals
33,000 staff to be trained
28 million PAYE taxpayer records
1.1 million employer records
3.5 million schedule D records

The original plan was for the initial COP system to be implemented in 14 pilot offices with the conversion of manual to computer records to start on 1 October 1983. That proved to be a Saturday so the system actually went live on the 3rd. The pilot system was to be evaluated throughout 1984 and, if successful, a decision would be sought to extend that system to the rest of the country by the end of 1987 or early 1988. By 1984, however, the experience gained was sufficiently encouraging for the replication decision to be made early (in July 1984) and for the system to be substantially extended in order to include CODA.

Within that revised timetable it has also been possible to develop a National Tracing System and, more importantly, to move away from the original concept of a large number of stand-alone mainframe configurations, four or five of which would be co-located in each computer centre, to a much smaller number of larger configurations with on-line communications between them. That was made possible by a combination of a clause in the original contract between the Government and ICL which allowed for hardware and software variation and a very close and integrated working relationship between the Revenue and ICL in the development and validation of new products. That collaboration led to the early development of the National Tracing System and to the decision to intercept the new Series 39 computers (developed by ICL under its collaborative agreement with Fujitsu) in mid-flight, first

Table 11.5. *Revised Timetable*

Decision to extend to rest of country	July 1984
Setting up COP in the remaining regions	April 1985–End 1987
Develop National Tracing System	End 1986
Analysis, design, & development of CODA	April 1984–End 1986
CODA system testing and integration with COP	July 1986–October 1986
CODA user testing and staff training	November 1986–March 1987
Introducing CODA	April 1987–June 1987
Completing CODA	End 1988–Early 1989

Table 11.6.   *Processing Centres*

West Midlands	Telford, Shropshire	Operational
Eastern Counties	Peterborough, Cambs	Operational
Wales	Cardiff	Operational
South East	West Byfleet, Surrey	Operational
N. Ireland and Scottish LPs	Livingston, Nr Edinburgh	Operational
Greater Manchester	Wythenshawe, Manchester	Operational
South Yorkshire	Wentworth, Sheffield	Operational 9/86
South West	Exeter, Devon	Operational 11/86
North West	Netherton, Liverpool	Operational 1/87
North	Faverdale, Darlington	Operational 2/87
London Regions (4)	Peterborough, Cambs	Operational 4/87
Scotland	East Kilbridge, Scotland	Operational 1988

moving development work to the new machines and then to live operations. The Series 39 (Estriel) was installed in the fifth processing centre to become operational and is currently being retro-fitted in the first four.

Control

The COP system has been developed at the development centre in Telford, Shropshire, by a team of Inland Revenue personnel augmented by expertise from the different suppliers. Management and monitoring techniques from each organization have been developed into a successful matrix of mechanisms with the aim of providing all the information needed to ensure that the product satisfies the requirement and that it is produced on time and within budget. Three main mechanisms are readily identifiable:

1. activity planning and monitoring;
2. budget planning and monitoring;
3. change control and configuration management.

All three have been inherent in the project from initiation although they have developed substantially to cope with a changing environment.

The process of activity planning is aided by a project control team using an automated project control system (Artemis). Individual managers remain responsible for their own plans (having enough discretion to exercise judgement but not being left without guidance or standards) but these are developed and validated using both the skills and experience of the project control personnel and the power of the computer. The structuring of activity into networks on the Artemis system allows validation of the logic (i.e. dependencies between activities) of the plan and enables plans for related areas of activity to be linked.

The management of change is an essential input to both activity and financial planning. The COP project developed an extensive change control mechanism—a change may not be made to a particular program, or design, or configuration or plan unless it has been approved in accordance with a change control procedure. This requires all those potentially affected to analyse the impact of the proposed change on the system and on schedules, staff and other resources. The impact statements which result from that consideration, with recommendations on implementation, are summarized for decision by a change control board. This mechanism provides for project-wide impact assessments of changes and can be used for consideration of speculative changes as well as firm ones.

Costs

In 1980 the estimated total cost of developing and installing Phase 1 of COP nationwide by the end of 1987 or early 1988 was £180 million (at 1980 prices excluding VAT). That was to cover hardware, software, consultancy support, and accommodation, as well as the cost of operating the computer centres as they came on stream. At 1986 prices the estimate for the full COP system including on-line data communications and national tracing and the extension to CODA by the end of 1988 or early 1989 is £319 million. Using the change in the rate of inflation as measured by the Retail Price Index as a crude indicator, overall costs look to have risen by 12% in real terms. However, these figures conceal very substantial changes to the original requirements as well as the introduction of major new features originally scheduled for the second phase of COP.

Current Developments

Success, of course, breeds demand for enhancements and for new projects. These usually involve overlapping timescales and come at a

Table 11.7. *Critical Success Factors*

Visible commitment at all levels
Tight but achievable timetables
Right mix of internal and external resources
Secure funding
Continuity
Comprehensive but dynamic methodology
Mechanisms (in place early) to:
Structure user specifications
Manage and cost change
Check any reliance on external agencies

time of increasing skill shortage and pressure on IT resources, combined with a continuous drive within the Department for reduced costs or offsets. These will, themselves, require changes to the management of IT. The reasons for the success of COP are summarized fairly succinctly in Table 11.7.

The move from a single project to multiple, overlapping projects within the same development centre will require similar but subtly altered success factors. That is a new story and a new challenge.

12

Strategies for Managing End User Computing

MARTIN LOCKETT

Oxford Institute of Information Management, Templeton College, Oxford

Introduction

End user computing is the largest growth area in information systems activity. The spread of personal computers combined with end user facilities on mainframe and minicomputers has been rapid. End user computing now pervades many areas of business which previously made little use of information technology. In the UK, this is reflected in the sales of business personal computers which have now overtaken those of mainframe computers in value. Another indicator is that in a sample of major companies the installed base of personal computers increased by 50% during 1986. This paper will analyse this growth of end user computing, concentrating on the management issues in larger organizations, in particular the formulation and implementation of an end user computing strategy.

Origins and Development

End user computing involves two main strands of activity which are increasingly difficult to distinguish. The first was the development of *mainframe* tools which could be used by staff outside data processing to analyse corporate data and to perform other information processing tasks such as modelling. The information Centre concept of central provision of the necessary training and assistance without applications development was popularized in many large organizations. However the spread of this mainframe-based end user computing was limited, as applications development still required significant computing knowledge, the user interface of mainframe systems made learning difficult, and the costs of end user computing appeared high to users, especially bureau services.

The second strand of end user computing has been the use of *personal computers*. In some companies, there were early attempts to use microcomputers for professionally designed systems but often these were criticized by users who saw them as unfriendly as mainframe systems and not meeting their real needs. Frustration with backlogs in systems development, combined with growing use of home computers for games and programming, meant that enthusiastic managers and professionals pioneered the use of personal computers in business to gain independence from the information systems function. By the mid-1980s however, information systems managers had seen the significance of personal computers and there are few large organizations without a personal computing policy and organization. Meanwhile, personal computer users realized that independence brought problems such as isolation from technical support. Even more important has been the desire to access and analyse the corporate data held on the mainframe systems from which independence was sought.

A third related activity has been the spread of '*office automation*', in particular word processing, which can no longer be seen as separate from either corporate information processing or end user computing. For example, word processing software on personal computers is replacing dedicated word processors in the office. 'Office automation' as a concept of creating an automated, paperless office is unrealistic at present as most 'automated offices' produce more paper than non-automated ones! Further, 'office automation' is in itself a technical rather than a business goal. Thus 'office automation' is merging into end user computing on the one hand and corporate information processing on the other.

Today end user computing involves the convergence of Information Centres, personal computing, and part of 'office automation'. The management of end user computing is particularly complex as it involves: (i) *highly dispersed activity*, with hundreds or even thousands of personal computers and other terminals in a large organization, split between many different locations; (ii) *new and rapidly changing technology*, which few users or even information systems staff can fully understand as hundreds of hardware and software products are released each year; (iii) *diffuse responsibilities* cutting across organizational boundaries, with unclear divisions between the appropriate role of information systems function and that of managers and staff in business functions; and (iv) a need for *organizational change* in both the information systems function and in business functions, as many information systems professionals are as ignorant as senior managers about how end user computing can and should be exploited.

Outline of Paper

The paper will first look at the *costs and benefits* of end user computing, both of which are higher than usually imagined. This, combined with the pervasiveness of end user computing, makes it more important to formulate and implement an end user computing strategy. Four major issues in such a strategy are examined in more detail: *cost-justification* criteria and processes; approaches to *applications development*; end user computing *standards and architecture*; effective exploitation of *corporate data.* Finally come some conclusions on the need for *organizational change* both in the information systems organization and elsewhere.

The paper is based on a detailed study of end user computing sponsored by Arthur Andersen in eight large UK corporations (see Lockett, 1986) as well as a wider range of contacts with both managers and information systems professionals. The research covered a variety of sectors: the main corporations studied were two banks, two retail chains, two brewing and leisure groups, and two manufacturers (vehicles and IT products). This enables comparisons between sectors and organizations, which in some cases reveal important differences. In particular it appeared that both highly centralized and highly decentralized organizations made less effective use of personal computers than those between these two extremes.

Table 12.1.   *Areas for an End User Computing Strategy*

Business goals

Main goals in business terms
Who decides on overall spending
Broad criteria for success

Cost-justification procedures

Originator of proposal
Basis of costing and benefit claims
Criteria for acceptability
Approval process
Who pays

Support organization

Level of support to users
Who pays for support
Staffing policy
Determination of standards
Internal consultancy role

Standards and Architecture

Who sets standards
Hardware
Software
Communications
Applications
Operations

Data

Sources of data
Data definitions
Control on access
Database operational responsibility
Data maintenance responsibility

Table 12.1. (*cont.*)

Development

Criteria for mode of development
Quality assurance
Validation
Documentation
Responsibility for development
Applications maintenance responsibility

Operational

Who is responsible for what
Maintenance
Backup
Recovery

Education and training

Types and objectives for users
How provided
Who pays for education and training
Education within information systems function

Evaluation procedures

When to evaluate
Criteria for evaluation
Who does evaluation
Checklist for user management
Organizational learning from evaluation

Costs and Benefits

Why End User Computing?

The spread of end user computing, particularly the use of personal computers, has arisen for a number of reasons. The biggest factor on the supply side has been the availability of quality *software packages*, which are relatively easy to use and adapt to individual or departmental needs. These packages include the major fields of:

1. spreadsheets and modelling
2. word processing
3. databases
4. communications
5. graphics

In addition, there is integrated software which combines two or more of these functions into a single package and a range of utilities which can be used for electronic diaries, phone dialling, and many other more or less useful activities. Emerging areas for software include desktop publishing, expert systems and applications for group working. These packages have enabled *user-developed applications*, which can meet individual and local needs more effectively than centrally developed systems. The *speed of applications development* can be much faster given such software packages, with the business advantages of speed of response to changing markets and a reduced time between investing in a new information system and getting the benefits, thus improving the return on a given investment.

Reduced costs are also possible but by no means certain. The incremental cost of a personal computer is lower than a minicomputer or mainframe, while calculations show that the cost of processing power for a microcomputer is around 1/30 of the equivalent share of a mainframe (see Ein-Dor, 1985). In practice this does not mean that personal computer solutions cost 1/30 of mainframe ones as personal computers are unable to tackle larger tasks and those involving wide access to data. Instead the main implication is that utilization levels need not be as much of a concern as for larger systems. Personal computers also give *flexibility* as they can be used for a wide range of tasks—including intelligent access to corporate databases, word processing, and spreadsheet modelling.

But the fundamental issue in end user computing is that of *local control.* Many users of personal computers and other forms of end user computing have adopted the technology in order to gain or maintain independence from what they perceive as centralized, unresponsive, and expensive data processing facilities. Organizational politics is a major factor in the choice of information technology approaches, and end user computing makes locally controlled information processing more viable. On the one hand, this can be significant in motivating staff who must take responsibility for their systems. On the other hand, it can lead to the proliferation of incompatible systems, not just using different makes of computer and duplicating development work but also unable to communicate data when needed outside a single department.

Costs of End User Computing

This might not matter if end user computing were cheap—but it is not. End user computing costs much more than most managers and information systems staff imagine—and in most cases is giving greater benefits. In the eight major corporations studied, the average investment in personal computer hardware alone was about £2.5 million. However the overall investment is probably at least five times greater than this, implying that many corporations have invested more than £10 million in end user computing. In most cases it is impossible to determine how much has really been invested as the expenditure is split between the formal information systems budget and a host of business function ones.

However the main costs involved in end user computing can be identified as:

1. workstation hardware,
2. software packages,
3. training,
4. software tailoring,
5. communications,
6. maintenance,
7. user support,
8. mainframe and data costs.

Most purchase proposals cover only the first two categories and often ignore all the costs of training, developing tailored applications from packages, and the increased demand on mainframe communications, processing, and storage. These extra costs are substantial. For example, in one bank the mainframes used for end user computing ran out of capacity within the annual budget cycle, while in the vehicle manufacturer online database queries used around 1/5 of central computing power. The total investment of an organization in a personal computer apparently costing £3,000 is £10,000–15,000 by the time all the above costs are taken into account. If the project involves extensive applications development or organizational change, the costs will be higher still. These costs imply that getting value out of end user computing should be a concern of both information systems executives and general management. While many of the costs are spread widely throughout an organization, the overall investment is at a level which would be seen as a strategic investment decision, especially when this investment is continuing and increasing.

Benefits of End User Computing

But, given this need for an end user computing strategy, few organizations have evaluated whether they are getting value for money or competitive advantage out of end user computing. In only one of the eight case study corporations had a systematic overall evaluation been carried out, though a smaller exercise was being undertaken in another. Very few users or managers interviewed could evaluate the costs and benefits of their use of personal computers—though all felt that they were cost-justified.

The potential business benefits from end user computing are in three areas:

1. efficiency
2. effectiveness
3. strategic (gaining competitive advantage)

Efficiency gains come from cost reduction and there were numerous cases of this. For example, staff in some areas were reduced or other costs saved. However it appeared that the major gains were in the *effectiveness* area, through increasing the quality, speed and value of work done. For example the manpower planning manager of one bank thought that two years previously he would have been unable to do 90% of his current work, and that the other 10% would have needed 25 staff rather than the 9 he had. This was a result of greatly expanded use of both mainframe Information Centre databases and personal computers.

Strategic gains in the form of enduring competitive advantage are more difficult to obtain through end user computing. The major reason, particularly in the case of personal computer based systems, is that it is quicker to develop systems to copy competitor initiatives. However systematic improvement in the effective use of corporate data has the potential for sustainable competitive advantage—for example linking point of sale information in a retail chain to end user computing analysis by buyers and merchandisers to improve performance and speed of response, especially with riskier products. More generally, the organizational capability to both develop and implement end user computing systems fast can give a more sustainable competitive advantage. Thus it is likely that end user computing could be a necessary but not sufficient factor for strategic gains in some businesses.

Looking at the evaluation of the costs and benefits balance, in the one formal corporate evaluation undertaken by a case study company, the benefits claimed by users were £1.9 million a year with costs of £0.9 million for 187 personal computers. However the costs reported were typically only basic hardware and software, and the report recognized that 'the hidden costs of these machines in software, maintenance, supplies, support, etc. are typically equal annually to their purchase cost'. The other study from part of one corporation estimated annual costs of £0.15 million compared with total quantifiable savings of £0.16 million a year as well as substantial non-quantifiable benefits, indicating low efficiency gains but potentially major gains in effectiveness.

In some cases, major business benefits have come out of end user computing. Several projects in different corporations had quantifiable benefits of over £¼ million a year. In a vehicle manufacturer, spreadsheet programs were used to allocate labour and balance the assembly line. In terms of efficiency, it took perhaps one tenth of the time used in the previous manual methods to do this work. In practice part of this efficiency gain was used to reduce the number of planners and part to increase the number of plans made from one to four or five. The effectiveness gains were in several areas: first, the labour allocations could be produced faster and optimized better than with manual methods, thus improving the efficiency of labour utilization in the whole factory; second, planning mistakes were reduced; third, printed job sheets were produced which were better received on the shopfloor than the previous scribbled ones; and fourth, there was an indirect positive effect on industrial relations as better labour planning reduced the number of conflicts arising from over-loaded work stations. While not of direct strategic impact, this use of personal computers contributed to strategic goals of cost reduction and speeding up lead times of new products.

So end user computing is both more expensive than users and information systems managers believe. However it also can lead to substantial business gains, partly in efficiency but mainly in effectiveness. The direct strategic impact on competitive advantage may be more limited, but in some areas end user computing may be a necessary if not sufficient factor.

Cost-justification

A Suggested Method

End user computing has been shown to be a high cost and potentially high benefit activity, raising the issue of policies for justification and financing of end user computing. Organizations use a wide range of methods—from not attempting any justification and allocating facilities administratively to giving business managers sole responsibility for any purchases. The method below was the one which came out as the most successful in the organizations studied.

First, it is important for the primary initiative for end user computing to come from the business area. The process of justification and purchasing should be user-driven. This ensures a higher level of commitment as well as making it clear that the responsibility for effective use lies with the users. In practice, there may be publicity or marketing campaigns by the information systems function to stimulate demand— though in most cases demand is soon so high that these campaigns stop!

Second, a cost-justification proposal should be drawn up with some clear criterion of what is acceptable. Different organizations tackle this in various ways—for example requiring a one year payback or a 25% rate of return. This proposal may be similar to other capital expenditure proposals. The end user computing support staff should be involved in this to ensure that the proposed scheme is technically feasible, meets corporate standards and has realistic costings.

Third, the final proposal should be approved both as a business case by the relevant management in the business area and as technically feasible and compatible with overall standards by the information systems function. When the benefits are expected to be in efficiency, this evaluation is not too difficult. However the evaluation of effectiveness benefits is much more difficult and imprecise. The extent of benefits will be uncertain and their existence risky rather than certain. In such cases benefits will need to be higher to justify going ahead than in more certain cases, and business management judgement of relative benefits and risks will be essential. Ultimately this means relying on business managers rather than information systems staff.

Fourth, it is usually best if the capital expenditure involved is undertaken by the information systems function and the equivalent of a leasing charge made to the user department. This helps ensure compatibility with standards as well as enabling overall control of capital spending. Personal computers probably should be depreciated over a period of three years (many companies use five years or more).

Is Evasion a Problem?

Such a procedure enables users to be responsible for both costs and benefits—making the use of end user computing esentially a business responsibility. If this does not happen, information systems staff will necessarily be making business decisions which they are not competent to make about who should get personal computers and other end user computing facilities. However in practice, such a procedure will be evaded to a significant degree. What will happen is that the cost-justification will be made to fit the required criteria if potential users feel a need for end user computing. For example, in the planning office described above, the manager planned to lose some staff in any case as a result of financial pressures on overheads but used these savings to justify his investment in personal computing.

This evasion of cost-justification controls need not be a problem. For while costs are under-estimated, so are some of the benefits as these may not be quantifiable in advance. Thus the core of the suggested procedure is not spurious precision in cost-justification but: (i) forcing a coherent business case to be made; and (ii) making the users of end user computing ultimately responsible for both costs and benefits and relying on their management judgement. Implementing such a policy may require some modification in line with different organizational structures and cultures but the basic principles can still apply.

Standards and Architecture

Gains from Standards

Corporate standards for end user computing and the link between these and the organization's overall information systems architecture are important dimensions of any end user computing strategy. The major gain from standards is not bulk purchasing with quantity discounts, though such cost reduction is useful. Rather, the gains from standards are organizational. Take package software for personal computers as an example. Two aspects stand out. First, limiting the range of packages in an organization reduces support costs. Put simply, adequately supporting two packages instead of one can require three people instead of one—you not only need double the staff for basic support of users but also a third person to work out how to communicate between the two products! Second, flexibility is increased and training costs reduced as staff moving from one area of the organization to another do not need to learn new packages. A further gain is that users do not have to spend the time evaluating the huge range of alternative packages if they are given no choice!

Although user resistance to standards is often believed to exist, in practice it is much lower than expected in most organizations. Most users want solutions rather than experimentation with computers—except perhaps for a few enthusiasts. If three conditions are satisfied, standards are likely to be welcomed rather than resisted:

1. Standards are *clear*, so that it is easy to define what is and is not allowed.

2. Standards are *functional*, such that the great majority of user requirements can be satisfied adequately with the standard products—even if the product is not the latest or best for a particular application. A further aspect of this is that the standards must fit organizational structure and culture. Thus in more decentralized organizations, standards should be more concerned with ensuring compatibility in areas such as communications and document interchange than with more detailed hardware issues. In more integrated and centralized organizations, the scope of standards may well be more detailed.

3. *Incentives* exist for following the standard, the most important of which is adequate support and training. Except for certain specialized applications, where there could be limited support for non-standard products, support for non-standard products should be refused—except to move towards the standard.

Scope of Standards

The areas covered by standards in an end user computing strategy fall into five broad areas:

1. *hardware:* what personal computers, printers, displays, terminals, and so on should be used. Standards here make maintenance and software support easier. For example, one end user computing support group reckoned 60% of its calls for help were for problems of getting printers to work with software packages.

2. *software:* the systems software and applications packages to be used, for example word processing and databases.

3. *communications:* how to connect personal computers/terminals and other systems together. A major choice here is between personal computer networks, departmental minicomputers, and direct micromainframe connections.

4. *applications:* standards for the development of applications covering not only areas such as validation, testing, and documentation but also the transfer of data from one application to another. This should cover not only personal computer systems but also the mainframe business systems which are used for data extraction and analysis. This is discussed further below.

5. *operations:* security, data protection, backup and other procedures to be followed. These should be relatively simple with clearly defined responsibility, which must be taken by users and their managers.

Architecture Links

The issue which must be of most concern for the future is bringing end user computing into an overall organizational information systems architecture. This will become an issue of increasing importance and poses a difficult set of choices. The personal computer has established itself as a basic workstation for both desktop end user computing and access to other systems. Increasingly, there is both the demand and the potential for integrating personal computer and mainframe systems, rather than just using a personal computer to emulate a terminal or download data. Such integrated applications require co-operative processing by personal computers and mainframes, hence standards are important not only for ensuring compatibility of basic communications between the two but also at the level of applications so that they can communicate with each other. Further aspects for standards include keyboard layout and screen designs.

Major information technology vendors such as DEC and IBM are now starting to develop such facilities, for example IBM's Systems Application Architecture plans. But substantial uncertainty remains over whether these attempts will succeed. Most organizations have standardized on the IBM PC or close compatibles until now because of the availability of hardware and software from a wide variety of sources. While any successful vendor must preserve organizations' heavy investment in IBM PC software and applications, future choices must be based on integrating personal computers into a broader information systems architecture. Thus personal computing and other forms of end user computing must be more closely linked to overall information systems planning in the future.

Applications Development

User-developed Applications

End user computing was initially seen as a way of decreasing user frustration and application development backlogs through individual users developing their own applications. In practice however end user computing tools are used to develop applications in three ways. The first approach is the 'true' user-developed application, in which an individual uses a personal computer or mainframe package to tackle individual needs. Many of these have been highly productive but require a combination of training and time—and it is time which is the constraint on most managers. In general, professionals doing quantitative analytical tasks have been more prepared and able to develop applications themselves.

The 'Grey Analyst'

The ability to design and implement solutions to individual requirements is a major gain from end user computing. Often these solutions meet user needs more closely than systems developed by professional analysts and programmers. However the time and training barrier has led to a second approach to application development: using a 'grey analyst'. In this, it is neither individual users nor information systems professionals who develop application. Instead it is a 'grey analyst'—someone in a business function who has little or no information systems training but develops systems for others. Typically, the 'grey analyst' has self-taught skills in personal computing, perhaps gained through home computer use. He or she will have come from a business department, developed these end user computing skills personally, and then be asked to tailor applications for other people or for the department as a whole. The formal organization structure does not recognize their existence but in practice they have been behind many of the innovative uses of personal computers. As they are on normal departmental budgets, they seldom appear in the spending figures for information systems.

The numbers involved often dwarf those officially supporting end user computing users. For example, in the headquarters of one corporation, there were three end user computing support staff for the whole of the UK—but a couple of floors above them was an equal number in just one department of fifty people. Yet despite the scale of the applications development by 'grey analysts', few organizations recognize their existence and importance in end user computing. By reducing the training effort and time needed to develop applications by individuals, they boost productivity. And coming from a business rather than technical background, they are better able to make solutions which fit the real needs of users.

Problems of the 'Grey Analyst'

However, as well as being a major asset in developing end user computing, the 'grey analyst' is also a potential major liability. The problems with individually-developed applications are often magnified when the 'grey analyst' is used.

1. *Over-enthusiasm:* individuals and 'grey analysts' get carried away and try to computerize activities even when there is no pay-off—the means becomes the end with good managers turning themselves into highly-paid, bad programmers.

2. The potential for *duplication* of development is immense as similar systems are developed and maintained in many parts of an organization.

3. There is *inadequate validation and testing* of systems which are then used to make significant business decisions. Spreadsheet output may look impressive but it is easy to make mistakes. One publicized case was of someone who added an item to a quotation but did not include it in the total which as a result was $100,000 short. He tried to sue the software company!

4. Applications *maintenance* becomes a major long-term liability. This is particularly true of spreadsheet models which are often re-used and need updating or enhancing in line with changes in the business or new individual needs. Lotus 123 and similar programs are excellent for fast development but break many of the rules for easy maintenance—data is mixed with logic, design is not structured and modular, code can easily be over-written and so on. When models are developed by a 'grey analyst', it is likely that no one else will understand how the system works. If the 'grey analyst' leaves—or is run over by a bus—the application may be unmaintainable. This is reminiscent of the past (and current) problems with larger applications which the information systems function is attempting to remedy in most organizations.

5. *Backup, recovery, and security* procedures are inadequate. This is not a problem for 'throw-away' applications which are only used once, but those which are used on a continuing basis often take no notice of backup and recovery issues when things go wrong. As 'grey analysts' develop systems which are relied upon for key departmental tasks, these issues must be a major concern.

IS Professional Development

The third approach is for information systems professionals to use end user computing tools and personal computers for systems development. End user computing tools can speed up and reduce the cost of many smaller projects. Obviously the scope of such systems is restricted but the business gains can be substantial. For example, in distribution there are often depots scattered around the country. For individuals in each depot to develop their own applications may well be less appropriate than a professionally-developed system which uses personal computers. In the longer term, such a system should be easier to link to others as well as to enhance in the future. It will also be easier to ensure compliance with corporate standards and architecture.

Another area of major value is the use of end user computing tools in prototyping. The development speed of spreadsheets and personal computer databases make it possible to design prototypes with limited data handling capacity but realistic screens and basic data handling. This has been used successfully in a number of companies. In some cases these prototypes are actually used as the specification for the final system—with more conventional languages used to replicate the screen designs of familiar personal computer packages such as Lotus 123.

Problems of IS Professional Development

However there are problems with this approach of professionally developed systems:

1. *Lack of end user computing knowledge* among information systems staff, in particular concerning personal computers. In the past many information systems staff have seen personal computers as little more than toys. While this attitude is changing slowly, the level of knowledge of end user computing tools is still low among many staff concerned primarily with mainframe system development. Thus end user computing solutions may be ignored even when relevant.

2. The old problem of *making systems meet user needs* persists. Given the gap between many information systems staff and users, there is no guarantee that systems developed using end user computing tools will meet user needs better. A key ingredient in success is information systems staff who can link their technical knowledge with awareness of business requirements and bridge the gap between information systems staff and users.

3. The creation of a *new systems development backlog*—this time for small systems using personal computers and other end user computing tools. Also the resources used in developing systems are more visible than when they are developed by individual users or 'grey analysts'. This leads to more obvious resource allocation conflicts in the organization than if the costs of applications development are hidden in many user departments.

Which Form of Development?

In practice an end user computing strategy should include all three approaches to application development. Professionally developed systems using end user computing tools are most appropriate where: (i) development speed and cost are important goals and the systems involved are relatively small scale compared with most data processing projects; (ii) gains will come from standardized applications, in particular when they are intended to be linked to corporate systems in the future; (iii) security, validity, and disaster recovery are significant issues; (iv) implementation will be in geographically dispersed sites performing similar functions.

Individually developed systems are most appropriate for purely individual and 'throw-away' use. The emphasis should be on training staff to use simple but effective tools and to have adequate low-level support which is readily available, preferably on site. Part of the training should be in identifying which problems should be tackled with end user computing tools, left as a manual task, or seen as a larger systems development project.

Managing the 'grey analyst' is the most difficult issue—but it must be faced. The 'grey analyst' is both an asset and a liability, requiring management by both business and information systems functions. A first step is recognition of the problem and the need to tackle it. Attempting to remove 'grey analysts' is no solution, so the emphasis must be on education and co-ordination. The aim should be to pass on the lessons an discipline of the information systems function to the 'grey analyst' for small scale systems development, combined with increasing their managers' responsibility for their work.

User groups are one potentially valuable method: the 'grey analysts' will usually be interested and meetings give the information systems function a chance to educate 'grey analysts' in areas such as disaster recovery and security. The contact between people in different business areas may also help to limit duplication of effort. More formal education programmes on small scale systems development may be useful in addition to the specific training for software packages which already exists. Clear corporate standards, including those for applications, can provide a focus for such education. On the management side, simple internal audit procedures can be implemented—with a checklist of five or six areas (such as validity, security, and maintainability) for systems for which a business manager must accept responsibility. Also effort must be put into developing methods for the recognition of suitable opportunities for the use of end user computing. Overall, applications development is an essential part of any end user computing strategy requiring a variety of approaches and management from both the information systems and the business sides of an organization

Data and Integration

The Data Bottleneck

In end user computing, there has been a convergence between users of mainframe based tools for data extraction and analysis and personal computer users who find that the data they need is held on corporate mainframes. Generally the software packages for personal computers are easier to use and more flexible than those on mainframes, but of course cannot cope with volume of data held on corporate business databases.

The result is that much of the data entered into personal computers for analysis actually comes from other corporate information systems and is rekeyed. Some estimates—which are probably realistic—are that at least 60% of the data entered into personal computers is from printouts of other computers. For example in one retailer, summarized data from corporate point of sale systems was rekeyed into personal computers for analysis to determine the week's order levels—and then sometimes put back into a mainframe system. Thus the availability of data from corporate systems is a crucial bottleneck for getting the maximum potential out of end user computing.

Resolving the Data Issue

Resolving this problem has two dimensions: *data* and *organizational*. Currently there are few fundamental hardware problems in linking personal computers to most mainframes and minicomputers, though costs can be fairly high. The block is in end-users flexibly accessing and analysing corporate data. Current 'micro–mainframe link' products are usually tied to a single mainframe database package and often require knowledge of the mainframe application itself. As a result, there is a need for continuing professional assistance for most users to effectively access corporate data. Technical developments of packages on both personal computers and mainframes will ease this problem—so identifying and implementing these should be a priority for an end user computing strategy.

But much of the data contained in corporate applications may not be in an appropriate form for analysis as a result of their past development. To take one example, in a major bank, data in corporate systems is held by account numbers—and it is difficult if not impossible to form a picture of the banks' customers. Also applications designed in the past to maximize performance may well use their own database structures—and make no provision for flexible data extraction for analysis. For the future it is vital that such facilities be built into corporate business applications. Thus specifications for new mainframe applications or major enhancements should require provision for data extraction and analysis. In the meantime, the best approach is usually to extract the relevant data from these applications on a regular basis, making it available in a standard database for which suitable micro–mainframe link software exists.

The organizational dimension is a necessary condition for effective end user computing and the exploitation of corporate data. While the idea of data management has been around for a long time, the growth of end user computing makes it even more of a priority. For example, if items in corporate databases have no common definition, analysis will be misleading. A discussion with managers in one retail chain showed the extent of this problem as there were about eight definitions of a 'delivery' in their systems—ranging from an order being submitted to the goods being bought by the final customer. Thus development of data dictionaries is a requirement, as is their effective implementation.

Further organizational issues are the definition of ownership of data, including responsibility for maintenance and both controlling and promoting access to databases. While part of many organizations' overall information systems planning, end user computing increases the need for data management. This again points to the growing need for end user computing to be considered as an integral part of overall information systems strategy.

The Need for Organizational Change

The management of end user computing involves both the information systems function and the business functions. The effective use of end user computing implies significant changes in organization and attitudes for information systems managers and staff. So what are the main organizational issues which must be faced?

Defining goals

There is a need to define the goals of end user computing within large organizations more clearly than is usually done at present. The reasons for this includes the significant expenditures involved both now and in the future, and to set the overall direction and priorities for end user computing in line with business strategy. Examples of the goals which could be pursued are enhancing professional productivity, faster response to new business opportunities, enabling business departments to develop their own systems, and access to corporate data across the organization. These will differ between organizations and should be linked to overall business objectives. From such goals, will come clarification of how the overall level of investment in personal computers is to be determined, in particular the extent to which it should be determined by user readiness to pay for personal computer systems. While the approach proposed here is for this to be basically user-driven within a framework of corporate standards, there will be a need to monitor overall spending and to evaluate the benefits achieved.

Integrating IS Organization

Another priority is for the information systems function to see end user computing as a whole and to integrate its approach to *personal computing, Information Centres,* and *office automation.* This has already been done in some organizations, but by no means all. But even in more advanced cases, there is evidence of a disturbing gap within the information systems function between those who are involved in supporting end user computing and those in more traditional areas of systems development and operations. One reflection of this is that it appears that, of any function in the business, information systems has gained least from end user computing.

Management Responsibilities

Making effective use of end user computing is primarily an organizational rather than a technical issue. Business managment must take responsiblity for the effectiveness of end user computing. While there is a gap within the information systems function, there is another gap between users and more senior managers in business functions. Much of the use of personal computers is by professionals and junior managers, whose superiors often do not really understand what their staff are doing. This is likely to lead to less effective use of personal computers not only because of missed opportunities as a result of managerial ignorance but also to ineffective use by the more junior staff due to the potential lack of connection between their work and departmental objectives. Thus managing end user computing must be a concern for management in user departments.

Role of the Information Systems Function

Given its growth and significance, end user computing is also of great importance to the information systems function. In practice this will mean that the organization of end user computing has five parts. The first part is *front-line support* for users who have problems, such as the existing help desk facility in many organizations. This should be as close to users as possible for maximum effectiveness. The problem now is apparently inexhaustible demands on support staff. Part of the job of such support staff must be to encourage and develop basic support skills within user departments, perhaps using existing 'grey analysts', thus leaving them with the time to tackle more difficult problems.

A second part will be the *education and training* effort necessary. Generally, there can be little doubt that training is an area to which greater attention must be devoted, particularly if companies wish not only to give an understanding of personal computers and applications packages but also to develop standards for the design and quality of applications themselves. A related issue is that of education, in this case on the potential use of personal computers and their management. Given that much of the use of personal computers is by professionals and junior managers, there is a clear need for this end user computing to be managed by those responsible for their overall work. There is a gap between these users of personal computers and many middle to senior managers. This is likely to lead to less effective end user computing not only due to missed opportunities as a result of managerial ignorance but also due to the potential lack of connection between the work of the actual end users and business objectives. Thus managing end user computing should be a concern not only of information systems staff and users, but also of middle to senior management in user departments.

A third part of end user computing organization will be *central policy-making*, product evaluation and architecture work. This will include the linking of end user computing into the overall information systems architecture of the organization. The staff doing this must be freed from the interuptions involved in day-to-day user support to enable them to do their jobs properly. However the danger is that their work gets isolated from the actual needs and priorities of end users. To prevent this, it is probably necessary for most of these staff to spend a limited time in such a central function. Also gains could be made by involving knowledgeable users, perhaps on secondment from their own departments, to work with such a group.

A fourth part of end user computing organization will be in *systems development* for applications identified as of general potential use. This will overlap the more general systems development effort, particularly if end user computing tools are being used for prototyping. The challenge here will be to identify these potential common applications and to develop systems which meet user needs.

The fifth and perhaps most significant will be *internal consultancy*, especially on the exploitation of corporate data. Given the importance of access to corporate data for the future potential of end user computing, enabling business functions to make use of existing information resources is a major task. This again is clearly a role linking together information systems and the organization as a whole.

Conclusion

This paper has analysed the main aspects of a strategy for managing end user computing. The message is that the spread of end user computing is a challenge for both the information systems function and user departments as well as senior management. Looking into the future, there can be little doubt that the demand for end user computing will continue to grow, though the pattern of use and consequent policy issues will gradually change over time. Henderson and Treacy (1986) have suggested that there will be an organizational learning curve in which education and support will reduce in importance over time, while concerns with integrating hardware and software into an overall architecture will grow and then decline somewhat. Meanwhile cost-justification and data management continue to grow in importance over time.

While such a picture appears to be broadly correct with respect to technology, cost-justification and data, there is less evidence that education and training needs will decline. Rather, the needs will shift from basic skills training in the use of personal computers and other end user computing tools towards the recognition of opportunities and education in effective use of corporate data. A gradual shift of operational responsibility towards divions and departments is also implied—with incentives to ensure compliance with corporate standards. This implies a growing focus on organizational issues rather than individual ones, in particular the relationship between the information systems function and user departments.

From the viewpoint of the information systems function, end user computing is most clearly at the borderline between information systems and the organization as a whole. To be effective, the information systems function must place a high priority on business understanding and communication with many levels of managers and staff. In short, end user computing is one of the areas where the need for information systems function to be linked to the business and for the consequent internal reorganization are most pressing (see Earl *et al.*, 1986).

References

Earl, M. J., Feeny, D., Hirschheim, R., and Lockett, M. (1986), *Information Technology Executives Key Education and Development Needs: A Field Study*, Oxford Institute of Information Management research and discussion paper 86/10.

Ein-Dor, P. (1985), 'Grosch's Law Revisited: CPU Power and the Costs of Computation', *Communications of the ACM* **28, 2**, pp. 142–51.

Henderson, J. C., and Treacy, M. E. (1986), 'Managing End User Computing for Competitive Advantage', *Sloan Management Review* **27, 2**.

Lockett, M. (1986), *The Use of Personal Computers by Managers and Professional Staff*, Oxford Institute of Information Management research and discussion paper 86/18.

SECTION FIVE

IT Strategy and Organization

FOREWORD

In earlier sections, several writers have either dwelt on organizational tensions that arise in this strategic era of IT, for example Seddon, or have stressed the fact that organizational issues outweigh technological matters, for example Lockett, or have seen the blending of technological and organizational factors as crucial, for example Scott Morton, or have called for more serious attention to be given to the education and development of IS human resources, for instance Gooding. Thus it seems appropriate that the final section of this book should focus on organizational aspects of IT and Strategy.

Indeed social and organizational matters have never been far from the concerns of both academics and practitioners working in the fields of computing and related technologies. There have been analyses of the impact of computers on organizations (Whisler, 1970), predictions of the effect of computing on managerial behaviour (Simon, 1977), treatises on the political aspects of information systems (Pettigrew, 1973), efforts to mediate the effects of technology on work and workers (Mumford, 1981), efforts to open up our perspectives on information systems (Mason and Mitroff, 1973) and work on more socially valid system development methodologies (Checkland, 1981) to quote a few examples and influential workers.

In 1987 as IT becomes pervasive in many organizations, as IT growth is explosive, and as IT becomes regarded as a strategic resource, practitioners, consultants, and the business school academics recognize that organizational issues of a much more managerial flavour are central to satisfying firms' expectations and needs. They are to do with structuring the IT function when technologies both multiply and converge, when some users achieve maturity in understanding different aspects of IT, when host organizations become more complex and when organizational change in many manifestations has become the norm.

Hubinette traces the recent organizational history of the IT function in Volvo. He describes the sensitive balances required between decentralizing and centralizing IT activities, the management control aspects of IT and the top management responsibilities. It is interesting to note that in Volvo, the concept of the IT organization extends beyond its legal boundaries into at least their dealerships and importerships. Finally Hubinette draws on Volvo's experience to predict the organization structure for IT in the late 1980s.

Another organizational concern today is the position of the IT Executive or IT Director—his or her role, tasks attributes and prospects. More organizations are creating the post of IT Director, many are renaming the senior IT post, and in strategic sectors numerous executive searches are scanning for vaguely-defined, illusory 'maestros' who can lead the IT function. Leadership seems to be one common requirement for this post, but this can incorporate developing strategies for IT, controlling the cost of IT, improving the performance of the IT function, accepting responsibility for IT in the firm, rescuing or turning round IT, representing IT on the board, bringing IT closer to the business and its managers, etc., etc.

Earl, Feeny, Hirscheim, and Lockett suggest an organizational model of IT leadership, based on interviews in leading UK companies. They find, once again, that organizational and business issues outweigh technological matters in the minds of both IT executives and top managers. An evolutionary pattern emerges for both the leadership and leader of the IT function. Underpinning this evolution is increasing investment by organizations in information management education.

This raises a third key organizational question and the one that was raised most often in general discussion at the conference which prompted this book. IT directors of large firms for whom IT is a crucial resource, increasingly are seeking guidance on, are experimenting on, and devoting much of their time to, the education and development of IS professionals and managers and of line and general managers who in future can and will exploit or depend on IT and IS. What seems a simple issue is beset by problems of skills shortages, labour market economics, career development, changing needs and conditions, and conflicts between the long term and short term. These factors are aggravated by an historical legacy—IS or IT has been seen as different from the rest of the organization.

In the final paper, therefore, Keen describes and analyses many of these human resource management tensions. However he goes further, as he also prescribes actions and programmes required to remedy a major skills gap. He acknowledges that some bold and determined top management intervention is required—and calls for some new approaches to education.

References

Checkland, P. (1981), *Systems Thinking, Systems Practice*, J. Wiley.
Mason, R. O., and Mitroff, I. M. (1973), 'A Program for Research on Management Information Systems, *Management Science* **19, 5**.
Mumford, E. (1981), 'Participative Systems Design: Structure and Method', *Systems, Objectives, Solutions* **1, 1**.
Pettigrew, A. (1973), *The Politics of Organizational Decision Making*, Tavistock, London.
Simon, H. A. (1977), *The New Science of Management Decision*, Prentice Hall, Englewood Cliffs, NJ.
Whisler, T. (1970), *The Impact of Computers on Organisations*, Praeger, New York.

13

Organization and Control of Development in Information Technology in Volvo

KARL-HENRIK HUBINETTE

Volvo Data AB

Volvo

Volvo's operations started in Gothenburg, Sweden 60 years ago. Its objective was to produce cars and trucks and the first 10 cars were built in 1927 by a work force of 66 people. Since that time the company has grown considerably and has expanded into several other activities besides car and truck manufacturing. Energy and Trading as well as Food, Aerospace, and Marine and Industrial engines have become important Volvo operations. The automotive part of the business is, however, still the largest part and provided two thirds of the Group's 1985 turnover of 86 billion swedish crowns (approx £8.6 bn).

Volvo's production base is Sweden and the majority of all the products are still made there. Out of the total work force of more than 67,000 people 74% are employed in Sweden. From all other aspects Volvo is a truly international company. Excluding the oil business, 82% of the sales revenue comes from sales outside Sweden and Volvo products can be found in practically all the countries of the world.

Over the years Volvo has acquired a number of other companies and it has reorganized its operations into separate subsidiaries. The Volvo Group now consists of more than one hundred operating companies wholly or partly owned by AB Volvo. In addition, a number of affiliated companies are part of the group.

Information Technology and Volvo Data AB

Volvo was an early proponent of the use of information technology; indeed many new technologies found their way into the Swedish market through Volvo as their first user. The use of data processing in the forms of unit record machines and later computers was organized in two separate staff functions. One, the Administration Techniques department, mainly responsible for development of systems and procedures, and the other, Volvo Data Center, in charge of data processing operations.

In 1972 a major reorganization of the Volvo company took place resulting in a separation of business responsibilities into separate divisions, with a substantial reduction of central head office services. At the same time a separate subsidiary was formed under the name Volvo Data comprising the two staff units mentioned above. Volvo Data was to operate as an allocated cost centre providing systems development services and data processing operations to the Volvo organization at cost. It was to operate in competition with other service organizations available in the market place and was expected to offer superior price performance mainly through economies of scale and possessing better knowledge of the Volvo business.

In addition to Volvo Data becoming the corporate service centre, several divisions and subsidiaries organized their own information technology departments. Some of these were fully organized data centres, including both systems development and computer operations, while others only comprised a systems development activity and left data processing operations in the hands of Volvo Data.

For the direction of Volvo Data as the Group's service centre the board of directors comprises senior managers representing the major users of Volvo Data's services. The role of Volvo Data in the Volvo organization has been defined as follows:

1. To be the service organization for information technology services in the Group.
2. To supply specialist competence in the area of information technology.
3. To market IT products to the Group companies.
4. To take responsibility for development, operations, and maintenance of IT services as requested by the individual companies.
5. To take responsibility for common IT products such as a communications network (the Volvo Corporate Network), and an electronic mail system (MEMO).

In addition to the conventional computer services, responsibility for telephone, telex, and radio services also has been placed with Volvo Data.

Today Volvo Data provides about 40% of the total Information Technology services for the Volvo Group. The total spending on IT services for the Group is estimated to be 1,100 m Swedish crowns (Approx £110 m). The processing power in the Volvo Data installation is about 140 MIPS and the storage capacity is close to one terrabyte (1,000,000,000,000 bytes). A large number of computers and more than 17,000 terminals are attached to the network. Volvo Data employs 600 persons.

Management Control Principles

Volvo is a decentralized organization where each company is responsible for its own results. In addition, the main units in Sweden are responsible for market planning. Group headquarters issues directives and guidelines for strategies and financial results.

In the area of Information Technology a number of standards and guidelines have been created to strengthen the Group's development of data processing tools in support of Volvo's business activities. The main reasons for the need of common standards and guidelines are the following:

1. the need for a holistic view on the use of IT
2. IT is a relatively expensive resource
3. IT is an area of very rapid development
4. the need for integration of information within the whole company.

Standards and guidelines are issued by the Group head office after review and acceptance by the EDP Committee. This committee consists of a number of senior executive directors representing Volvo's main business units. The committee meets three to four times a year to review important aspects of Information Technology development.

So far the following standards and guidelines have been issued:

1. Volvo policy for the use of data processing
2. Rules for profitability calculation of data processing projects
3. Data Processing security
4. Standards for selection of computer equipment
5. Recommendation for office automation
6. Control and Organization of the Volvo Corporate Network
7. Rules concerning ownership of computer applications.

These standards and guidelines are prepared by the Group EDP-coordination, a staff unit placed within Volvo Data but reporting to the Group head office.

The Impact of Standards and Guidelines

An individual company's adherence to common standards and guidelines is influenced by the impact on the profitability of the individual company, the availability of alternatives, and the influence on the company's ability to fulfill its business objectives. Some of the documents are more mandatory than others, but the final decision concerning adherence to standards and guidelines is always taken by the local management.

Standards and guidelines dealing with communications and computer equipment are in effect unconditional in most cases. Access to the Volvo Corporate Network and the use of it is regulated by detailed specifications as to which organizations it may serve and for which purposes it may be used as well as the different types of equipment and communications modes that are allowed. In the computer area there are firm recommendations as to which suppliers to use and the various families of computers to employ.

For the systems software area we have recommendations concerning standard software packages as well as maintenance and support services offered by Volvo Data which may prove to be advantageous to the individual company having their own computer center. There are also recommended system development methodologies for use within the Group. Here, however, the size and scope of the local operations plays an important part in deciding whether or not to apply the centrally used procedures.

Management of Common Application Systems

In the development of Information Technology, a number of application systems for common use have emerged supporting the business administration. The first systems were developed for processing in the Volvo Data Center but later, as computers were installed at the market units, systems were made for local installation. Today a portfolio of a dozen different systems is installed completely or partly in our major importerships and dealer systems are installed in more than 100 dealerships. This whole concept of distributed common systems was made possible by an early standardization of computer equipment for the importers.

Common systems have been planned and developed through the main product units in Sweden, sometimes supported by user interest groups or tried out by pilot installations. Several hundred man years have been invested in common systems development.

The product units are responsible for both product planning and market planning at a strategic level and the development of common systems has been seen as a way of introducing common administrative practices to the market organization. The benefits of these systems will be realized at different levels of the organization in dealers and importers as well as in the main units in Sweden.

Vertical business integration and the need for detailed information at different levels of the organization have been driving forces for the development of common systems. Two examples may be used to illustrate this point.

Availability of spare parts and accessories for cars and trucks is a problem of optimizing warehousing and distribution. Capital tied up in storage of parts centrally, at importerships, and at dealer level, accounts for a large part of the cost in the parts distribution area. Improvements in logistics requires detailed information concerning parts requirements through the whole distribution chain. Data about available parts both at dealer and importer level, as well as up to date information concerning the actual demand, must be at hand in order for the main Parts department in Sweden to optimize the total logistics planning. Common definitions as well as common procedures are an absolute requirement. The Parts division has therefore sponsored the development of distributed systems both at dealer and importer level. The systems communicate information between dealer and importer and are also linked to the Parts division in Sweden. In this way, Information Technology will make it possible to use information as a resource to improve the profitability of the parts business at all levels and also to keep competitive prices for the customers.

Another example is the handling of warranty claims on new vehicles. It is important that the verification and acceptance of warranty claims be made in a uniform manner all over the world. It is equally important that information about product quality in the form of demands for warranty repairs is communicated uniformly and quickly to the production unit in Sweden. The product units in Sweden have led in the development of common and integrated systems for dealers and importers in order for this important aspect of consumer relations to work correctly and efficiently. The benefits are obvious: the dealer and the customer will know immediately if a claim will be accepted; the main units will have immediate information concerning product quality and may be able to correct a fault in the production line thus reducing future claims.

Successful development of common systems puts great demands on system quality and requires a great deal of co-operation from all levels of the organization. Good planning and adequate assistance in the implementation and education phases are very important in order to succeed in the common systems area. Even more important is quality. The systems offered must be at least as good as anything offered on the market. Correctly managed, however, the benefits are evident in any large organization which is geographically or organizationally dispersed.

Problems/Opportunities in Management Control of IT

The continuing proliferation of data processing in our organization further compounds the problem of management and control of IT. In Volvo we have more than a hundred mini and maxi computers installed in our various companies. In addition, system development staff have been distributed into the user organizations and the users themselves are taking increased responsibility for the introduction of information technology in their respective organizations. This trend is especially prominent in the widespread use of personal computing both on main-frames and stand-alone PCs.

The different maturity levels among the users and the user management are reflected in their ability to control and supervise the use of information technology. At the same time, data processing is evolving from being primarily a technology for cost reduction to becoming a business too, the use of which will have a profound impact on the organization's ability to survive and prosper in a competitive environment. There is, however, a growing understanding in the board rooms and in the executive suites that information technology may have a great impact on the business itself and that the conventional DP organization and its managers cannot be expected to handle the strategic planning of IT on their own. The realization that IT is an integral part of the business strategies and should be handled by the business managers, however, provides opportunities to establish a more efficient management control procedure for IT. There is a growing acceptance on the part of company management that a well thought out and formulated strategy for the use of information technology is necessary. Also there is a realization that information can be an important company resource and that the proper use of this resource is dependent on accepted standards being followed throughout the organization.

In most organizations there is now an opportunity for establishing better procedures for management and control of IT. Management should take the full responsibility for the role that IT will have in the organization and determine the criteria for performance and effectiveness. The DP organization can then concentrate on being a professional support centre responsible for maintaining high efficiency in computer and communications processing and having the technological expertise required by the business. In addition, DP should evaluate new technologies and play the role of advisor on how to effectively make use of these new developments in the business area.

New areas in Information Technology such as Computer Integrated Manufacturing, Local Area Networks, Manufacturing Automation Protocol and the heavy investments required in these areas further underline the need for good management and control in order for the business to reap corresponding benefits.

Outlook to the Future

There are no signs that the present development in Information Technology will stop or even slow down within a forseeable future. We can expect mainframes to become larger and larger with expectations for increased price/performance. Mini computers will be found in many places in the organization, sometimes as stand-alone equipment but more often communicating with large mainframes through telecommunication networks. The PC explosion will perhaps not be an explosion but a steady increase can be expected.

The overall problems in the use of the development in technology will be in the areas of Management and Control, and User Maturity. Management will have to direct the utilization of IT as it directs the use of other resources in business, and the user will have to accept responsibility for decisions concerning the support he or she will need. This will influence the way in which IT support is organized. Systems development, maintenance, and part of the processing will be under control of line management and organized as a part of its normal responsibilities. Technological competence, the major part of the daily processing, and the custodianship of common resources will be in the hands of a IT service department. Overall co-ordination of IT strategies and responsibility for corporate planning in this area will become a staff function closely attached to executive management.

These changes already can be distinguished for some organizations but for most companies the restructuring of automation services will take place over the second part of this decade.

14

Information Technology, Strategy, and Leadership

MICHAEL EARL, DAVID FEENY, RUDI HIRSCHHEIM, and MARTIN LOCKETT

Oxford Institute of Information Management, Templeton College, Oxford

Introduction

In late 1985 and early 1986, we investigated the information management education experiences and needs of ten large UK firms. From this survey, we discovered some interesting traits and trends in the strategic management of information technology (IT) and information systems (IS). Indeed what emerged was a tentative evolutionary model of the leadership of the IT function and of the IT Executive. We have presented this model subsequently to a number of IT Directors and Chief Executives who generally have been able to position themselves on the model, trace their own evolution, and provide further anecdotal evidence to support our findings. Although the model is soon to be tested more rigorously on a larger sample, we believe that even at this tentative stage it indicates the organizational dynamics that surround the strategic application and management of IT and suggests how organizations and IT executives can prepare and develop for the 'IT Age'.

The Survey

The research had as its general goal a broad survey of the IS educational needs of major UK businesses. Although there have been a number of papers on the educational requirements of IS personnel (Numamaker *et al.*, 1982; Buckingham *et al.*, 1986; Capper, 1986) and key issues (including education) of the IT executive (Earl, 1983; Dickson *et al.*, 1984; Martin 1984), there is apparently less knowledge of the precise areas where education is needed and what vehicles or approaches are most suitable. After some deliberation it was felt that the most appropriate approach to studying these issues was a field study involving a number of key IT executives, and those senior executives at or near board level who were seen to be major sponsors of the exploitation of IT.

Ten IT executives were identified as leaders in the field, whose views were likely to be most valuable in understanding the concerns and needs of not only the current genre of IT executives but also the future. Their thoughts and beliefs were felt to be indicative of successful and future-oriented IT executives.[1] Thus, a small but carefully selected sample of key individuals, interviewed in a face-to-face manner, was felt to be a better research design and capable of producing more meaningful results than a large and varied sample. Moreover, the ability to undertake personal interviews with a small number of individuals was considered a better vehicle for obtaining meaningful data than mailed questionnaires. However, in selecting the interviews, a stratified sample of industry sectors was attempted, so that the respondents represent financial services, manufacturing, retailing, and transportation.

A semi-structured questionnaire was constructed covering both the role of information systems within the business, and perceptions on educational considerations. The first part of the questionnaire provided background information on the IS environment: the nature of the IT function in the organization, the background and activities of IT executives, key and future concerns and the like. The second part specifically addressed executive education: the kind and form of IT education, its value, what improvements could be made, and so on. As it was felt that views on these matters should come from both the IT executive and one of the IT function's major sponsors, a second questionnaire was developed and aimed at this senior executive. This questionnaire was largely a subset of the first, reflecting a more general business orientation and consistent with the level of the individual being interviewed. It was felt that a general business perspective would be gained by interviewing the IT functions' sponsor. Data from this second individual provided an interesting 'check' on the data obtained from the IT executive.

Respondents were given freedom to respond to the questions asked as they wished. Some interviewees answered the questions in a matter-of-fact, objective way; others were more perceptual and subjective. The degree of objectivity–subjectivity in question responses varied between questions and interviewees. Interviews lasted at least one hour, and in some cases they were much longer. No tape recordings were used, with all information being unattributable so as to preserve the confidentiality of the interviewee. Organizational details were also kept in confidence.

Of the ten organizations visited, in four, both the IT executive and his sponsor were interviewed. The ten organizations are all very large companies whose IS budgets range between £2 million and £261 million. The organizations are labelled A to J in the analyses that follow.

[1] The determination of these organizations was a subjective exercise involving the opinions of a number of academics, IS professionals and suppliers who were knowledgeable about the IT executives of major corporations in the UK.

Survey Findings

The more revealing data we collected were prompted by the first part of our interview questionnaire, namely the concerns, priorities, activity patterns, career histories, and development programmes of IT Directors. The more direct evidence on information management education is reported in Earl *et al.* (1986). Figure 14.1 summarizes the details of the IT Executive interviewed in terms of personal background (whether they were hired from within or without the firm) and IT background (whether they had come up through the IT function or not).

IT background

		IT	Non-IT
Company background	Internal	3	3
	External	4	0

Fig. 14.1.   Details of IT Executives

Of the ten IT executives interviewed, three have general management backgrounds, whilst seven spent their careers mostly in the IS field. Six of the companies appointed their IT executive from within, while four went outside to hire theirs. The average length of time the IT executives have been in their present positions is four years, with a range from one to eleven years. Respondents were then asked in what areas they were spending the most time. The second part of the question asked where they thought their time should be spent.

Answers varied considerably in terms of how they categorize heavy time-consuming activities and what proportions of time were spent on each. Some discussed their tasks in terms of IS strategy, IS marketing, internal services, and internal IT organization. Because of the unstructured nature of the answers, it made sense to divide the stated tasks into two broad categories: *Inside IT* and *Beyond IT.*[2] The former relates to those activities and tasks specifically associated with keeping the IT function running on a day-to-day basis. The latter includes such activities as IS strategic planning, working closely with senior management in discussions and committees, liaising with other organizations and such like. Four out of ten felt that most of their time was being spent 'inside IT', while five were 'beyond' oriented. One felt that the breakdown was of the order of 50% 'inside IT', 50% 'beyond'. It was unanimously agreed,

[2] The terms IT and IS at this level of analysis are often used interchangeably. The spirit of our usage is that IT refers to the technologies and the function and IS to the applications and systems.

however, that more than 50% of their time *should* be spent on 'beyond' tasks. The IT executive from company G was typical of this opinion. He noted that although about 60% of his time was spent on 'inside IT' tasks, 25% is the figure it should be. Figure 14.2 represents how the ten IT executives spent their time, placed along a continuum of *Inside IT* to *Beyond IT.* Figure 14.3 summarizes how IT executives felt their time should be spent in comparison to how they were actually spending their time.

Fig. 14.2. Where IT Executives' Time is Spent

	Normative	
	Inside IT	Beyond IT
Inside IT		A D G J
Beyond IT		I B C E F H

(left axis label: Reality)

Fig. 14.3. Where Should IT Executives' Time be Spent?

While in the previous question there was unanimity regarding where IT executives ought to be spending their time now, their views of the future differed. Four out of ten respondents felt that in the future there would be a need to shift emphasis back to 'inside IT'—on the surface, a peculiar belief. The IT executive of company A, for example, stated that he 'should be less concerned externally in the future but spending more time managing the boundary personnel'. A similar view was stated by the IT executive of company C who noted the need to 'move from marketing towards how to manage the IT function'. There is an apparent shift from planning and control to the organization and structure of IT and IS. Figure 14.4 summarizes where the IT executives felt their time should be spent in three years' time.

Respondents also were asked how they saw the strategic importance of IS within their companies. The vehicle by which this was to be obtained was through the McFarlan and McKenney 'strategic grid'.

The 'strategic grid', a widely known and used model to classify the strategic importance of IS, attempts to map the strategic importance of current systems against the strategic importance of systems being

Future

		Inside IT	Beyond IT
Now	Inside IT	A	G J
	Beyond IT	B C F	D I E H

Fig. 14.4.   Where Should IT Executives' Time be Spent in Three Years' Time?

developed, ranked on a scale of low to high. Four broad scenarios or categories are possible: 'support', 'factory', 'turnaround', and 'strategic'. We asked about the strategic grid in an attempt to test the importance of IS and to see if it related in any way to educational needs and practice. Unfortunately, when applied, the strategic grid did not show itself to be a particularly effective vehicle for discussing the IT function. The notion of comparing the strategic importance of current systems with the strategic importance of systems being developed to provide an archetype of the IT function appeared largely unrealistic. Many of the respondents felt it was a disingenuous way of categorizing the IT function since virtually every company had systems in all four categories. Most respondents thought that while it was impossible to classify themselves as belonging to any one category, they did note that different categories provided an interesting (although not necessarily meaningful) way to think about the strategic importance of IS. It is likely, however, that the grid may be more helpful when applied at the level of the strategic business unit rather than across the organization as a whole.

In attempting to map the various companies along the grid, it is possible to note that while all have systems in each category, a number have rather more in the 'strategic' category; companies F, H, and I. Company G is moving from 'turnaround' to 'strategic'; company B is moving from 'support' through 'factory' to 'strategic'; companies C and J, from 'factory' to 'strategic'. Figure 14.5 attempts to classify the organizations, very generally, along the grid.

It is not unusual for users and general managers to have different views and opinions of IS than those held by the IT function. Thus we asked IT Executives if their views on the strategic importance of IS were shared by management at large. We also tried to verify the view by asking the chief officers interviewed for their opinion.

Generally speaking, there was felt to be broad agreement between senior management and the IT executive, although in some cases there was a sense that senior management still had not recognized the

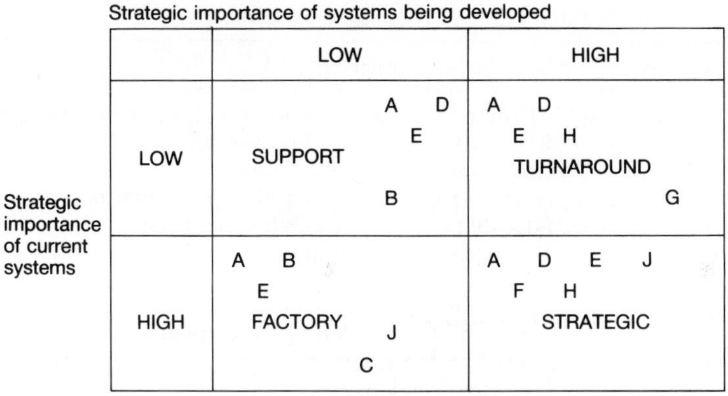

Strategic importance of systems being developed

		LOW	HIGH
Strategic importance of current systems	LOW	A D E SUPPORT B	A D E H TURNAROUND G
	HIGH	A B E FACTORY J C	A D E J F H STRATEGIC

Fig. 14.5. IS Strategic Grid

importance of IS. Companies F, H, and I, who were thought to be most advanced, largely 'strategic' along the 'strategic grid', seemed to have the greatest sense of shared senior management and IT executive view. Companies A, B, C, and J noted that management was aware of the importance of IS but that this had not fully percolated through yet. Companies D, E, and G raised the concern that management had not yet recognized the strategic importance of IS; they were more concerned with sorting out problems than strategic direction.

It is interesting to note that for the most part, there was a shared conception on this question between the IT executive and the chief officers interviewed.

Respondents then were asked what they saw as the main concerns with the use of information technology in their business. Perhaps not surprisingly, there was a wide range of concerns expressed by the respondents. Some felt the major problem rested with the users—more specifically, their inability to come to grips with new technology and its uses. Others felt systems development, in particular their rate of delivery, was the key concern. Broadly speaking, it is possible to classify the concerns into four general areas: technological constraints, systems development, user understanding and relationships, and organizational change. One respondent felt that technological constraints were the main concern; two thought it was systems development; three saw it as user understanding and relationships; and two noted organizational change as the key issue.

Respondents subsequently were asked if they would scan a list of twenty-two issues and rank them in terms of importance. The list is a composite of the many issues which are commonly talked about within the context of IS management. Table 14.1 lists the issues, and ranks them in terms of overall importance.

Table 14.1.   *Key Management Concerns with IT*

Rank order	Management concern
1	Aligning information systems with business strategy
2	Relations between IS and user departments
3	User awareness and education
4	IS project management and implementation
5	Identifying opportunities for the use of IT
6	Top management support for IS
7	Information systems security
7	Integrating diversified technologies
9	Information systems long range planning
10	Location of IS function in organization structure
10	User involvement

Of key concern among the respondents was the area of IS and business strategy—particularly, aligning information systems with business strategy. This issue was felt to far outdistance all others in importance. Often related to, or subsumed within this, was concern over how managers could spot opportunities for exploiting IT for strategic gain and how top management could be assisted in creating a strategic vision of IT.

The second most important concern was the relationship between IT and its user departments. Third place was user awareness and education. Fourth was IS project management and implementation. Fifth was identifying opportunities for the use of IT and sixth was top management support for IS/IT.

It is interesting to note that not one IT executive respondent mentioned budget constraints on IT, technological constraints, or coping with new information technologies as a key managerial concern. Nor were data management control, developing end-user computing or cost justification of spending on IS projects perceived as important issues. To summarize, it is the broader business and organizational level issues which were felt to be of key importance.

From all these questions, a picture emerges of IT Directors having quite diverse backgrounds and careers, some spending much of their time inside the IT function and others being external agents of change. Most IT Executives see managing beyond the IT function as where their time should be spent, no doubt because IS strategy formulation and user relationships and eduaction are their key management concerns. However, future issues are seen to be different leading to a 'retreat' back into the IT function. Finally all the companies surveyed would claim that Information Systems are strategic; thus the trends emerging may be seen to typify a 'strategic' sample of UK firms.

Thus today's patterns of IT Executives are diverse, but tomorrow's seem to converge. In seeking to understand this apparent paradox, we began to detect patterns and associations in the survey data. These suggested a dynamic model of leadership of the IT function once a firm recognizes that IT is potentially a strategic resource. The evolutionary process about to be described might be termed a stage model of strategic leadership of IT.

The Suggested Model

The model was suggested when we compared some of the qualitative descriptive and anecdotal evidence with the responses to the interview questionnaire. We emphasize that both the associations we are about to suggest and the 'softer' evidence behind them are tentative and require further validation. In other words, the data at most is suggestive and the model interpretative.

It appears that in companies where top management begins to realize that IS are vital to their business, the organization moves through three evolutionary phases in its emphasis on managing the IT function—in some ways these are leadership phases. These are depicted, with metaphors, in Fig. 14.6 and are associated with one significant factor throughout: the investment in management education increases with each phase. The phases collectively may be called 'the new age' and thus we attach a prior phase (the question mark) to cover those firms who have not yet realized the strategic importance of IT.

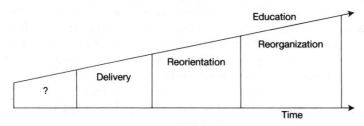

Fig. 14.6. The New Age

The data associations, albeit trends and not correlations, that particularly prompted the model were the following:

1. The background of the IT/IS executives.
2. The desired and actual patterns of the IT/IS executives' time spent in managing the function.
3. The priorities they attached to key issues.
4. The amount of education commissioned.

The soft benchmarks which seemed indicative were:

1. The anecdotal evidence on the organizational dynamics of managing the IT function.
2. The interest and support of the chief executive.
3. The career aspirations and concerns of the IT executives.
4. The use of external IT consultants.
5. The degree of access we were given to general managers.

Our feeling that the model may indeed be a valid description of how organizations strategically manage IT is partly based on two subsequent sources of support. About fifty account executives, from an IT supplier, have been exposed to the model and generally have been able to place their clients on the evolutionary path and provide rich anecdotes to back it up. Second, a number of IT executives and chief executives recently exposed to the model observed that it described their own organization's experience rather well.

In the first phase, top management begins to realize that IT is important to the business and must be taken seriously. Typically, however, there is a concern about the current performance of the IS/IT function and thus a desire that the basics are satisfied. This includes ensuring basic business systems are satisfactory, systems development projects are completed to specification and budget, DP operations are efficient, hardware and infrastructure policies are consistent, and users are satisfied with the service. Often this phase is initiated by replacing the DP manager with an external recruit who has substantial professional computing experience as a DP manager, or within a computer manufacturer, and is perceived to have a good track record. The emphasis is on *delivery* and accordingly the IT executive (although he may still be termed DP manager) spends most of his time on matters internal to his department. His job is to restore credibility for the function and/or create confidence in user and top management that the function is supporting current needs and is run efficiently. Education is sparse and mainly provided for DP personnel to improve their skills, techniques, and delivery management.

In the second phase, top management (or the Director ultimately responsible for IT) changes the focus of attention. Now the priority is to exploit IT for competitive advantage and align IS investment with business strategy. In short it is in this *reorientation* phase that 'the business is to be put into computing'. The common reaction therefore is to appoint an IT executive or director over the DP manager. This new post is filled typically by an insider—a senior executive who has run a business or been active at a senior level in business development, marketing, or some such strategic activity. The incumbent has limited or long-ago experience of DP but is respected by general management and can mobilize forces for change.

The phase two IT executive therefore spends—or seeks to spend—much of his time outside the function, trying to interpret business strategy, to raise user management awareness of new strategic opportunities afforded by IT, to create procedures and organizational devices which will ensure senior management commits to, and steers, IT, and to learn what other firms are doing. The chief executive may well promote IT but the substantive leadership and the initiation of actions to reorient the thinking about, and approach to, IT rest on the IT executive. Over time he tends to bring in strategy and technology consultants to advise, to recruit senior managers below him and to realize that top management, user management and some of his staff require education on IT in the new age.

This education may comprise at least three forms. Top management is encouraged to go to executive briefing events. User management may be provided with awareness courses on both the new technologies and the strategic opportunities and implications. Finally, the IT executive has continually to educate himself. He does this by frequent participation early on in IT manufacturers' event, attendance at an occasional course or conference, but largely by individual tuition. This is by three mechanisms: visiting other organizations, bringing in consultants and eventually often building an ongoing relationship with one or two well known experts whom he meets from time to time—as one IT executive put it 'my guru'.

In this third phase, the IT executive (by now IT director) is now concerned with managing the interfaces or relationships between his function and the rest of the organization. Some areas will be strategically dependent on IT, other business units looking to IT more in a support role. Some departments will have significant IT capability, particularly with the advance of end-user computing, and some functional and business executives will be driving IT and IS and themselves. At the same time, the IT executive may be thinking 'now I've done the reorientation job I should be moved back to a real business position, preferably very near the top'. Unfortunately only he now understands the complexity of IT functional leadership and the ambiguities he has to ride. For here he is having to redesign the IT organization to relate to the different environments in the company. He has to know when to let user areas have more autonomy and where to intervene for the good of the whole. Issues of data management become more complex than ever before. And a situation has been created where top management and user management want to direct and influence the use and, in some ways, the delivery of IT as well. This is where he is spending equal amounts of time inside and beyond the function.

Education in the reorganization phase grows in importance. There is much more action-oriented and business- or function-specific education of business management. The IT staff are having to update themselves on the new IT age in technological, organizational, and business terms. IT and IS may well be topics on the agendas of most management education and development activities in the company.

There is one important 'misfit' to this pattern. It is the occasional IT professional who lives through each of these phases and not only survives but grows and advances with them. It may well be that these misfits do not fit the *personal* dynamics of the model because they *anticipate* each phase and lead their organization accordingly. However the *organizational* dynamics of the model still fit their companies and the 'benchmarks' we suggest still apply—not least the investment in, and changes required of, education. It is just that the 'misfits' have been able to lead their organizations in the right way at the right time.

Table 14.2. *Managing the New Age*

Factor	Phase		
	Delivery	Reorientation	Reorganization
IT Executive	External IT	Inside business recruit	Same Person
Management focus	Within IT/DP	Into the business	The Interfaces
Priority concern	Credibility	Strategy	Relationship
Education needs	Skills	Awareness	Information Management
CEO Posture	Concerned	Visionary/ Champion	Involved
Leadership	The Board	The Function	Coalition

Conclusion

When a firm recognizes that IT is a strategic resource, a leadership issue arises. Whether the 'awakening' is inspired by top management or IT management, someone has to alter the basis of IS/IT activity and change attitudes towards it. The vision and push may come from 'the top' but the initiatives and action usually are driven by the IT function—a function which is barely formalized and recognized. The challenge is immense because most of the leadership has to come from behind (i.e. from the function) in organizational climates of doubt and hostility, in a rapidly changing technological environment, by relatively immature specialists managers, in an era of 'hype' and competition.

The sort of leadership required appears to change over time, becoming ever more complex and ambiguous. The astute leader anticipates the changes and leads the organization from one stage to another, recognizing that the leadership task and process must evolve. If this evolution does not occur or if the IT Executive cannot cope, a new leader may be found. However leadership does not only require a leader, it depends on a subtle mix of formal and informal management structures and processes. For smooth stage management of this evolution, management education seems to be important. In the delivery stage it is functional and technical; in the reorientation stage it is widespread and business oriented; in the reorganization stage it is advanced and continuous for by this time most key managers have become information managers.

We suspect that many large firms are in the reorientation phase. It is here that they are learning about strategic exploitation of IT and IT strategy formulation. These are not simple matters and may take some time to understand and manage (Earl, 1987). Yet the reorganization phase may be still more complex and comprise a host of technical, business, management and organizational questions we still do not appreciate or understand. However, our model is still tentative enough, without speculating on the detail of these matters! Nevertheless, we can be sure that in the late 1980s the vital questions for information management will be organizational.

References

Buckingham, R., Hirschheim, R., Land, R. and Tully, C. (eds.) (1986), *Information Systems Education: Recommendations and Implementation*, Cambridge University Press, Cambridge.

Capper, L. (1986), 'A Philosophy for the Teaching of Computer Science and Information Technology', *The Computer Journal* **29, 1**.

Dickson, G., Leitheiser, R., and Wetherbe, J. (1984), 'Key Information Systems Issues for the 1980s', *MIS Quarterly* **8, 3**.

Earl, M. J. (1983), 'Emerging Trends in Managing New Information Technologies', in Piercy, N. (ed.), *The Management Implications of New Information Technologies*, Croom Helm.

—— (1987), 'Information Systems Strategy Formulation', in Boland, R. J., and Hirschheim, R. (eds.) *Critical Issues in Information Systems Research*, J. Wiley & Sons.

——, Feeny, D. F., Hirschheim, R., and Lockett, M. (1986), *Information Technology Executives' Key Education and Development Needs: A Field Study*, Oxford Institute of Information Management research paper RDP 86/10, Templeton College, Oxford.

Martin, J. (1984), *An Information Systems Manifesto*, Prentice–Hall, Englewood Cliffs, NJ.

McFarlan, F. W., and McKenney, J. (1983), *Corporate Information Systems Management: The Issues facing Senior Executives*, Irwin Press, Homewood, Ill.

Nunamaker, J., Conger, J., and Davis, G. (1982), 'Information Systems Curriculum: Recommendations for the 80s', *Communications of the ACM* **25, 11**.

15

Rebuilding the Human Resources of Information Systems

PETER G. W. KEEN

International Center for Information Technology, Washington DC

Introduction

For the next decade, the main management problems concerning telecommunications and computers will relate to people, not technology. Firms face three main challenges:

1. To build a new level of management awareness so that business executives lead, not delegate, the development of IT.
2. To mobilize the entire organization for an era of radical change in work, structure, and business practices created via IT.
3. To reposition the Information Services (IS) function to handle a far broader range of roles, responsibilities, relationships, and skills.

These three challenges are interdependent, and in each area senior management vision, and policy and education are critical resources. They are especially critical once IT is recognized as a strategic resource.

This paper focuses on the third issue: building the skill base needed in repositioning the IS organization. It provides specific recommendations for action:

1. Bring together the generally disparate units handling systems development and voice and data communications.
2. Identify the critical roles IS must fill to meet its mission over the next 3–7 years.
3. Define the new career trajectories and provide needed lateral development and education—and re-education.
4. Re-evaluate recruiting options and recruiters.

The Traditional IS Skill Base

In most organizations, IS—or 'Data Processing', 'Information Services', 'Information Systems', etc.—has been built around the traditional core of technical work: designing, developing, and running large application systems. The mainstream career path has been from computer programmer and/or systems analyst to project leader to 'manager'. There have been clear differences in relative status within IS:

1. *System programmers* have for a long time been the technical elite, because of their knowledge of the most complex aspect of business computing: mainframe operating systems.
2. *Application development* has been the central activity in terms of both how work is organized and managed and career opportunities.
3. *Operations* is definitely lower status.

The Information Systems and Telecommunications organizations have developed along very separate paths. Telecommunications has largely been built around voice services and operations, with relatively little overlap of skills with IS, even though more and more aspects of computing are interdependent with telecommunications. As a result, in many, perhaps even most organizations, IS professionals know relatively little about communications, most voice specialists are unfamiliar with data communications, and many telecommunications experts do not understand high-volume, large-scale transaction processing.

This adds up to a recipe for disaster. The entire direction of Information Technologies (IT) is towards 'integration' of computing and communications. This makes it vital that voice and data communications and information systems be brought under the same organizational umbrella.

That is easy to accomplish. What is far more damaging to Information Services is that its traditional skill base and corresponding career structure are too narrow and inflexible to meet the new demands it faces:

1. *System programmers* are only one part of a technical service unit which has to cover a bewildering range of technologies, where there is little experience and rapid change. Just a few examples are shown in Fig. 15.1.
2. *Application development* is no longer the dominating aspect of IS work. End user computing, office technology, personal computers, packaged systems, distributed processing, electronic publishing and the like are transforming the role of IS from building systems to supporting product and service innovation.
3. *Maintenance*, far from being lower in status than development, often requires the very best technical talent. In an era of online customer service and electronic support for more and more aspects of business, the quality of operations, reliability, service, and efficiency depend increasingly on old computer systems that were never designed to handle today's volumes and demands for fast, reliable service. 'Maintenance' is really management of a critical business capital asset.

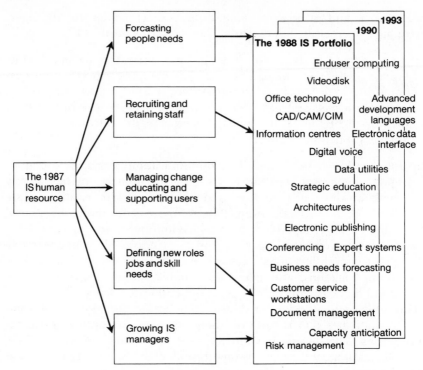

Fig. 15.1. Examples of Emerging Technologies and Their Uses Requiring New Skills

4. *Operations* similarly have become a strategic skill area. When a bank's ATM network or an airline's reservation system is down, so is its business. The complexity of such systems makes diagnosis, troubleshooting and emergency action a new element in business planning and decision making and needs new skills.

Roles Versus Tasks

Building the skill base has to begin by defining the roles IS must fill. On the whole, IS professionals' work and career development have been based on tasks, rather than roles. The difference is important for IS. Tasks relate to what people do and the content knowledge they need; roles relate to how they operate. The task of traditional systems development mainly required knowledge of COBOL, particular hardware and operating systems environments and techniques for design, coding and testing. Technical experience was the main criterion for career growth.

Many types of system development now require a far broader set of attitudes, skills and processes than before:

1. Close interaction at all stages of development with nontechnical 'users'.
2. Business and functional knowledge.
3. Understanding of nontechnical aspects of the context of the system: work, workers, and working, ergonomics, organizational procedures, etc.
4. The ability to communicate and listen well, and to act as an educator and a consultant.

Thus the *role* of development support is broader than the *task* of applications development.

For many IS professionals, the new requirements create ambiguity and stress. In particular, the more senior ones have spent up to twenty years learning their craft, only to hear that the rules are being changed. How do they adapt? How does management help them do so? Almost all the training they are given focuses on tasks and technology. Whenever the technology changes or a major new vendor product is launched, they are given a course or a manual. Job ads provide a check list of the desired task skills: 'At least five years' experience with CICs, MVS, COBOL. Knowledge of DB2 and C desirable.' The receive much less help on the nontechnical components of their new or emerging roles.

Role Analysis

The new IS skill base has to be defined in terms of roles, not technical tasks: 'what is the mix of skills and experience we need to operate effectively to support the business, to build a real dialogue with users, to maintain technical excellence and to provide first rate operations and service?'

It is obvious that technical experience is just one requirement in IS work; it is essential in such areas as operations, maintenance, and large scale applications but almost irrelevant in others, where technical currency is key: many aspects of data base management, digital communications, and optical storage are examples. In telecommunications, the technical experience of senior staff has often shifted from being an asset to a liability; their knowledge base mainly relates to voice communications in a regulated environment when what is needed now is the ability to manage digital communications and its integration with computing in a multi-vendor context in a period of massive technical uncertainty. Again, their role, not just their task has changed.

Their are two main dimensions, each of which has two subcategories, relevant to all existing and emerging IS roles:

A. Technical
  1. Breadth of technical experience
  2. Currency of technical speciality

B. Business/Organizational
  3. Business and functional knowledge
  4. Organizational skills.

A simple and reliable base for assessing the balance among the four very different skills needed in a particular role is to rate the demands on a scale of 0–5, where:

  0 = irrelevant, no need for this skill
  1 = of very minor importance; a small degree of exposure, experience helpful but not required
  2 = minor importance
  3 = basic competence/qualification needed
  4 = high level of capability required
  5 = absolutely essential; a critical requirement.

Roles can then be classified by generating two totals—one combining the two technical subcategories and one for the business/organizational ones. Ratings (hypothetical) are shown in Table 15.1 for four very different—and important—IS roles:

The four resulting role categories are defined on the following basis as summarized in Fig. 15.3.

Table 15.1. *Hypothetical Ratings of Importance of Technical and Business/Organizational Skills in four different IS Roles*

	(1) Data communications technical support	(2) Office technology analyst	(3) Application development	(4) Business unit IS planning
A. Technical				
1. Breadth of experience	3	2	4	2
2. Currency of specialization	5	3	4	2
Total: (T)	8	5	8	4
B. Business/ Organizational				
3. Business/ functional knowledge	3	4	3	5
4. Organizational skills	1	5	2	5
Total: (B/O)	4	9	5	10
Role category:	Development support	Business support	Technical services	Business services

1. *Technical services:* Here the score for the two technical aspects of IS work are greater than for the business/organizational ones, which add up to less than 5. This means that the business/organizational ratings averaged out to 'of minor importance.' The example shown above was for data communications technical support. There, currency of specialized knowledge is vital, with reasonable breadth of experience. Organizational skills—communication, the ability to act as a translator between the worlds of business and technology, understanding of work and workers, etc.—are entirely subordinate to technical excellence.
2. *Development support:* Here, the technical components of the role are rated higher than the business and organizational, but the latter are of more than minor importance (i.e. the score is greater than or equal to 5). Traditional applications development put little if any weight on nontechnical skills and much of the career ambiguity IS professionals now face comes from the acknowledged need for knowledge of the business and organization. It can be very hard for experienced systems development staff to acquire this late in their careers.
3. *Business support:* Many of the new IS roles require strong business and organizational expertise and only limited technical skills. In many instances, breadth of experience is either not obtainable because the technology or application is so new or not valuable because the pace of change makes it obsolescent. Both technical experience and specialization are less important than their business and organization counterparts in many areas of support to end user computing, office technology, and business product and service development.

   Business support roles are ones where there is a need for business fluency and technical literacy—this is indicated by the 'B/O' score being greater than that for 'T', which in turn is five or greater.
4. *Business services:* The fourth role category requires only limited technical capability and mainly related to such areas as setting priorities for business unit IS plans, customer service, financial analysis, etc.

Baseline Analysis of Roles

Figure 15.2 summarizes the role categories. It contains some important implicit message for IS professionals:

1. The main career directions are towards Development Support and Business Support, in client service, through the equivalent of account management and in project co-ordination.
2. For people whose training and experience have taken them along a largely technical path, it is very hard to move across categories; many

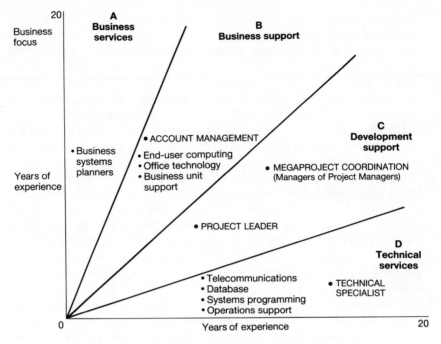

Key

A. **Business services:** Strong business/organizational skills; technical skills of minor importance

B. **Business support:** Strong business/organizational skills; fairly strong technical skills

C. **Development support:** Strong technical; fairly strong business/ technical

D. **Technical services:** Very strong technical; business/organizational skills of minor importance

Fig. 15.2. Summary of Major Role Categories

project leaders are being pushed towards Business Support and lack adequate people management skills and knowledge of business essentials.

3. We no longer have room for average technicians; IS people either have to build business and organizational skills or make sure they maintain technical currency.

4. There are no career 'paths' now, only career trajectories.

5. We are changing the rules on IS people:

Experience may no longer be an asset,

Old skills are not as valued as before,

Seniority does not mean qualification,

The 'hybrid' roles that involve a mix of technical and business/

organizational skills create career ambiguity; there are no precedents, measurement of performance is hard, and IS professionals run the risk of losing their technical edge while not becoming 'real' business people.

The starting point for repositioning IS is to develop a set of appropriately defined roles. 'Appropriate' relates to the firms' business plans and the mission for IS within the plans over the next 3–5 years, defined in terms of priorities, service and relationships with IS's clients. The specific basis for identifying new roles and redefining old ones is the IS strategic development portfolio: the planned major development projects in the IS capital budget.

This baseline analysis does not take more than a few weeks to develop; the goal is to identify roles not write detailed job descriptions. Examples follow of a role description, developed in a major bank and the main roles the bank identified; over half of these are new.

EXAMPLE OF A ROLE DESCRIPTION

ROLE CATEGORY: Development support
ROLE: Systems Asset management

Description:
This is a very new role, that has to be carefully positioned and explained. It changes the status of 'maintenance' from the bottom of the ladder to an elite position. The role of a system asset manager is to take responsibility for a key operational system and to make sure that it is economically effective and efficient. This means trouble-shooting, restructuring bad design, cleaning up code, assessing opportunities to improve technical performance and operational efficiency, etc.

Level in the organization:
Relatively senior. Generally at the level of project manager. In a few instances the person in this role is the equivalent of the megaproject manager (sytems reinvestment for DDA and VISA processing might be future instances). The most technical of the development support roles.

Importance to the bank's competitive plans:
Vital. The investment in old systems that were not designed to handle today's volumes and that are poorly documented and structured is immense. Many of these are basic to customer service (ATM code is an obvious instance). Maintenance and operations costs for such systems are growing in absolute and relative terms. They have to be managed as an economic asset and the best development staff assigned as a privilege and career opportunity not as a perceived punishment.

Recruiting source:
From within Development Support and on occasions Technical Services.

Background and skills needed:
Experience with the system or group of systems is essential. Needs solid development skills and experience. Needs fairly good business knowledge about the

context of the relevant systems and ability to work well with user department staff.

Type of contract:
Mainstream of IS. Generally, taking on this role means that the person intends to move up through Development Support or into Technical Services roles and not into Business Support.

Education and personal development priorities:
Structured methods, systems redesign and reinvestment tools.

Career quadrant:
Estimate of skill needs (0–5):

Broad technical experience	4
Currency in technical specialization	4
Business/functional knowledge	3
Organizational/personal skills	3

ROLE SET FOR A LEADING BANK

Business Services
  Business measurement and performance analysis
  Capacity anticipation
  Business unit planning support
  Economic planning: Funding, costing, and pricing analysis
  High-payoff opportunity analysis
  Corporate information architecture
  Vendor relationship management
  Human asset planning
  Work environment planning

Business support
  Systems account management
  Customer marketing and service support
  Education and training support
  Computer-related risk assessment
  Business systems standard and policies support
  Information lilbrary co-ordination

Development support
  Megaproject co-ordination
  Project leadership
  Development support
  Systems asset management
  Quality assurance

Technical services
  Architecture and integration planning
  Computing utility specialist services
  Computing utility operations services
  Specialist technical support
  Technology scanning and evaluation

The example role description includes assessment of recruiting source(s), type of contract, and education and personal development priorities.

Each of these is an important element in moving from the baseline analysis of roles to human resource planning; the baseline often mainly reveals the gap between available skills and needed ones. The issue is then how to close it. There are three main areas when management can take action:

1. recruiting policy—and choice of recruiter,
2. lateral development and movement in and out of IS from/to business units,
3. education and personal development.

Recruiting

IS units have always been short of good development staff and technical specialists. To a large extent, that problem has been compounded by the emphasis placed on technical 'aptitude' and on experience. Firms have tended to recruit graduates with technical degrees and to head hunt for people already in the IS field. Firms that invested heavily in entry-level training often found that they were largely creating a pipeline into other companies who would pay a premium for the people they grow.

It is surely time to rethink recruiting. The old assumption was that the technology was hard to learn—and by implication, the business was easier to learn. It is no exaggeration to say that now *any* person with strong analytic ability—needed to manage the constant process of learning and personal development that marks the shifting IS roles, technology, applications, and business demands—is useful to and usable in IS.

The liberal arts major who can easily handle the unstructured nature of support of office technology, the accountant who can develop pricing strategies, or the financial staff member who can help end users develop their own systems on personal computer, can easily learn enough about the relevant technology to be effective. They will rarely be able to, or want to, become Development Support Specialists working on large scale COBOL projects or designing complex data bases, but they are far more likely to feel comfortable in their support and service role than a traditional applications programmer pushed into it—and out of his or her chosen career niche.

Figure 15.3 complements the role descriptions given above. It shows two career time boundaries, one at roughly 4 years and one at 7. IS recruits have plenty of opportunity to find their own niche and to explore the variety of role categories in their first four years, with very little career risk. They are unlikely to become square pegs in round holes because every skill can be usefully employed.

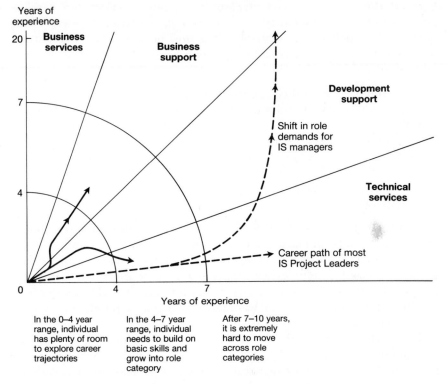

Fig. 15.3.   Career Time Boundaries

In the 4–7 year range, they need to learn their craft and sharpen their sense of career direction. Very roughly the development priorities are:

Business Service: solid grounding in business planning, knowledge of a functional area and exposure to business unit(s) at a fairly senior level.

Business Support: exposure to the business at a nuts-and-bolts level, development of organizational skills and close working relationships with the user community.

Development Support: experience on large-scale projects, education and experience with software productivity methods, development aids and project management methods (especially user-led ones).

Technical Services: continued indepth education in their chosen field of expertise, membership of professional societies, and exposure to relevant developments in related fields, so that they do not get locked into a narrow area that leads to technical obsolescence.

If people can grow into their roles over a four-year period, it is no longer essential that they fit the traditional profile when they are recruited at entry level. Of course, a computer science graduate is more likely to want to move along a Technical Services career trajectory but the opportunity is there to shift towards Development and Business Support. Similarly, the senior secretary assigned to IS to help train office staff in word processing may well build a much broader knowledge of office technology: electronic publishing, optical storage, document interchange, intelligent OCR, etc., etc.

This argument goes against the established belief that computer people are somehow 'different' from others and technical aptitude is a basic requirement for entry to the field. Obviously, most aspects of Technical Services do involve unusual and idiosyncratic skills. Data modelling, network design, and programming at the 'hacker' level are just a few examples. The new importance of the support roles must not divert attention from the equal importance of first-rate technical talent in an environment where the business is online, so that technical risk is now business risk and quality of customer service a function of quality of computer and communications operations.

That said, broadening the recruiting sources is the only way both to locate good people in a market of scarcity of qualified staff in traditional tasks and to bring in the new attitudes, knowledge and aptitude required for the hybrid support roles. There is plenty of evidence, albeit fragmented and anecdotal that this approach works. For example:

1. One of the top five computer manufacturers successfully imple mented a program of internal recruitment. It selected a small group of secretaries, junior clerical workers and others who were 'non-except' personnel—hourly wage earners with no degrees or professional qualifications. They were moved through a 20-week training program which taught them the best of structured analysis and design techniques. They were then moved into IS, where a review two years later showed they were rated as significantly above average in their performance. The firm has since repeated the program several times, with the same result.

2. Several firms in the petrochemical industry, which has generally been a leader in IS organizational developments and in the application of effective development tools (an example is Exxon's SADT—Structured Analysis and Design Technique) have moved away from their earlier recruiting of computer science graduates into Technical Service roles because of the vital need for infusion of business attitudes.

3. Many banks now have a strong cadre of Development Support Specialists with strong technical expertise in data management, advanced personal computing (mainframe–micro links, specialist development languages like C, and local area networks rather than just spreadsheets). These people have never been in IS and have no formal technical training. They are finance or accounting staff who have shaped a new Business and Development Support role, largely self-directed.

Many firms are also recognizing that, since knowledge of the organizations—and credibility with users—is a primary requirement in many Support roles, the best source of recruitment into IS is from elsewhere in the company. Technical currency and experience is largely organization-independent. A systems programmer is probably close to being fully effective on joining the firm; his or her knowledge of IBM mainframe operating systems translates directly to the new context. It takes at least two years and probably closer to four to build organization-dependent experience. Figure 15.4 shows the relative impact of the difference in terms of both the productivity of recruits and the cost of losing existing staff; the salary for the systems programmer is higher than for the office technology support role, but the true cost of growing and of having to replace the latter is far higher because of the hidden cost of building organizational experience (the figures shown are only hypothetical, but reasonable).

Clearly, IS units can and should recruit aggressively from inside the organization. They will still, of course, need to bring in people from outside, especially for Technical services and many Development Support roles, where technical aptitude or experience are at a premium. If the recommendation made earlier is accepted, they will place a special emphasis on bringing into Business Support, at the entry-level, people with business not technical training.

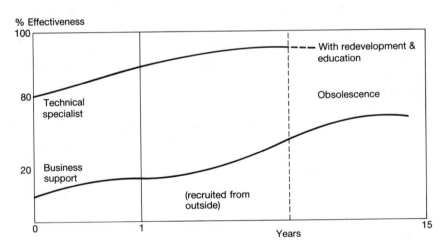

How effective is this person (or role):   When hired?
                                          after 1 year?

What is it worth to keep him/her 1 extra year?
What 'maintenance' is needed?
How much more effective would a business support individual recruited from within a business unit be than one brought in from the outside?

Fig. 15.4.   The Recruit's Learning Curve

All this makes the IS recruiter an important element in recruiting. In general, the middle to senior level IS manager and project leaders who meet with potential hires, explain the firm and the organization to them and evaluate them, come out of the old career tradition; too many of them are not natural managers and not sensitive to nontechnical issues—or in some cases to the need for people management skills. They will naturally tend to recruit in their own image and attract recruits who are on the same wavelength as themselves. With the best will in the world, the old guard of IS can be a substantial blockage to changing the IS culture. It may be more effective to have users play an active role in recruiting Business Support staff.

Lateral Development

Just as recruiting from within the organization brings in business and organizational skills onto which some technical ability can be built, moving IS personnel out into users areas for a six-month to two-year period builds Support skills on technical ones. The best IS organizations have increasingly moved their best people out—but have not got them back. They are a net exporter of talent.

The two-way flow in and out of IS has to be brought into balance. Senior management support is needed, though, to make this happen and to speed up the cross-fertilization of IS and business people. Movement into and out of IS has to be seen as career enhancement not some form of punishment.

Figure 15.5 illustrates the problem of career ambiguity. 'Fast-track' managers or outstanding supervisors who are pulled off their main-stream business trajectory to work on assignment to IS are likely to see themselves falling behind their peers while at the same time not becoming an IS professional—or accepted by IS professionals. Similarly, an applications programmer with a solid technical resume will feel that he or she is less marketable or promotable by being moved into the area of 'amateur' computing.

Senior management has to establish that IT is now so central to the firm that a subset of the future management cadre will be routinely given the lateral development that creates hybrids. Just as Development and Business Support within IS balances technical fluency and business literacy, there is no longer room for technically illiterate business managers in key positions.

It is largely too late for the 40-year olds to get lateral development. This means making a senior IS project leader a neophyte finance analyst, or a senior finance executive a bungling pseudoprogrammer. The ideal time for the cross-cultural assignment seems to be 2–3 years after the entry-level position, when the individual has learnt the IS craft

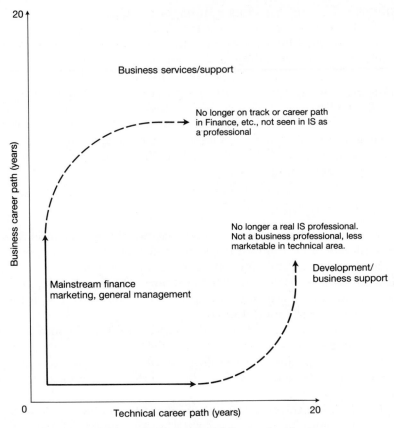

Fig. 15.5.   The Problem Of Career Ambiguity

or functional area basics. A six-month to two-year transfer is early enough not to disturb career development and late enough to build on proven mainstream skills. When the person returns to home base, the individual is credible in both cultures and adds something special and valuable in his or her career trajectory. But, unless senior management endorses or even enforces this very new philosophy of lateral development, there is minimal incentive for people to make the move and maximum career ambiguity in doing so.

Education

Most IS professionals are undereducated for their roles—old or new.

They need to be treated like machines. Firms look after computing and communications machinery very well. They generate forecasts, monitor products, and spend substantial money on maintenance. They need to maintain IS people, too; investment in education is the equivalent of maintenance. It is essential to IS professionals in avoiding depreciation of their skill base. There are three types of education, which; have to be related to the individual's role and career trajectory:

Maintenance: 'I need to know about this to keep up in my job'.
Development: 'I must acquire this as part of the knowledge to move ahead in my career.'
Innovation: 'This is not something everyone in my job needs but is important for my own personal growth'.

Education programs for IS people need to be largely individually determined, because of the new roles, the lack of precedents for promotion and career development, the breadth of skills, technologies, and applications they imply, and the lack of any standard career path and hence education program. What, for example, is the career path for the applications programmer moved into a Development Support role in an Information Centre? What does he or she need to know? The job has never existed before, and will be shaped by the individual's initiative, personality, and ability.

Very roughly, Maintenance education mainly relates to updates on emerging technologies, and to education on business basics and design, development, and implementation methods. Development Education is more concerned in most instances with advanced technical training for Technical Service roles and management education in Support roles. That education has to be provided *before* it is needed in the individual's work. Many IS project leaders are having to acquire management skills through vicarious trial-and-error, *ad hoc* learning. They often recognize they lack managerial skills and even managerial attitudes but all they can do is try, and hope.

The following list sketches out examples of education topics needed to build the new IS cadre. For someone in Business Support, a program on managing change and on understanding the human side of systems, 'Technology and People', is Maintenance. For someone in Development Support, it is not so immediately relevant but may be needed later as Development Education. It may be irrelevant to most professionals in Technical Service but be an innovative option for, say, a IS data base specialist interested in trying to work with Marketing to use data modelling as a tool for product development (this example is especially relevant to financial services and airlines where 'products' are increasingly information-based).

Education in IS

Topic Areas:	Maintenance? Development? Innovative?

Topic Areas:
Technology and people
Digital telecommunications
Practical state of the art in network
  management
Development productivity tools
Selecting a 4th generation language
Business data modelling
Systems management skills
The effective consultant
Architecture and integration
Competitive uses of IT
Financial dynamics of IT

Barriers to Education

IS professionals need to spend 10% of their time—half a day a week-on education. They rarely do so, because of the many barriers:

Logistics: They are too busy to take three days to two weeks off from work to attend a course.

Quality: There is a vast range of available external courses but they vary widely in quality and it is hard to assess them from the brochures.

Topics: The courses are rarely well tailored to the individual's needs.

Management: Access to education for junior people in IS often depends on the importance their supervisors place on education and monitoring their own staff.

Cost: Quality education is expensive in terms of direct costs and the indirect ones of travel and time away.

These barriers can obviously be removed by:

1. A formal policy requiring all IS professionals to spend 10% of their time on education.
2. A formal plan for education based on individuals' stated needs in terms of Maintenance, Development, and Innovation, their supervisors' assessments, their role definitions, and a survey of the best education programs being provided by universities, vendors, and consulting firms.
3. In the longer term, the use of Information Technology to improve the logistics and cost of education through video-conferencing, which reduces travel and scheduling demands, allows the cost of education to be shared by a number of units (or firms) through point-to-multipoint communications and to allow the far too small supply of

top rate educators to reach a wider audience than at present. Video-conferencing is immensely underexploited as a vehicle for accelerated education.

Summary: Recommendation for Action

Repositioning the IS organization for its new, broad, business-focused mission is essential—now. The ability of firms to exploit IT depends increasingly on people, not money, hardware, software, or tools. The key steps to take are:

1. Bring together telecommunications and information systems—if that has not already been done—into an overall Information Services organization.
2. Carry out a baseline analysis of the roles implicit in the firm's business plan and explicit in the IS mission and its capital project portfolio.
3. Use the role definitions to establish the equal importance and prestige of maintenance and operations and to give clear signals to IS staff about the new skills they must build—with support from management through lateral development and education—and the new expectations about service, performance, and career development the roles imply.
4. Encourage IS professionals to think through very clearly their own skill base, education needs, and career trajectory.
5. Set up a process for lateral development and movement into and out of IS.
6. Set up a process for internal recruitment.
7. Re-evaluate entry-level recruiting (and recruiters) in relation to role needs.
8. Establish an ongoing education plan, with responsibility for it clearly defined; this is not a part-time or *ad hoc* assignment.
9. Recognize that, if your firm is typical, the middle-level IS managers and project leaders are likely to be a major blockage to change. They have moved through an obsolescent technocentric career path, lack management education, are often unconvinced or even ignorant of the need to shift from a focus on traditional systems development to service and partnership with 'users', and are also lacking in knowledge about emerging technologies, end user tools and user-centred or user-managed project development methods. Getting them to buy in to the principles and recommendations made here is a priority and may not be easy. A prerequisite is to make sure they get education in the basics of management and of the business.

IT and Strategy:
Reflections and Directions

16

Information Management: Some Strategic Reflections

MICHAEL J. EARL

Oxford Institute of Information Management, Templeton College, Oxford

The purpose of this *denouement* is to reflect on some of the themes evident in the book, particularly taking into account discussions at the conference which begat this volume and ten months' experience since then. Some directions for research and practice are offered *en route*.

Perhaps six issues stand out in the summer of 1987. These are represented by the following questions, each a paraphrase of observations increasingly heard in recent months.

1. Are claims about *competitive advantage* and IT overdone?
2. Is IT beginning to run out of *corporate support*?
3. Is *information systems strategic planning* worthwhile?
4. Is *innovation* the key?
5. Isn't it *organizational issues* which are crucial?
6. Has any business solved the *educational challenge* in information management?

These questions are discussed in turn.

Competitive Advantage

Whilst many practitioners admit that IT is being used as a competitive weapon they frequently are sceptical about deriving any marked competitive advantage from IT. Four doubts seem to underpin this scepticism.

First, they opine that 'we are just not like American Hospital Supply ... or Merrill Lynch ... or Thomson Travel, etc.' 'our customers are not so naive ... we are not so information dependent ... we can't sell our product like packaged holidays.' These are not necessarily simple regrets that their particular business cannot just emulate one of the exemplar strategic information systems, but they are frequently claims that their businesses are quite different, more complex and perhaps more 'serious'.

However one often finds that these sceptics and their colleagues, have not attempted a serious analysis of the competitive forces they face and highlighted where competitive advantage opportunities may exist—to be followed up, of course, by detailed investigation using opportunity frameworks of analysis. What often seems to be overlooked is that the American Hospital Supply success was built (incrementally over several years) around both supply and demand factors that were special to them and their sector. So every organization has to ask what are the special factors *they* face. This point is developed later.

The second concern is that competitive advantage seems to be ephemeral. 'We introduce a new banking product and the others copy it within weeks'. There are a number of issues here. In particular, it is useful to refer to King's distinction between competitive weapons, which he portrays as ephemeral tactical uses of IT in the market place, and strategic uses of IT, which are aimed at achieving sustainable comparative advantage. It is likely that many, if not most, competitive strikes achieved through IT will be ephemeral if they are not conceived of, and implemented, strategically. IT and information are but one or two factors in the multivariate context of the marketplace. A competitive idea conceived around these two factors also must be sound in terms of other competitive forces, timing and industry dynamics for it to achieve sustainable competitive advantage. Ghemawat (1986) has argued that for competitive advantage to be sustainable, whatever its base, any one or more of the following factors must be favourable to the initiator: benefits of size, superior access to resources or customers, or restrictions on competitors' options. In other words IT capability and creativity may offer potential competitive advantage, but they are not sufficient in themselves if sustainable competitive advantage is the aim.

The implication of this observation therefore is, again, that detailed analysis of competitive forces is required before embarking on, or approving, any IT-based competitive strike—if it is to be mroe than an emphemeral weapon. Just as important, however, given that IT-based competitive weapons could just turn out to have more strategic potential than first conceived (and given that much innovation is incremental and/or by chance), is the need to appraise and re-appraise IT-based competitive weapons to see if they can be further exploited for sustainable advantage. Good questions to ask include: are we managing complementary competitive forces to get the most out of this IT weapon and can the weapon be modified or enhanced to build around the conditions of the marketplace now prevailing? Our investigations at Oxford often find that managements have not realized the full strategic potential of an IT-based weapon, because they have not properly or creatively analysed its possibilities for enhancing or limiting existing competitive forces at work.

Of course it could be that in some sectors 'competitive advantage' is mostly ephemeral. As one retailer put it, 'we often create a new product or standard of service which the customers value and the competitors admire. One year later everybody has copied us and all we have done is innovated for the sector'. There would seem to be at least four possibilities raised by this third doubt:

1. This is the natural state of the sector, only to be expected in very competitive markets, and the truly competitive advantage strike through IT would be to radically change the market structure and basis of competition. (However, the retailer quoted may be pursuing a differentiation strategy by perpetually being perceived as innovative and the market-definer.)

2. To reject all uses of IT for competitive edge, however ephemeral, might eventually create competitive disadvantage—especially if this particular player was creating a perception of innovatory leadership. Indeed the rivals presumably felt disadvantaged if they continually strove to copy the innovator.

3. The IT strikes that initially create competitive edge may have further potential within them. King hints that it is information that often provides added value, whereas it is the technology that often seems to be the initial base for the competitive move. Indeed there seem to be several well known cases of firms who have changed the basis of competition through a strategic information system, but subsequently have failed to maintain their advantage because rivals have not only followed them but have improved the system or service and leapfrogged the now complacent first mover.

4. Detailed strategic analysis—as argued earlier—was done neither originally nor once the competitive weapon was in place and its effect observable.

The fourth common doubt about competitive advantage is more one of outright senior management rejection or disbelief. 'Competitive advantage was invented by the business schools and consultants to raise the profile of IT and all it has done is create unrealistic expectations which can't be met' was the comment of one IT Director recently. Certainly, we should all discount the hype of recent years, but there is sufficient evidence of equilibrium in market places being disturbed by IT developments to give the competitive advantage serious thought and attention. At Oxford in the last year, we have had two companies seek help in information management education because they have been disadvantaged by rivals using IT competitively. A third company with whom we have been working now realizes that it is not achieving its IT plans quickly enough as both its rivals and customers embrace IT boldly and rapidly.

Indeed we find increasingly that executives who are close to competitive forces can quote very quickly examples of suppliers, rivals, customers, or new entrants who are making IT strikes. Commonly these executives do not realize how much time and effort will be required either to react or to make similar moves. Indeed this is one of the attractive features of IT as a competitive weapon. It cannot always be copied quickly and easily.

Furthermore there often turns out to be a more profound gap in the doubting companies thinking and actions. Their existing business strategies are not being supported by either existing information systems or applications under development. For many firms today, lack of relatively humble, basic operational systems to support their overall business strategy, or new strategic thrust, or critical success factors is a major capability exposure. Such systems may be just as strategic as some clever exploitation of new technology delivering a value added service to a new customer set. In other words in sectors where business is either being redefined by IT or is dependent on IT, poor systems can be a competitive disadvantage and impair survival. So before dismissing the concept of IT for competitive advantage, top managers might ask three questions:

1. How would we be caught out by our rivals?
2. Do those close to the competitive forces know of any competitive uses of IT in the market place now?
3. Are our business strategies properly supported by information systems?

Overall, the four doubts about competitive advantage discussed here suggest the following directions for practice and research:

1. *Non-IT factors* must also be analysed when considering use of IT for competitive advantage; researchers need to inform us more about the salient conditions for success and how they relate to IT.
2. Competitive advantage may be ephemeral; to be sustainable it may have to be worked for continuously, manipulating both IT and non-IT factors; IT researchers perhaps need to guide us—as both King and Feeny have started to in this volume—on what are the *unique and sustainable* qualities that IT and information bring to competitive strategy.
3. When formulating business strategies, executives should ask what new strategic options does IT offer and what IT systems support do our new strategies demand; researchers therefore need to continue to develop *frameworks* which help the search for opportunities and IS strategy formulation *methods* which bridge the gap between business strategies and systems development.

Corporate Support

For many years it has been fashionable to quote lack of 'top management support' as an impediment to successful development and use of information systems. This term can mean many things to all concerned—and yet it seems to describe something that is commonly missing in the information systems area. More recently, there has been concern about 'middle management buy-in' (Keen, 1986), recognizing that major change facilitated by IT requires the understanding, support, involvement, and action of rafts of executives across companies. There is in 1987 emerging, I detect, a more subtle but equally important problem: *disappearance of 'corporate support'.* What does this mean?

First there is the funding question. In many companies who would place themselves in the turnaround or strategic quadrants of McFarlan *et al.*'s (1983) strategic grid, expenditure on IT has been growing at 60 to 100% p.a. compound in the last three years. For many others, growth rates of 20% to 40% p.a. for several years are common. Now this raises four doubts at corporate levels: (1) can we afford for this to continue? (2) We thought it was for one or two years and then would fall away. (3) Which other function is growing like this? (4) Have we seen the benefits yet? Each of these doubts can be addressed at some length—but the overall impression is clear. Many corporate managements neither expected, nor are content with, ongoing expenditure on IT at current levels. Thus IT management has a challenge to manage corporate expectations and achieve politically a balance between efficient management of IT as an expense and effective managment of IT as an investment! The help that researchers and consultants can give therefore would seem to be to:

1. Offer some guidance on what revenue and capital expenditure on IT can be expected in different sectors and situations over time—not current norms but predictive frameworks based on technological economics of supply and use.
2. Develop better, but practical, methods for evaluating the economic impact of IT investments both *ex ante* and *ex post.* One suspects that more strategic management of IT might help on both these appraisal problems, particularly qualitative as well as quantitative evaluation, but organizations probably need numbers for comfort.

The second corporate support problem is 'understanding'. It has been fashionable to talk of 'IT awareness' and I would doubt if there are many corporate managements of large organizations who have not been made aware of the importance of IT by sundry events and experiences. However, there are many IT executives who worry that 'there is corporate awareness of something but little understanding of what is involved and what they should do'. At the same time of course, 'I don't want the board telling me how to do my job and run the function'. This often seems to be an extreme case of the R&D management problem. Companies recognize R&D is important, know little about it, and hope they can leave most of the worrying to the R&D division, as long as it does not ask for too much money. The difference is that information systems and IT are pervasive, require management involvement at all stages, and are more exposed to day-by-day pressures.

What IT managers ask for is informed corporate attitudes when IT proposals are made, business-oriented direction and guidance, constructive support for technology policies, and relevant evaluation of performance. Often they feel their corporate managements deserve far worse IT than they are getting and that the same arguments and discussions about the need for, or importance of, IT are repeated every other year. Increasingly therefore IT Directors find themselves 'educating and re-educating' their corporate colleagues about IT and its management. Indeed a very recent trend seems to be requests to consultants and academics along the lines of 'could you come and talk to my chief executive about IT and what he should be worrying about'. This sort of request was common three to four years ago—perhaps there is a cycle at work, a point developed later. Equally, of course, IT Directors become lonely in this context and also find the need to test out their thoughts on gurus and advisors, sometimes as a validation test before engaging corporate management, sometimes to act as a general manager in the absence of the real ones who are sufficiently informed.

There are no obvious research needs suggested by this phenomenon. However, there is a clear requirement of management education and development. It seems likely that education can achieve awareness and some understanding—but the recurring lack of corporate understanding discussed here would seem to be borne of inexperience and inattention. In other words, in an information era, should not every manager in a sense be an information manager and have had experience of using and managing IT at different levels throughout his or her management development? In this way information management might be perceived by managers as no different than any other management activity.

The final corporate support problem relates to the cyclical phenomenon raised earlier. It often seems that major, stepped—even strategic—changes in the profile of information management occur in a rapid transition process driven by a very few pioneers who saw a need, opportunity, or threat, sensed the timing was right and relatively speaking moved mountains. They probably fully understood neither the scale nor the consequences of their initiative.

Three or four years on, a new scenario dawns. The pioneering group has moved on—dispersed around the organization, changing jobs, with only the IT Director remaining in place. As the spending on IT grows, the benefits are flowing but are often camouflaged by other factors. Some systems are still awaited and yet the IT function is becoming impatient for resolution of one or two vital technology policy issues. In short, original corporate support and drive is now found to have evaporated. It may now either be replaced by quite formal structures, which ask all the old questions again, or alternatively be nowhere to be found, so that the organizational infrastructure has gone. The IT Director now has to educate a new team and redevelop his host organization, but it seems a one-way process.

Meanwhile in the same period, the senior management of IT function has become both more business-oriented and more professional. At the same time, senior executives in different functions, divisions, and business units have been involved in the new IT initiatives. Both these groups know IT is important, the drive must continue, a strategy is necessary, etc. But corporately there are at best doubts and at worst no common understanding. So the challenge is how to tackle this cyclical phenomenon. The answer may well be that corporate support should be seen as a critical success factor in information management *but* that it should come from, and therefore be cultivated in, the component business units, divisions, and functions of the corporation. In other words, any top management doubts or challenges should be answered by the rest of the corporation and not just by the IT function. The IT executive therefore cultivates champions and allies all over the business.

Strategic Planning

Galliers reports from his study that most companies attempt some form of strategic IS planning, but their experience is recent and limited. There is a diversity of approaches in use, but few focus on competitive use of IT, and there is little concern with, or evidence of, which approaches suit which conditions. It seems likely therefore that strategic IS planning will evolve in a similar fashion to strategic business planning. Organizations embark upon it for a variety of partly thought-out reasons, but it takes time to sort out the appropriate methods and evaluate the benefits.

So we are at an experimental stage. Seddon reports that ICI has tried most of the well-known approaches to strategic use of IT and to strategic systems planning. Earl implies that firms should be selective in using whatever methods help, but select the methods to fit the purpose, the business or sector, and previous experience. What seems clear therefore is that consultants and researchers need to help practitioners by evaluating which methods work, which work in what circumstances, and what factors are critical for success. King, Earl, and Galliers have all made useful steps in these endeavours in this volume.

What has been happening in practice recently? My own experience is that more firms have felt the need for formulting IT/IS strategies (including many who hitherto have made strategic use of IT), many organizations have not progressed with their plans too much in twelve months, most businesses have found their business strategies inadequate—too vague, immature, uncertain, or general—as a foundation for IS strategy, and rarely has anyone found stunning competitive advantage opportunities in the process. In the meantime, demands on the IT function—and threats or doubts—have grown, but have not surfaced or been addressed through formal IS strategic planning.

It is quite difficult to make sense of this scenario. There is comfort to be drawn in that organizations still report that at least benefits of top management support, improved IS understanding of the business and better dialogue between users and specialists emerge from these planning experiments. However, one is reluctant to resort to 'the benefits are in the planning not the plans' observation. The following clues may be relevant:

1. Much of the need felt for IS and IT strategies comes from the IT function. There is a desire for direction and order. However both types of strategy are concerned with connecting IT to the business. Thus the business must be involved. It seems clear therefore that the goals and expectations of both the business managers and the IT function must be explicated and appropriate methods selected, for in the past providers and users have not always had identical views and goals.
2. Progress with plans often seems impeded by three related factors. Too much detail is sought, the emphasis is not strategic, and neither the right quality nor quantity of resource is used. However, as I report in this volume 'it does take time'.
3. Inadequate business strategies do point to the need for what I called top-down approaches to be concerned with 'clarification'— clarification of the business and its strategy. This means that top-down methodologies will be more business-oriented than techno-logical, must comprise validation steps with top management, but must also be able to help firms interpret business directions into IS opportunities and demands. Conventional business stategy methods are likely to fall short, and traditional IS planning techniques to be too low-level. Development of top-down clarification methods is still required.
4. The continued demands placed on IT, however, suggests that by whatever mechanism requirements arrive on IS development lists and

issues enter IT management agendas, they should be subjected to strategic questioning first. In other words, if ongoing IS planning and IT policy formulation is not tested at all against business strategy, most planning for IT and IS will continue to be reactive and tactical—and strategic opportunities and directions will be a matter of chance.

5. If strategic systems planning seems to produce few competitive advantage ideas for IT, either the current methods are deficient or planning is not an appropriate process for idea generation. This is discussed in the next section.

Innovation

Runge and Earl emphasize in Chapter 7 that seeking competitive advantage from IT is in many ways a process of innovation. The formal apparatus of most traditional IS management seems at odds with the conditions that Runge discovered were necessary to discover and implement new opportunities from IT. The textbooks on industrial innovation seemed more instructive. More recently Lockett has suggested that pursuit of innovation through IT needs an R&D management approach. So we can predict that information management rhetoric will be peppered with key words of 'innovation', 'entrepreneurship', 'creativity', and 'change'!

These concepts all embrace issues which are essentially organizational and easy to say and difficult to do. It is instructive to recap some of the lessons from our 'Oxford IT innovation studies' so far:

1. Product champions and sponsors matter.
2. Hybrids or IT-experienced line and staff managers help.
3. Formal planning and control can hinder.
4. Softer systems development and project methods help.
5. Ideas are often incremental and accidental.
6. Customers and competitive forces stimulate ideas.

Guidelines for the innovating IT Director therefore might include the following:

1. Organizational development is part of the brief. It is necessary to work with general management and the personnel function to help place and move champions and sponsors around the organization. The IT Director may also have to identify them and promote education for them.
2. It is also necessary to develop hybrids. Schemes which give all management trainees worthwhile IT experience and/or promote job rotation—including non-IT managers moving into the management positions in IT—are necessary. If the IT function seems to suffer a balance of trade deficit, as Keen has noted, then at least there seem to be compensating benefits for the organization as a whole.

3. Flexibility in information management is important. It is vital for many organizations that systems development priorities can be changed, there is a discretionary budget for wild hare projects, and experiments, and some risks, are taken.

4. It is important to recognize when tight methods and controls are necessary and when more relaxed, informal approaches are required. All too commonly, prototyping has lost its original experimental intent (Earl, 1978) in systems development, technology policies and standards are sought where they are not necessary, and cost constraints applied too early in technological and project life cycles.

5. Caution must be exercised when dismissing, or becoming frustrated with, the level of systems maintenance and enhancements and frequency of user requests. If many innovations are incremental and by chance, there may be as much potential competitive advantage latent in existing systems as there is to be found in new technologies and their development. Thus tools which facilitate maintenance and enhancement may be very valuable.

6. If innovations are often inspired from the outside, we have to open up the IS arena. The IT function has mainly been isolated from the market place for three decades. Those close to competitive forces—marketing and purchasing executives—have ignored, abandoned, or despaired of IT. Just as R&D are often advised by innovation scholars to build closer links with marketing and production, so must the IT function. And since customers are often the source of ideas, the IT function might treat all user departments as 'customers'—which implies bringing marketing concepts into information management. Certainly the current trend of appointing account executives is a signal that this is happening.

The tenor of all these guidelines of course, implies some quite radical management changes of structure, recruitment, performance measurement, reward, controls, and relationships. General management literature can help us here, for example Burns and Stalker (1966) on the Management of Innovation, and more recently Quinn (1980) on strategic change, and Maidique and Hayes (1984) on hi-tech management. But as in all studies of *information management* we have to be clear what is different from the general case and interpret it for our special situation.

Organization

IT Directors' concerns about organization are fairly fundamental; they are usually connected with improving the effectiveness of IS. Conveniently, they fall into three levels of analysis: organization, department, and individual.

In large UK organizations in 1987, there seem to be rapid changes being made in the structure of the information systems function. Whilst in general there appears to be a trend towards decentralization, particularly of responsibility for planning and development of information systems, movements in various directions are taking place. A complementary pattern, for example, is the centralization of telecommunications activities and with it therefore certain aspects of computing and other services. Equally, whilst in the early 1970s certain IS departments were converted into commercial profit centres, some have been 'floated off' and others brought back into the host organization. In at least two cases, group-wide information services departments are being fully decentralized overnight and in many others various hybrid federal arrangements are evolving.

In short, the structure of many information systems functions appears to be *unstable*. In this volume it is interesting to note that both Seddon and Hubinette dealt in some detail with organization structure in their accounts of corporate information management. However I wonder whether the issue of organization structure for IS has always been a concern—and furthermore always will be. There are so many factors and tensions which lie behind the question what is the appropriate organization for IS—and these change quite quickly over time and vary across enterprises. For example technological change and adoption, strategic importance of IT, host organization structure, and the current state of organizational relationships all influence what is appropriate at any time. Thus it may be helpful not to think of organizational structure for IS, but the organizational *arrangement*, which implies that an arrangement has to be worked out for all the different information technologies to fit the state of these influential factors at any time. The 'arrangement' may comprise quite a mix of relationships and structures and be continuously evolving.

This is a research area which has been neglected since the 1960s and we now have in Oxford a major project investigating the structure and management of the IS function in European companies. Some of the thinking just described is emerging from our work. Certainly it seems important that we seek to understand (a) what is the appropriate organizational arrangement for different circumstances, (b) what factors help make different arrangements effective, (c) whether there are any universal success factors to be followed in designing the effective IS arrangement.

At the departmental level, a host of concerns exist. Many are raised by Keen in this volume. I detect four crucial gaps in information resources in many UK companies. First, in many firms, including large organizations strategically dependent upon IT, there is a shortage of senior project managers. IT projects today can be large, complex in business terms, sophisticated in their use of technology, and demanding politically. In large IT departments, project managers are the key line position. Even if users are 'leading' projects, the continuous management usually falls on the IT function. Besides the observations of IT Directors, the advertisements for project managers and the increasing number of publicized write-offs or law-suits concerning IT projects, suggests that (a) we need to develop more project managers and (b) IT project management is still in need of study and development. Some healthy prescriptions, of course, can be found in Matheson's paper in this volume. And it may be that if we can understand the needs of IT project management better and develop appropriate methods, the project managers can be found and/or developed.

A second gap appears to be, curiously, lack of systems analysis skills. In several companies I know, there is a paucity of either experience or ability in analysing business and management information systems requirements. I have been tempted to ask 'Where have all the systems analysts gone?'

Possibly the skills have decayed through a decade and more of rewriting systems and maintaining them. There is emerging a new breed of IT personnel who are experimenting with and applying new techniques and applications—expert systems, boardroom communications, computer graphics and, of course, various forms of end-user computing—but often they are pushing solutions or supporting existing technologies. Possessors of the political and social abilities, the technological competence, and the business know-how which are required for detailed, radical systems analysis in areas untouched by IT for some years appear scarce. They may have to be provided by specialist consultancies as much as by in-house departments, if critical mass and optimal usage are to be achieved.

The third capability gap is what Keen and others have called hybrids. In some ways they need the skills listed above for systems analysts but crucially the hybridization is between technological competence and business know-how. Since the place for hybrids is not in the IS department but in user areas, technological *confidence* will do but business knowledge is essential. Their task is to be the product champions and sponsors referred to in the discussion of innovation. Also they are prime candidates as user leaders of projects, if they have the appropriate management skills.

In my view, hybrids must have been full-time workers in IT at some time. However as long as they retain an interest in, and sympathy with, IT it does not matter how long ago. The key requirement is that they can see where IT can contribute, they can appreciate what resources are required and know how to acquire them, and they can see an IT project through to implementation. The only development route therefore is for hybrids to spend a significant period of time in the IS department in their career development. They will not learn enough if they are enthusiastic do-it-yourself personal computer—or whatever—users.

The final resource gap is IT specialists who understand enough about the main but different branches of IT. Keen emphasises in Chapter 15 the need for professionals competent in DP and telecommunications. Another gap is in DP and automation technologies (especially manufacturing). In both cases, knowledge of old telecommunications (speech only) or old automation (instrumentation and controls) is too remote from IT. So the gap has to be filled by retraining and by a crash education programme for younger generations on IT, broadly defined.

The individual level issue of organization is the IT Director. Earl, Feeny, Hirschheim, and Lockett partially address this in Chapter 14. There are three problems: the job description, the job specification and the supply.

A number of corporations profess to be unsure as to whether they need an IT Director. Questions of status, title, position, and purpose lie behind this uncertainty, all complicated by the structural instability of the IS function discussed earlier. There is of course no general resolution of this uncertainty. The need for, and activities of, an 'IT Director' vary with the strategic importance of IT, the organizational structure and practices of the corporation, the history of information management in the organization—and to a degree the fit between the possible incumbent and his/her IT colleagues and organizational peers.

Three principal tasks seem to be expected of IT Directors:

1. business leadership—connecting use of IT with business needs and strategy,
2. technology leadership—working out appropriate technology policies for the business, keeping up with and co-ordinating information technologies,
3. functional management—having executive responsibility for the IS function and guiding its evolution.

The emphasis changes with the variables mentioned above, and thus so does the balance of personal qualities and experience required. Indeed over time, as Earl, Feeny, *et al.* suggest, the priorities change and thus so may the incumbent. Notwithstanding, we do have some evidence that cumulative information management experience and sufficient technological expertise are at least as important as business understanding.

What is becoming very clear however is that in organizations where IT is embedded in their business and sector, these IT Directors do need to have close access to, or be a member of, the board or executive committee. Recently I have met two IT Directors of companies in what I call the delivery sector—where IT has become the means of delivering the good or service and the sector's infrastructure is IT—who have no presence at board level. In one case he is under severe cost constraints when more investment is vital. In the second case the IT function is likely to be rationalized into an emasculated rag-bag of management services.

What is also evident is that several organizations have resisted appointing an IT Director, because no appropriate person can be found. They may well be right—for the golden pragmatic rules could be (a) be sure you need an IT Director and (b) only appoint one if the appropriate person can be found. In short, we need to understand much more about IT Directors and then begin to develop them more formally.

Education

In this volume, several authors have stressed the challenges of information management education. As Keen has tackled the problem of re-educating the information systems community itself, I will focus on the organizations as a whole.

Despite vested interests as an academic, I will be unambiguous. Management education is crucial to successful information management! Much of it is bad and ill-designed; we believe our experiments and research in Oxford are showing what is needed and possible. I will summarize our experience with statements on needs, approaches and success factors.

The needs inventory across the organization can be described as:

1. Refocusing—raising executive management awareness and understanding of how important IT is for the business.
2. Retooling—developing management or applications skills and knowledge to follow up any new initiatives identified in refocusing.
3. Reskilling—educating and training the IS community on technology, management, and business skills for the new IT era.
4. Reinforcing—building top management understanding, confidence, and commitment to support the effects of the other programmes.

Our experience indicates that an information management education programme for a corporation should begin at the refocusing level. By taking executive management teams from divisional or SBU level, a relevant, homogeneous, topical attack can be made on strategic implications of IT, strategic management of IT and getting manageable tranches of the organization behind it. This is the level to start in order to keep a business perspective and work through a level of organization which can be mobilized for change. Of course, if the business is organized centrally and functionally, it is important to begin at the corporate executive level.

Refocusing is most effective therefore where it is organization-specific. It is enhanced by workshops and case sessions relevant to the firm's business. Above all it is facilitated if there is some external stimulus which galvanizes management interest—a competitive threat or opportunity, for example. And it is only ephemeral in effect if it is not connected to follow-up activity in the firm. Finally, the full benefits of refocusing often take two to three years to be felt in terms of sensible, sustained executive management attention to IT.

Normally such refocusing highlights gaps in management of information resources or applications knowledge which need to be remedied. Examples of such retooling have included project management, strategy formulation, marketing information systems, and advanced manufacturing technology. Here the need is for in-depth, practical knowledge to help in identifying and developing new applications or to improve management execution of IS activities.

Since retooling needs are often identified out of refocusing, they too tend to be organization-specific. Also the demands can be specialized and for a few. Thus retooling can be expensive in cost–volume terms. To ensure the value, there is no alternative but to find educators who really do know about, and have experience of, the specialist areas. It is a mistake to believe that these different education needs can be bought at a one-stop service establishment!

Reskilling has been dealt with substantially in Keen's contribution to this volume. However there is one need he inevitably did not address. It is essential that senior members of the IS function have the same experiences as do executive managers in the refocusing events. Otherwise not only are gaps of understanding created, but opportunities to build bridges missed. Likewise key IS professionals need the same exposure as any users receive in retooling events, for the same reasons *and* because it is at this level that they will be working together.

Reinforcing is particularly necessary in developing and husbanding corporate support of IT. It is common for consultants and IT manufacturers to target top management for information management education—for obvious commercial reasons. However, apart from awareness benefits, these events often have limited impact. What is normally required from top management is support for, and understanding of, what is being aimed at with IT and how it is being pursued. This is much more effective if the reinforcing event is organization-specific, builds on the refocusing, retooling, and reskilling initiatives, and builds a shared vision and common language with those actually driving, developing, and using IT. It is thus likely to come later rather than sooner in the sequence of events. If corporate support, as argued earlier, is cultivated within the business, top management can be re-aligned subsequently. The main exception to this is in centralized, single-stream corporations where the board or top management are then primary targets for refocusing, followed by reinforcing.

The final experience in executive education is paradoxical. There are some organizations where management education is declared to be 'counter-cultural'. It is often unwise to dismiss cultural traits. However in this case, there are two points to be made. We find that whether organizations are turning around information management or seeking and building the IT-strategy connection, management education is a critical success factor. It enhances understanding, builds bridges, constructs common languages, helps change attitudes and discourse, and sets the scene for management initiatives. In short, it begins to change the culture. That is the second point!

Conclusion

This denouement began with six contemporary questions. It concludes with six matching aphorisms, each of which has implicit maxims for practice and directions for research.

1. IT alone cannot create competitive advantage; it needs non-IT as well.
2. If IT is to support corporations, it needs corporate support.
3. If information systems strategic planning is to work, it too must be planned.
4. If innovation from IT is required, so are innovative management practices.
5. If IT is to serve organizations we need to know more about organizing IT.
6. If education is the challenge, re-education is the key.

References

Burns, T., and Stalker, G. (1966), *The Management of Innovation*, Tavistock.

Earl, M. J. (1978), 'Prototype Systems for Accounting, Information and Control', *Accounting, Organisations and Society* **3, 2**.

Ghemawat, P. (1986), 'Sustainable Advantage', *Harvard Business Review* September–October.

Keen, P. G. W. (1986), *Competing in Time: Using Telecommunications for Competitive Advantage*, Ballinger, Cambridge, Mass.

McFarlan, F. W., McKenney, J. L., and Pyburn, P. (1983), 'The Information Archipelago—Plotting a Course', *Harvard Business Review* January–February.

Maidique, M. A., and Hayes, R. H. (1984), 'The Art of High Technology Management', *Sloan Management Review* **26, 1**.

Quinn, J. B. (1980), *Strategies for change: Logical Incrementalism*, Dow Jones–Irwin.

AUTHOR INDEX

291

SUBJECT INDEX